HOW "INDIANS" THINK

GONZALO LAMANA

HOW "INDIANS" THINK

THINK

COLONIAL INDIGENOUS INTELLECTUALS AND
THE QUESTION OF CRITICAL RACE THEORY

THE UNIVERSITY OF
ARIZONA PRESS
TUCSON

The University of Arizona Press
www.uapress.arizona.edu

ISBN-13: 978-0-8165-3966-6 (paper)
ISBN-13: 978-0-8165-4026-6 (cloth)

Cover design by Leigh McDonald
Cover illustration from Guaman Poma's *Nueva corónica y buen gobierno* (1615)

Publication of this book is made possible in part by funding from the Richard D. and Mary Jane
Edwards Endowed Publication Fund, Dietrich School of Arts and Sciences, University of Pittsburgh.

Library of Congress Cataloging-in-Publication Data are available at the Library of Congress.

Printed in the United States of America
♾ This paper meets the requirements of ANSI/NISO Z39.48–1992 (Permanence of Paper).

You write in order to change the world, knowing perfectly well that you probably can't, but also knowing that literature is indispensable to the world. . . . The world changes according to the way people see it, and if you alter, even by a millimeter, the way a person looks or people look at reality, then you can change it.

—JAMES BALDWIN, *THE NEW YORK TIMES*,
SEPTEMBER 23, 1979

CONTENTS

PREFACE AND ACKNOWLEDGMENTS

THIS BOOK is about race-thinking and coloniality in the early seventeenth-century works of two important Andean Indigenous intellectuals: Felipe Guaman Poma de Ayala and Garcilaso de la Vega, el Inca. It studies the ways in which they conceived the tensions and contradictions of the colonial world and how they sought to change it, making new futures possible. My project was initially driven by curiosity. Trained as a scholar sensitive to the cultural (epistemological, ontological) differences separating Indigenous and Western worlds, I could see the role these distinctions played in these intellectuals' texts, but it was also clear to me that there were many elements in them a two-cultures interpretive frame failed to explain. I first attempted to make sense of these elements through an in-depth study of sixteenth-century Spanish theology. While theology certainly helped, it was not enough. Thinking that the discrepant elements pointed to a questioning of cultural differences, I turned to critical approaches to Andean societies and to decolonial theory. They helped me but once again were not enough. My third attempt resorted to critical race theory from both African American and Native American thinkers. In them, I finally found images and vocabulary that resonated closely with the material with which I was working. This coincidence brought into sharp focus the role race-thinking and feeling had in shaping social interactions in the turn-of-the-century Andes. Despite their many disagreements on matters related to colonial rule, Spaniards agreed on the basic distinction that made of native actors "Indians": the latter had a "material intelligence." Incapable of abstract thinking, Indians could not know the true conditions of their own existence. Therefore, Spaniards concurred that Indians' acts and ideas were expressions of their primitive level of cultural development, not the result of reasoned choices—and thereby they were a problem for Spaniards to solve. This book fleshes out these early racial ideas and feelings along with Garcilaso's and Guaman Poma's responses to them. It argues that their texts aimed to change the world by altering how people made sense of it, one pair of eyes at a time. As such, they were Indians of a very special kind—activist intellectuals.

Many people have contributed to making this book possible and to them, I am indebted. If having to revise one's writing in search of clarity is difficult in its own right, it gets even more difficult when one writes in a language that is not one's own. For her fine copyediting work and sharp observations, which often pushed me to develop unclear ideas, I am grateful to Emily Metz-Cherné. I also thank the anonymous readers for their comments and wise advice and the editorial team at the University of Arizona Press for their professionalism. In particular, I was lucky to work with Kristen Buckles, an intelligent and sensible editor, always supportive of my project and determined to make it come through.

During the multiple incarnations of this manuscript, I benefited from comments I received at conferences and in more sustained dialogues. For that, I want to thank especially Jorge Coronado, Sara Chambers, Ananda Cohen Aponte, Fernando Rabossi, Tom Rogers, Sebastián Ferrero, Kenneth Mills, Catherine Poupeney Hart, John Beverley, Fatimah Tobing Rony, Mark Possanza, Andrea Cabel García, Andrea Noble, Sebastián Zubieta, and Jasmine Rault. Other colleagues not only offered me suggestions that helped me move forward but also proved to be long-term sources of inspiration and support. For this, I am grateful to Orin Starn, Sara Castro-Klarén, Patricia Seed, and Walter Mignolo.

The repeated rethinking of the main arguments of this book carried with them equally repeated moments of frustration and discouragement. I am very thankful to Karen and Paul for patiently helping me stay fit to carry on during the process. My family also proved indispensable to navigate the ups and downs of the writing journey. My sons, Marcell and Sebastian, were constant sources of joy who reminded me of what is really important in life. My wife, Gabriella, not only gave me smart advice that put momentary setbacks into (the right) perspective but also helped me articulate inchoate intuitions. Having you all in my life makes me smile.

Some of the material included in this book has appeared in previous publications. Earlier versions of parts of chapters 2 and 3 have come out in *Revista de crítica literaria latinoamericana* 2015, 103–16, under the title "Conocimiento de dios y razón natural, historia local y universal en la *Nueva corónica y buen gobierno* de Guama Poma de Ayala," and in Catherine Poupeney Hart et al. (eds.), *El Perú en su historia*, 149–66, published by Editions Le Manuscript, under the title "Colonialidad y teología en la obra de Guaman Poma de Ayala." Also, chapter 5 includes a revised and expanded version of "Signifyin(g), Double Consciousness, and Coloniality: The Comentarios as Theory of Practice and Political Project," which has appeared in *Garcilaso de la Vega in Dialogue with Today's World-Making*, edited by Sara Castro-Klarén and Christian Fernández 2016, and is hereby reprinted by permission of the University of Pittsburgh Press. The indexing of this book has been done by Amron Gravett, Wild Clover Book Services.

Finally, I am grateful for the financial support that made this book possible. Support from the University of Pittsburgh's Center for Latin American Studies and the University Center for International Studies allowed me to carry out archival and bibliographical work. Also, funding from the Richard D. and Mary Jane Edwards Endowed Publication Fund made it possible for this book to appear in paperback. In this age, when everything one does seems to be ruled by financial considerations, I express my gratitude for the dissemination of knowledge being deemed as valuable in itself. On the same note, and in a more distant but not less important way, I thank my home country, Argentina, for giving me the opportunity to study at an excellent, free public university, the Universidad de Buenos Aires. It may seem like an outdated idea, but I firmly believe that education should not have a price tag on it.

As it is true and necessary to say, all shortcomings and mistakes are mine alone.

HOW "INDIANS" THINK

INTRODUCTION

THE DISCOVERY, conquest, and colonization of the Americas marked the beginning of a change of global magnitude. Before 1492, the world was composed of different economic and cultural areas that were unevenly connected or not connected at all. Europe was marginal to the circuit centered on India and China while the Americas were a separate unit. After 1492, the world began the long process of becoming a single interconnected system. The European ascendancy that would be the end result of this centuries-long transformation started with the exploitation of the labor, resources, and knowledges of the Amerindian peoples who in turn would have to increasingly share control over their own lives. What from the Western point of view was the beginning of modernity, for those on the receiving end was the start of modernity's Janus's sister, coloniality. A long history of having to deal with the West, both in terms of the material processes of cultural and economic transformation it unleashed and in terms of the narratives justifying them, began after Europeans found their way to the Americas.

From the start, the Spanish conquest and colonization went hand in hand with the emergence of accounts about it. These narratives were by no means univocal. In fact, almost from day one, navigators, conquerors, friars, and royal officers disagreed much about their goals and the best ways to achieve them. There were celebratory accounts, those who praised the conquerors' deeds; there were critical accounts, those who condemned the very same acts; there were moralizing tales, which defended the task of persuasive conversion above all reasons; there were others who justified the use of force and the obtaining of riches; and there were also those concerned with the legality of it all. In all these accounts, the images of the Indigenous peoples played a central argumentative role: depending on how they were cast, specific Spanish actions were justified or condemnable. Thus, if Indians were sinners or people with no good form of government, then it was easy to cast a conquest as a great civilizational feat; if they were meek people with properly organized republics, then the same conquest was portrayed as a regrettable sequence of atrocities and spoils.

The internecine Spanish disagreements, including the heated debates about the rights and procedures of the Spanish conquest, have been thoroughly studied.[1] What has not received equal attention is a common trait present in all Spanish narratives. It was a shared assumption that started in the early stages of the colonial process and evolved as colonial rule advanced, securing Spanish superiority, and as such became central to Indigenous actors, too: the Spanish were convinced that *Indians did not know—and did not know that they did not know.* That is, Spaniards thought that Indians were not just ignorant but also were unaware of their ignorance. By contrast, while I do not know nuclear physics, I do know that I do not know it. This awareness makes me accept my inferiority vis-à-vis nuclear physicists. Indians, Spaniards concurred, not only did not know the conditions of their own existence but also were blind to their predicament. They therefore had to be taught all that they were ignorant of and made aware of their conceptual limitations, which were composed because Indians were not good at thinking. Indians were consequently a problem for Spaniards to solve. These ideas, which made of natives actors "Indians," grounded Spanish colonialism. The practical consequences of these seemingly simple observations, including the way Indigenous actors responded to them, will acquire full meaning as the book progresses. For the time being, I present snapshots that trace their historical development to provide some context to the time period on which this study focuses—the moment when colonial rule was solidly established in the Andes and Indigenous intellectuals penned their views of the whole thing.

From 1512 on, while Spanish colonialism was still circumscribed to the Caribbean, the Crown mandated that all conqueror companies read a text called *El requerimiento* to the native peoples they encountered the first time they contacted them. The text requested political submission to the Spanish kings and recognition of Christian superiority. The ritual updated Indians about their "true" history and the "true" conditions of their existence—what they did not know and did not know that they did not know. The text started, "We notify you and make it known to you, as well as we can" ("os notificamos y hacemos saber, como mejor podemos"). Indians were informed that God had created the world and all men, who had since dispersed and populated it, and that the pope was his representative and as such he had granted the Spanish king power over the Americas. It followed that the Indians present for the reading of the text (also children of the Spaniards' god) were vassals of their majesties—they just did not know about it. Now that they were being informed, they had the option of welcoming the representatives of the king and the queen "as subjects are obliged to do" ("como súbditos lo deben hacer"). If they did, then a peaceful future awaited. If they did not, and therefore refused to accept reality as it really was, then the use of force was justified (and as the document concluded, it would be the Indians' fault as they had been duly notified).

El requerimiento, a product of the aforementioned internecine Spanish disagreements, was the object of many critiques since its very inception. However, its key assumptions did not fade, only evolved. The idea that just informing Indians about the order of things would do the trick was revised and factors that prevented that information from being absorbed were considered. For instance, Indians could be too proud to accept the truth (a direct result of their ignorance of their being ignorant). In the Andean case, the 1534 official account of the conquest of the Incas penned by Francisco de Xerez, secretary of the head of the conquering company Francisco Pizarro, resorted to this rationale to justify the use of force against the Inca king, Atahualpa, in 1532. The latter never used force against the Spaniards, but the Spaniards captured him and slaughtered most of his retinue. Xerez's justification in a last instance was that Atahualpa had been too full of himself to accept Christianity as the true religion and the Spanish king's authority; therefore, force had been the only way to disabuse him. After the massacre, Pizarro made sure to get the point across. He told Atahualpa, "Once you have seen the error in which you have lived, you will know the benefit that you are receiving" ("cuando hubiedes visto el error en que habéis vivido, conoceréis el beneficio que recebís") (Xerez [*1534*] 1985, 113). Note the visual metaphor: it was because Atahualpa had been unable to *see* reality as it really was (he just saw it as he thought it was) that he had not welcomed the Spaniards. Only after acquiring that capacity would he be able to realize the good that came to him from having been conquered and disabused. In other words, Atahualpa (and other Andean ethnic lords as the conquest progressed) not only had to face the material reality of being conquered but he also had to put up with being told that being conquered was in his very best interest. To top it off, Spaniards saw Indians as incapable of grasping this thought (at least not yet)—they on the other hand knew (and saw) it all.

It would be reasonable to expect that these Spanish ideas about Indians applied only to first contact cases—that, decades after native actors had been informed of the true conditions of their existence, the assumption that Indians were doubly ignorant would fade away. But, the argument did not disappear. In fact, it grew more complex as the colonial regime settled—and it revealed itself hard to crack. In an ironic reversal, when Indians tried to disabuse Spaniards of their faulty understanding of reality, they faced an uphill battle. Repeated examples of everyday colonial interactions, from casual dialogues between Indigenous rowers and Spanish sailors to those between friars and native lords, made plain that no matter how much Indians worked to dispel the idea that they were doubly ignorant, Spaniards ended up even more deeply confirmed in their beliefs. In fact, the Indians' refusal to accept their inferiority was considered further proof—it was simply evidence that they had not yet reached the level where they could see themselves and the Spaniards for what they truly were.

Consider for instance the following conversation between a Spanish friar who defended Indians from Spanish abuses, the Dominican Domingo de Santo Tomás, and an anonymous cacique (ethnic lord). The dialogue took place some thirty years after Atahualpa's capture, when Spanish colonial rule was firmly established. As he walked by an Indigenous town high in the mountains, Santo Tomás exchanged some words with an ethnic lord that exemplified the obstacles facing conversion: "Asking once in a given province a cacique whether he was Christian, he told me: 'not yet, but I am beginning to.' And as I asked him what he knew of [being] Christian, he told me: 'I know to swear God, and play cards a little bit, and I am beginning to steal'" ([1560] 1995, fol. 68, 140).[2] This extraordinary dialogue preceded a revealing explanation: "As I understood it, that sinner had to think that, in the same way that there was nothing else to being a tailor than what they saw tailors do, which is to sew, and the same happens in other trades, he thus thought that there was nothing else to being Christian than what they commonly saw Christians do" (Santo Tomás [1560] 1995, fol. 68, 140).[3] I will analyze the intricacies of this exchange and others like it in more detail in the following chapter. For the time being, I want to point out that the friar turned the ethnic lord's amazing wit and abstraction—his ironic comment about what it meant to be Christian and implicitly about what Spaniards thought that Indians could think—into an example of Indian inferiority. For Santo Tomás, it is because he (like all Indians) was able to see only what was in front of him (bad Christians lied, played cards, and stole) that the ethnic lord misunderstood what it was to be Christian. And, because he did not know that he did not know, the cacique thought his answer was funny and smart while in reality it was comic and pitiful. In short, Spaniards were unable to see Indians as capable of being funny, ironic, self-reflexive, and critically reflective about what Spaniards had to say about themselves and about Indians. From a native point of view, however, the world was upside down: while it was Spaniards who did not know that they did not know, they thought it was the other way around. In their day to day, Indigenous actors thus faced a catch-22 scenario. If they adopted Spanish ideas, they had to live upside down and confirmed their inferiority. If they tried to express their disagreement to Spaniards, setting their lives back on their feet, they were deemed even more inferior—stuck in the evolutionary line Spaniards led, Indians were not even at the point of having accepted their own ignorance.

The ideas this dialogue exposes were by no means extraordinary. Toward the end of the sixteenth century in the Andes, a solid argument that formed the core of what Spaniards thought about Indians had crystalized: Indians (still) did not know and (still) did not know that they did not know because they had a limited mental capacity. They could not see the world for what it really was because their thinking prowess was too close to the ground. It stopped with what was visible to them. They were not capable of abstract thinking. This *inteligencia material* (material intelligence), as another clergyman succinctly put it, prevented them from developing complex understandings of the world around them. That was what made them Indians. Whatever they did or thought, including the cacique's abstraction and amazing intelligence to speak the truth through irony, could rightly be dismissed. The Spaniards saw the acts and ideas of Indians as expressions of their primitive level of cultural development, not as the result of reasoned choices. In fact, Spaniards concluded, there was no such a thing as Indian agency. Indians did just what was natural to them, not what they had consciously chosen to do, because choosing implied knowing and Indians did not know. The reasoning—expressions of an emerging form of race-thinking and feeling way before the idea of race came into being—applied to all sorts of Indian matters, from religion to art, from sex to labor, from clothing to grammar and vocabulary.

The other side of the same coin was the image Spaniards had about themselves. They considered themselves at the pinnacle of abstraction—the ones who knew the most and could see reality for what it really was. They had the experience and intelligence that came with being at the forefront of the evolutionary line and, equally important, were aware of the Indians' double ignorance—the fact that they still did not know that they did not know. They saw themselves as adults to strange children who could not grasp the complexity of reality at all. These images (or rather imaginings) grounded Spanish ideas of superiority over Indians and set the stage on which Indigenous intellectuals acted.

INDIGENOUS ACTIVIST INTELLECTUALS

Most of what one knows about this complex historical process, about the ideas being discussed and the arguments being used, comes from Spanish sources. This is due to the simple fact that the Spaniards wrote extensively about it from the start while the Indigenous actors did not.[4] Indigenous voices, when they can be recovered, are often accessible only through the careful canvasing of colonial archives. Because they were recorded in specific files related to specific affairs, these voices did not express comprehensive views of the colonial system. This is precisely what makes the few texts penned by Indigenous intellectuals in colonial times—such as those I will examine in this book—so important. They allow one to see how some of those who inhabited the colonial world in a disadvantaged position thought and felt about it.

In colonial Peru, the two most important Indigenous intellectuals were Garcilaso de la Vega, el Inca, and Felipe Guaman Poma de Ayala. Garcilaso was the son of an Inca princess and a Spanish conquistador. He was born in Cuzco, the capital of the Inca Empire, where he received a formal education. At age nineteen, he moved to Spain where he eventually became a writer. He published his most renowned work, the *Comentarios reales de los Incas* (henceforth *CRI*), in Lisbon in 1609. Guaman Poma was the son of a woman of Inca descent and an ethnic lord of an Indigenous group of the Peruvian highlands, the Yarovilca. He worked with Spanish clergymen, was active in legal matters, and spent his entire life in the Andes. His *Nueva corónica y buen gobierno* (henceforth *NCBG*), a 1,189-page manuscript, was finished around 1614.

Written in impeccable Spanish, Garcilaso's *CRI* described Inca culture and narrated its history from the origins of the Inca Empire until the Spanish arrival. Guaman Poma's *NCBG* presented the precolonial and colonial history of Andean Indigenous peoples while also offering a sharp account of the injustices that characterized the Spanish colonial regime in the Andes. He wrote in a Spanish that showed the influence of his native tongues and in fact used different Indigenous languages throughout the text.

While indispensable to the study of colonialism in the Andes, the relevance of these two intellectuals goes beyond that. Garcilaso and Guaman Poma are in a way comparable to thinkers like Aristotle or Plato. All of them are vital for understanding the modern, interconnected world in which we live, the centuries-long result of the Western expansion that started in 1492. At the same time, they are unlike each other. Plato and Aristotle are at the core of how the West thought about itself and the Rest; Garcilaso and Guaman Poma are at the core of how the Rest thought about itself and the West. They were Indians writing in the Andes, not Greeks at the heart of Europe. In other words, if Plato and Aristotle are indispensable to understand modernity, including the origins of its enlightenment project, Garcilaso and Guaman Poma are indispensable to comprehend coloniality, including the origins of colonial race-thinking.

Scholars have long recognized the relevance of Garcilaso's and Guaman Poma's works, their defense of Amerindian civilizations, and their critique of the Spanish colonial regime.[5] As thinkers in between cultures (or epistemologies), they directed their sophisticated efforts of cross-cultural communication both to make readers understand the Indigenous world and to achieve practical political goals. Garcilaso's *CRI* stressed the rational nature of Inca society and history to correct demeaning Spanish representations of the precolonial empire and to implicitly criticize the unreasonable state of culture and society in the Andes at the turn of the century. Guaman Poma's *NCBG* described in detail the cultural and religious achievements of Andean Indigenous peoples, offered an indicting critique of the Spanish conquest and the colonial system, and explicitly asked the king for a number of remedies. Both authors argued forcibly for the preeminence and authority of the members of their own Indigenous lineages to be recognized and given a central place in the colonial system.[6]

This interpretive frame brings to light the cultural complexities and the political engagement of the *CRI* and the *NCBG* and also helps correct the Spanish-centric image of the history and workings of the colonial system. However, there are elements in both texts that escape the two-cultures frame. For instance, Guaman Poma consistently addressed his readers as *cristiano lector* (Christian reader) regardless of whether he was addressing a Spaniard or an Indian. This address neither privileged the king as primary reader and provider of solutions nor fit the cross-cultural, native/Western opposition. Furthermore, in addition to good Indians and bad Spaniards, which fits the critique of the evils of Spanish colonialism, there were plenty of bad Indians and good Spaniards in the *NCBG*. Similar observations can be made about the *CRI*. If Garcilaso wanted to offer a positive image of Inca culture and history prior to the conquest that answered demeaning Spanish images of the precolonial past, why did he also include numerous stories that are neither about the precolonial past nor about Incas but about Spaniards and Indians (Indians, not Incas) in colonial times? Or, if he wanted to portray the Incas as the embodiment of what precolonial civilizations achieved through the exercise of reason alone, why did he include detailed stories of divine intervention—only to discredit them by saying they were in fact not true historical accounts, just "fables"?

As I will show, these seeming tensions result from trying to fit under a single interpretive roof (one that houses two cultures) critical projects that were twofold. Both intellectuals understood the problems of the colonial system as springing not only from cultural or epistemological differences between Western and Indigenous civilizations, which a cross-cultural lens captures well, but also from differences caused by emerging Spanish race-thinking and coloniality. Guaman Poma and Garcilaso distinguished forms of discrimination based on culture from those based on race and coloniality not only because they were different but also because they demanded different answers. Both thinkers were well aware of the fact that the demeaning images Spaniards had about native peoples played an important role in the colonial system. They therefore worked to correct the record and, in an effort of cultural translation, explain how Indigenous societies really were. But, improving the image could only go so far. The way in which Spaniards saw Indians and what they thought the latter were able to think, was at the core of colonial forms of discrimination—this problem required correcting not the record but the gaze of those who could not see but thought that they could see. Both intellectuals understood the frustration ordinary native actors had when their repeated attempts to get through to Spaniards, to have them hear them and to take them as equal human beings, failed. Their texts aimed to bring this latter set of problems to light for all readers to see and to change the ways in which colonial actors saw each other and, as a result, the world in which they lived.

Guaman Poma addressed all readers as "cristiano lector" to trouble the distinction between natives and Europeans that grounded the colonial order.

In that way, he made all colonial actors equal. Their knowledge and thinking powers were the same—whether they acted well or not showed the "right" understanding of the world or not had nothing to with their ethnic origin. That is why Indians and Spaniards could be good or bad—they were all equally Christian readers. Garcilaso tackled the emerging Spanish race-thinking by interspersing between his narrative about the Inca kings numerous stories about colonial times in which he made visible how Spaniards thought about Indians and what Indians could do with those ideas—including the distinction Spaniards established between what were "true" historical accounts (their own) and "fables" (those of Indians). Both authors intended to help their readers make sense of the colonial present in ways that counteracted the effects of the emerging Spanish race-thinking and coloniality and offered new, alternative futures. Although they did this in different ways, ultimately their goal was the same: to turn the readers themselves into instruments of change. In other words, they were Indians of a very special kind: activist intellectuals.

As such, Guaman Poma and Garcilaso were part of a larger group of Indigenous actors that dealt with the impact the colonial system and its discourses had on their lives. A key trait of Spanish colonial narratives was that Europeans were active parts and agents while native actors not only had no initiative but they also had no agency. In the intellectual arena in particular, Spanish accounts produced the myth of a *Lettered City* (Rama [1984] 1996). According to it, everything that was really happening—the many incarnations of the project of modernity—sprang from the pens of white thinkers who lived in cities. The Indigenous countryside was an illiterate, static space into which, as modernity forayed, the light of Western writing and knowledge superseded superstition-laden oral traditions and rudimentary ways of recording information. Scholars of the colonial Andes have challenged this basic setup in different ways. They have long questioned the civilizing tale, denouncing the violent repression and destruction those forays entailed. More recently, they have begun challenging the oppositions at the core of the myth—the divides between urban and rural, written and oral, Spanish and native, agent and agentless, subject and object. The challenges tend to follow two paths: some zero in on the colonial archive to correct the image of Spanish colonialism we have inherited while others focus on coloniality, the still-present effects of that colonial beginning.

Combing the colonial archive shows that, if there ever was a *Lettered City*, there was also a *Lettered Mountain* (Salomon and Niño-Murcia 2011). There were literate natives across the rural landscape—many, in fact—and they were far from isolated islands in a sea of illiteracy. For one thing, literate Indigenous actors mingled with their Spanish peers in the legal and ecclesiastic terrains and the ways in which the parties teamed up did not necessarily follow the Spanish/native divide. In fact, the very image of a Spanish *Lettered City* is wrong—in colonial cities, natives were *escribanos* (notaries), petitioned before courts, and actively participated in ecclesiastical affairs. What is more, this was not a matter of a small group of elite natives that were somehow functional to the system, the exception that proved the rule. Written documents were just "the tip of an iceberg" (Ramos and Yannakakis 2014, 4)—the visible material result of large processes of communal deliberation, organizing, and planning. The networks through which knowledge was acquired and circulated were neither necessarily formal nor in Spanish hands alone. Some native intelletuals owned large libraries; others borrowed books from and loaned them to priests or Spanish letrados. Some went to *colegios* (already established schools); others set up their own schooling systems. And, in fact, Western knowledge did not simply supersede Indigenous knowledge—they coexisted well into colonial times. Indigenous intellectuals continued their work after the conquest in order to help the survival of their communities, the rights of their ruling lineages, or the preservation of their history. To do that, they resorted to both kinds of knowledges and both systems of recording information, Indigenous and European.[7]

Garcilaso's and Guaman Poma's ideas contribute to this revision of the colonialist image about intellectual work and agency in two important and related ways. First, they suggest that the idea of Indigenous knowledge has to be expanded. What native actors knew and Europeans did not was not only related to the precolonial past, to different epistemologies or ontologies, but also to a knowledge about the colonial present born out of the colonial encounter. It was Indigenous and it was something that distinguished Indians from Spaniards but it did not require precolonial roots. And, it was not a knowledge of the workings of the colonial system—it was a knowledge about coloniality and whiteness (see next sections). Second, Garcilaso's and Guaman Poma's texts tell that resorting to the colonial archive to recover Indigenous intellectual agency has its own risks. It certainly helps overcome the Spanish narrative; if it were for the latter, one would forever be in the *Lettered City*. At the same time, because of the very nature of legal documents, colonial archives reveal largely one kind of Indigenous thinking: that of making the best out of the system. In litigation over land, water, or political rights, ecclesiastic legal procedures, deeds, or petitions, intellectual practice was about the capacity of maneuvering, of working with what was given, not of transforming it.

To question the effects of the *Lettered City*'s ideas, other scholars resort to revising the long-term conceptual frame. Central to this endeavor is the notion of "coloniality" coined by Peruvian sociologist Aníbal Quijano. Going beyond the traditional focus of dependency theorists, the concept of coloniality points out that colonialism involved as much domination and exploitation, political control and wealth extraction, as a structure of discrimination that justified them. Race (understood as encompassing racial, ethnic, and national distinctions) was a colonial/modern invention that originated in the sixteenth century and is still at work. One of its effects was the subalternization and destruction of non-Western knowledges that did not directly help colonial exploitation and their eventual transformation into objects of scientific study (Quijano 1992, 2000, 2014).[8] Building on this general frame, the question becomes how to conceive responses to coloniality that foster a decolonial (or postcolonial) agenda. If the coloniality of power was/is "an energy and a machinery to turn differences into values" (Mignolo 2002, 13), then the critical project is the return of the other knowledges the West began silencing in 1492, an act of epistemic delinking (Mignolo 2007b). This project involved the erasure of the hierarchical difference instituted at the moment of inception of the coloniality of power that made anything Amerindian inferior, reestablishing "a dialogue between equals inhabiting a single creation" (Castro-Klarén 2016, 205).

Guaman Poma's and Garcilaso's views of colonialism add to this project the need for scholars to rethink both what was specific about the exercise of power at the moment when coloniality was coming into being and how to best respond to it. Both Andean thinkers understood colonialism as involving a structure of discrimination that turned them into objects of study. In this way, they aligned with current scholars' ideas. They were dissimilar in that they thought that the project of changing the colonial order of things did not necessarily involve the return of repressed knowledges or a statement of equality achievable through cultural translation. Garcilaso and Guaman Poma knew that vindicating other knowledges would only go so far for different reasons. For one, they were recognized and protected as were all things Indian that involved no idolatry or amoral practices. In fact, they were useful tools through which colonial administrators promoted "the demand to return to that utopian past that never was" (Smith 2009, 101).[9] As such, they could be dead ends functional to the colonial order. Then, there was the fact that they would still be seen as expressions of a material intelligence; therefore, change had to do with undoing the proto-racial structures set by whiteness (I will return to it shortly), not with validating knowledges derived from other cultures or epistemologies. At the heart of the coloniality of power, as far as the two Indigenous thinkers were concerned, was not the transformation of preexisting differences into values but the denial of the conceptual moves and postindian imaginations of those who were also thinking and the simultaneous demand that Spanish imaginings be taken for the real thing. In short, their texts were organized by a principle that required specific pedagogical strategies. Central to this principle was the paradoxical fact that Spaniards and Indians were alike and inhabited a single creation but yet they did not: Indians knew that Spaniards did not know that they did not know and did not want to know about the conditions of their own existence. At the heart of this distinction, and of the strategies needed to remedy it, was the question of what it meant to be Indian, something Garcilaso and Guaman Poma were heavily invested in redefining.

"INDIAN" AND OTHER KEY CONCEPTS

"Indian" is a contentious word and in many ways the wrong one to refer to persons belonging to any of the native peoples of the Americas. Besides being a misnomer, a result of Columbus's errors and limitations, it betrays the complexity of the political-historical and cultural-native landscape and it was not used by native actors to identify themselves (they used instead the name of the group to which they belonged). One could conclude then that Indians did not exist except in the Spaniards' eyes and, in consequence, that using it reproduces colonialist discourse.[10] Terms like "native," "Indigenous," or the actual ethnic affiliation would be preferable. However, Garcilaso and Guaman Poma used the word *indio* (Indian). Why? I argue that they did so because they thought that—to paraphrase the quote that opens this book—to alter how colonial actors saw the world, it was better to resignify the word "Indian" than to write it out.

What exactly did it allow them to tackle that other options did not? To answer this question, I first need to introduce terms coined by twentieth-century activist intellectuals that will also be important throughout the book. In particular, key ideas of W. E. B. Du Bois, James Baldwin, and Gerald Vizenor help bring to light the complex ways in which Garcilaso and Guaman Poma thought about the problems they saw in the colonial world and how to fix them centuries before the terms to describe those problems became available. What all these thinkers, colonial and contemporary, have in common is their understanding of social relations as being mediated by the ideas that different actors hold about the self and others and the unequal awareness these very same actors have about the work of that mediation.

The first relevant concept is W. E. B. Du Bois's idea of the "veil." In an oft-quoted passage of "Our Spiritual Strivings," Du Bois describes the "Negro" at the beginning of the twentieth century as follows: "Born with a veil and gifted with a second sight in this American world, a world which yields him no true self-consciousness, but only lets him see himself through the revelation of the other world. It is a particular sensation, this double-consciousness, this sense of always looking at one's self through the eyes of others, of measuring one's soul by the tape of a world that looks on in amused contempt and pity" ([1903] 1990, 43). Du Bois's use of metaphors of seeing and not seeing to conceptualize race relations in the twentieth-century United States is doubly significant. On the one hand, it resonates with the language Spaniards used in Peru at the turn of the sixteenth century to describe Indian inferiority and their expectations about Indians. Indians were unable to see themselves and the world as they really were, Spaniards argued. The latter's expectation was that Indians would progressively measure their worth with a Spanish tape, see the world with the Spaniards' eyes, and acquiesce—as if it were reasonable to be asked "how does it feel to be a problem?" (DuBois [1903] 1990, 41).

On the other hand, the discrepancy between those expectations and the experience of the world by a person of color results in the tension of a double consciousness and the emergence of a second sight. If, as Shawn Michelle Smith argues (2004, 40–42), the veil can be thought of as a double-sided site of racial interaction, then it has two sides, two different visual dynamics, and two different degrees of awareness. Its doubleness expresses then as much the particular perception of the world of a person of color as that of a white person—while the latter sees only the images that he projects on it, the former can see through the veil, accessing a second sight. Like the cacique speaking with Santo Tomás, Indians for Garcilaso and Guaman Poma were those who did not mistake the Spanish images about them for the real thing and were aware of the force those images had on Spaniards. Both Indigenous activist intellectuals used the term "Indian" to promote a sense of commonality knowing perfectly well that in any other regard there were no Indians except in the Spaniards' eyes. Following Garcilaso's and Guaman Poma's cue, each time I use the term "Indian" I will be adopting either the position of Spaniards talking about native actors or of the two Andean intellectuals' take on it.

This answer solves one problem but may open another: for different reasons, the term "white" is no less problematic than the term "Indian." Scholars who address questions of race and identity formation in the colonial Andes point out that white, as referring to a skin color or a race, is an anachronistic term. In general, identities were more fluid and context- and performance-dependent than later biological ideas of race imply (Burns 2007; Díaz 2017; Fisher and O'Hara 2009; O'Toole 2012; Rappaport 2014; Rappaport and Cummins 2012; Van Deusen 2015). "Spaniard" would not work any better. It was rarely used, and the difference was not about nationalities.[11] "Christian," as conquerors most often called themselves, failed to convey a clear-cut difference seventy years after the conquest. To express this tension between a difference that was neither essential nor based on skin color or phenotypes but was real, James Baldwin's ideas about "whiteness" and "blackness" are useful. For Baldwin, whiteness is primarily "a state of mind." It is not a matter of skin color—races do not exist, he states repeatedly—but of how certain people think about themselves and their others. Whiteness as a state of mind is something close to a state of self-delusion sustained by the stories white Americans tell, both to themselves and to their others, about themselves and about their others. One example would be the idea of morally exemplary whites facing sexually voracious blacks. For Baldwin, these images and stories are colonial in origin—Europeans began to think of themselves as white at the same time that they began to think of enslaved Africans as "niggers". Both were constitutive of each other and inseparable. Blackness, on the other hand, was for Baldwin a "condition," the result of having to face whiteness, a special kind of resilience and awareness that surviving the former demanded.[12]

These distinctions help understand social dynamics in the colonial Andes at the turn of the sixteenth century. On the one hand, they explain the repeated Spanish resistance to acknowledge that Indians could think as much and in the same ways as Spaniards. In the example of Santo Tomás and the ethnic lord, at stake were as much the stories about Indian inferiority the Spaniards told as the stories Spaniards told about themselves that made them different and superior. Had the friar acknowledged that the ethnic lord was intelligent and what he said about being Christian was an acute critique and not a misrecognition, he would have had to acknowledge that there was little he had to teach Indians and that he was not the benevolent father he thought he was. His world would have been turned upside down. On the other hand, for Garcilaso and Guaman Poma, being Indian was not an essence but a "condition," the result of having to live in a social context where whiteness was the norm. Each Indigenous thinker defined this social condition in a specific manner. For Garcilaso, being Indian was both being aware of how the nascent Spanish race-thinking worked—the images they had of Indians and how they conditioned (primarily) Spaniards' acts—and being able to use that awareness to their advantage. Like the ethnic lord in dialogue with the friar, Garcilaso told the truth to Spaniards, but unlike him, he showed native actors how they could get Spaniards to do what was (actually) in their best interest without the Spaniards noticing. For Guaman Poma, Indians were those native actors who refused to see the colonial system through the lies Spaniards told about them and managed to keep a clear sense of what was right and what was wrong and why. They saw the world as it really was and knew how it should really be while Spaniards did not. His goal was to teach those who saw the world through whiteness, regardless of the color of their skin, to see the world anew.

Both ways of proposing to be Indian parted company with Spanish imaginings of Indians in another important regard: in the *CRI* and the *NCBG*, Indians are "an active presence" and as such are "postindians" (Vizenor 1999). Although I will stick to the label "Indians," I will do it with Gerald Vizenor's ideas in mind. For him, Indians, as they commonly appear in American popular culture and scientific ethnographies, are an "absent presence." They exist but only insofar as they fit white imaginations of natives. All the labels that mark Indians in the imaginative repertoire—like victim, primitiveness, despair, melancholy, or the noble warrior—share the idea that Indians are predictable, a known quantity. There is no room for surprise. Indians also are stuck in—and belong to—an imagined past white people have created for them. *What* Indians may actually think is replaced by *how* Indians think, which is determined by their culture (as defined by scientific and popular discourses about it). The term "postindian," on the other hand, refers to ways of being Indian that escape white imaginings. Postindians are not expressions of what native peoples truly are—their true essence untouched by the evils of the West. To the contrary, they emerge out of their awareness of what Indians are expected to be. As such, postindians make interventions and exist as active presences—they are "unexpected" (Deloria 2004) native actors who refuse to be predictable, known quantities.

In colonial Peru at the turn of the sixteenth century, being Indian was not a simple matter. Spaniards talked at length about Indians because, for strange reasons I will explain in the next section, they were seen as a problem. Explaining what characterized them, what made them Indian, was needed to achieve a good diagnosis of the problem and determine the right solutions. The characterizations varied somehow. To some, Indians were pure children; to others, they were deceitful devils; to all, they were remnants of a past that had existed before the conquest, maladjusted to the modern project Spaniards embodied. Garcilaso and Guaman Poma flipped the temporal coin: because Indians were forced to live in a world that was upside down, scripted by whiteness, they could see what people who thought of themselves as white could not. And, unlike the latter, they were aware of it. This awareness meant that Indians were already in the future—they were postindians waiting for Spaniards to catch up and realize that *they* were the ones who failed to grasp how the world really was. In other words, these two activist intellectuals knew that to be an active presence, Indians had to be "experts in the fine art of staging [conceptual] jailbreaks" (Smith 2009, 90). That is why, for them, changing the state of culture and society in colonial Peru hinged upon altering the gaze of people (regardless of their origin or the color of their skin) who saw Indians. Until such a transformation could take place, other avenues of change, such as political reform, would only have limited effects since they would be bound by the same basic constraint.

HISTORY ON THE GROUND: COLONIALISM IN THE ANDES UP TO THE 1600S

A final element is needed to provide a full picture of the meaningful context in which Guaman Poma and Garcilaso intervened: the crazy discrepancy between what Spaniards said about Indians during these decades and what natives actually did. As it happens, the history on the ground behind nascent Spanish race-thinking and feeling is quite remarkable—no matter how much Spaniards wrote about them, Indians did not exist during this time. The Spanish colonial enterprise was messier and weaker than what words like "conquest" and "exploitation" evoke. Spanish colonialism on the ground was fraught with constant conflict, both because of the diverging interests and goals of the different Spanish factions and because of the sustained challenges Indigenous peoples posed. As a result, Spanish desires of ascendancy were repeatedly undermined by the success of Indigenous initiatives. Furthermore, not only was Spanish superiority often questioned by Indigenous peoples' competition in social, political, and religious arenas but also the lines separating Spaniards and natives were often blurred as the internal cleavages among the two resulted in shifting cross-group alliances.

From the moment the Spanish conquistadors set foot in the Inca Empire in the early 1530s until the 1550s, there were open wars between Spanish factions, often allied with different Indigenous groups and Inca factions, in addition to fighting directly between Spaniards and Incas. The result of this untidy cultural and political process was "domination without dominance" (Lamana 2008). In the following two decades, the different Spanish and Indigenous political, religious, and economic projects continued to tangle and clash, just in less violent ways. Debates and polemics were the order of the day including fundamental matters like the rightfulness of the Spanish conquest and rule, who should have control over Indigenous labor, and the kind of government the territories should have (whether it was to be governed by Spanish-conquistadors-turned-feudal-lords or by an alliance of ethnic lords and Spanish friars). During these years, Indians successfully lobbied for their political interests. To boot, they also participated actively in colonial markets, established their own commercial enterprises, limited the Spanish exploitation of Indigenous labor, and used the Spanish legal system to their advantage.[13]

It was only in the 1570s that, thanks to massive reforms implemented by an energetic viceroy (Francisco de Toledo), the colonial system began to resemble a two-tier regime with clear relations of subordination. Toledo's reforms strengthened state control over conquerors, friars, and ethnic lords; organized the colony around a system of two republics, one of Indians and one of Spaniards; and enforced the subordination of the former to the latter. Toledo also put a practical end to arguments about Spanish dominion, imposed demanding labor obligations from Indigenous peoples toward Spaniards in recognition of the latter's civilizing task, propped the mining industry (the heart of the colonial economy), and promoted a much stricter approach to Indian Christianity than the one prevailing during the early decades (by then the large majority of the Indigenous population had officially converted).[14]

At the turn of the century in the Andes, when Guaman Poma and Garcilaso were busy writing, the most urgent matters Spaniards discussed were problems that Toledo's reforms had caused: the fall of the Indigenous forced labor pool and accusations of Indian idolatry. Toledo's colossal reorganization of Indigenous labor and mining production initially resulted in a vast multiplication of wealth, which, in due time, gave birth to commercial enterprises that ended up competing with the mining centers over the labor of the Indigenous population. At the same time, to face the increased demands, Indigenous peoples developed their own patterns of resistance and adaptation, which involved complex migrations, varying economic strategies, and shifting political and settlement patterns that baffled colonial administrators and dodged their control. As the main Indigenous population centers subjected to labor levies progressively dwindled—and with them the mining boom—a hot debate ensued among Spaniards over what had caused the situation and what were the best remedies. Miners, clergymen, royal administrators, commercial entrepreneurs, encomenderos—each and every imaginable interested Spanish party voiced his opinion. The Crown changed course more than once, and royal decrees were issued only to be suspended by viceroys or simply ignored.[15]

The situation was similar in what concerned accusations of Indian idolatry. The stricter approach to Indigenous religious manifestations favored by Toledo was formalized in doctrinaire terms by the 1582–83 Third Ecclesiastical Council of Lima. The numerous texts the council produced changed the lines separating Indigenous and Christian religious beliefs and practices. What until then had been commonly seen as expressions of Indians' natural intuition of Christian truths and/or steps on the path toward a full Christianity were thereafter seen as proof of the fact that the devil had tricked Indians into imitating Christian truths to defile them. As a consequence, Indians were deemed idolaters. Progressively, vigilance over native religious practices, the destruction of Indigenous religious sites, and the denunciation of any unorthodox religious ideas became the norm. The change in attitude toward Indigenous religious practices and beliefs, which started as individual efforts by specific clergymen in their own areas of influence, eventually snowballed into one of the most infamous and violent forms of colonial oppression: the campaigns of extirpation of idolatries that regularly crisscrossed the Andean landscape during the seventeenth century. Reports and manuals proliferated describing (and in fact defining anew) what Indian idolaters did, why they did it, and the best courses of action to remedy the problem.[16]

All these turn-of-the-century Spanish arguments about Indians' true nature were used as fundamental elements to diagnose problems and offer solutions. Whether Indians were idolatrous or disappearing had to do with the Indians' faults and their incapacity to cope with the challenges the modern project posed. Indians were discussed, portrayed in this or that light, and considered ubiquitous known quantities, or absent presences. Guaman Poma and Garcilaso sought as much to challenge the repertoire used in the conversation (images of

Indian laziness, idolatrousness, lack of ambition, pusillanimity, etc.) as to change its fundamental frame of reference: the *CRI* and the *NCBG* said that *those who saw the world through whiteness were the problem, not Indians.* Because the former could not see reality as it really was, the colonial world was upside down. Until they were able to realize this, *they* were the absent presences.

STRUCTURE OF THE BOOK

This book is composed of six chapters grouped into four parts. The first part consists of a single chapter that fleshes out Spaniards' ideas about Indians in the Andes in the late 1500s. The second part has two chapters that study Guaman Poma de Ayala's *NCBG*. The two chapters of the third part examine Garcilaso de la Vega's *CRI.* The conclusion brings together the material previously examined and draws implications for the field.

Part 1 presents an overview of sixteenth-century Spanish ideas about Indians in the Andes—ideas that centered on questions of thinking and vision. Regardless of their political sympathies, Spaniards saw the colonial order as justified by the Indians' inability to see reality as it was and to think about it in abstract terms. Indians were beings with a material intelligence. These ideas, present in theological treatises as much as in fictional texts, expressed what were in practice expressions of race-thinking and feeling before the idea of race came into being in the West. As such, they provided the context in which Garcilaso and Guaman Poma wrote their texts.

Part 2 focuses on Guaman Poma de Ayala's work. It argues that the *NCBG* presented a critique of Spanish colonialism through a decolonial use of Spanish theories. By using theological ideas common in Spain but rarely (if ever) considered in the colonies, Guaman Poma divided colonial society not between Indians and Spaniards but between those who could see reality as it really was and those who could not, those who acted inconsequently and those who did not, regardless of their skin color or origin. He thus questioned the cornerstone of the colonial regime—the existence of racialized taxonomies of human capacity. His main goal was not to denounce Spanish abuses against Indians, which were well known to Spanish authorities and whose denunciation was part of the intra-Spanish political debate, or to move people to do the right thing, but to challenge the assumptions commonly used by those who reported the abuses and offered solutions. He aimed to change the way in which those who thought of themselves as white saw the world, one pair of eyes at a time.

Part 3 examines Garcilaso de la Vega's work. It suggests that the *CRI* was a paradigmatic example of what double meanings by subaltern thinkers could achieve. At one level, the text mimicked the Spaniards' rhetorical styles, authoritative sources, and favorite tropes thereby appearing to be a reassuring example of what good natives were able to write. At the same time, it unsettled Spanish racialized ideas about Indians and provided native readers with conceptual tools to foster their survivance. The *CRI* is two texts at once. Its main narrative plot is about the Inca past but its innumerable stories, which interrupt the main narrative, are about the colonial present. The latter offered a conceptual ethnography of the veil at work and provided spaces for action that different peoples' awareness of the veil opened up. In all cases, the *CRI* brought to the forefront the kind of abstraction Indians were allegedly incapable of having. For Spaniards to access Garcilaso's critique, they would have had to question their own ideas about themselves and their colonial others. That is, they would have had to accept that Indians could outthink them—a reverse catch-22.

Part 4 concludes by summarizing the main findings of the book. First, the chapter reverses the lens used in the introduction and examines what was specifically colonial about the very beginnings of the Western global expansion. Why did race-thinking and coloniality in the Andes acquire the specific forms they did? Second, it compares the ways in which Garcilaso and Guaman Poma theorized race-thinking and coloniality and imagined postindian futures. Which were the most salient commonalities and differences between them? Were their ideas exceptional at the particular moment and place of enunciation or were they expressions of a more extensive way of conceiving the colonial system that was present at other points in time?

NOTES ON TERMS, TRANSLATIONS, AND QUOTES

He/She. It is standard practice in English to alternate the gender of the third person (he/she) so as not to privilege one over the other. I decided not to do it when discussing sixteenth- and early seventeenth-century texts because it would have been untrue to the gender ideas of the time. Thus, when referring to potential readers of the texts discussed in this book or to theological ideas about humans, I have chosen to use "he."

Translations. All translations are mine. In the case of biblical quotes, I have chosen to translate from the Spanish *Biblia del oso*, which the authors discussed in this book would have known, instead of using English versions, which they most likely would have not.

Quotes. To make quotes accessible to readers who want to check the larger context of the *NCBG* and *CRI*, I have used widely available editions of each text. However, I have reviewed the wording these editions offer against the originals and have made corrections wherever I found them necessary (at times to amend transcription errors, at others to change the punctuation). All quotes are in English; if under two lines, they are followed by their original Spanish version in the body of the text; if longer than two lines, the original is in a footnote.

PART I

SPANISH IDEAS ABOUT INDIANS

It's a point so blindingly obvious that only an extraordinarily clever and sophisticated person could fail to grasp it.

—JOHN BERCOW

A MATERIAL INTELLIGENCE

TO SET their interpretive context, studies of the *NCBG* and the *CRI* often highlight their engagement with two main concerns: the Spanish debates about the rights and procedures of the Spanish conquest and the defense of the standing and cultural achievements of the Amerindian civilizations.[1] Both matters were indeed related as they played important roles in justifying Spanish colonial rule. The story is well known. On the island of Hispaniola, in a sermon on Christmas 1511, the Dominican Antonio de Montesinos lashed out at conquerors for their un-Christian treatment of Indians. The ensuing polemics involved a scrutiny of both the Spaniards' actions and the achievements of the precolonial civilizations, evolved as Spaniards expanded beyond the Caribbean and conquered the Aztec and Inca Empires, and peaked toward 1551–52 with the famous Valladolid debate between a representative of the so-called "party of the Indians," Fray Bartolomé de Las Casas, and a representative of the conquerors' position, Juan Ginés de Sepúlveda. The former cast Indians as primitive proto-Christians that had achieved significant degrees of civilizational development, rejected the use of force by the Spanish wolves against the Indian lambs, and sought to set strict limits to the rights and procedures of the Spanish presence in the Americas. The latter cast Indians as barbarians who deviated from natural and human law, justified the use of force, and considered the validity of the rights and procedures of the

Spanish conquest to be as clear as water. The debate reached no conclusion and settled little. The two opposing views of the colonial project continued to fight each other for years. In the Andes, an alliance of friars and Andean lords arguing for a strong native participation in political affairs faced the idea of a medieval-style order in which Spanish conquistadors-turned-lords would rule over their Indian vassals. The conflict was not settled in practice until the government of the Viceroy Francisco de Toledo (1569–81), which chose a third path neither side liked much: to strengthen state control. By the late sixteenth century, colonial rule had settled in the form of a two-republics system that defined the rights of Indigenous peoples and their obligations toward Spaniards in recognition of their civilizing task.

There is no question that Garcilaso and Guaman Poma were well aware of the fact that Spaniards held contrasting ideas about the colonial enterprise and valued precolonial civilizational achievements differently—and they framed their positions accordingly. However, I will argue in this chapter that what mattered the most to these two activist intellectuals—and to the larger group of Indigenous thinkers of which they were but two visible exponents— was what Spaniards thought that Indians could think. Despite their strong disagreements about mostly any colonial matter related to Indians, Spaniards agreed that Indians' limited mental prowess, their material intelligence, was what made native actors "Indians." Indians were material creatures, incapable of abstraction; Spaniards in contrast were airy, the masters of abstraction. The metaphors used to explain this condition were often visual—Indians could look but not see, unlike Spaniards. And equally, if not more importantly, while the former did not know that they did not know, the latter were aware of the former's double ignorance.

These ideas grounded the Spaniards' certainty of superiority over Indians. Colonial normalcy was contingent on having all parties acquiesce to them. That is why examining how these ideas played out in everyday arenas offers a window into the fledgling forms of early colonial whiteness and the ways in which the latter constrained both Spaniards and Indians. To flesh out these Spanish ideas about how Indians thought, I will begin by studying debates about conversion in the Andes in the second half of the sixteenth century. Then, I will explore texts written by laymen, showing the life these ideas had on an array of issues, including those as far removed from conversion as love and painting. Lastly, I will finish with brief examples of the impact of these ideas on royal and church policies as they were shaping in the early 1600s.

KNOWLEDGE, ABSTRACTION, AND AGENCY

Colonial arguments about conversion matter because conversion played a key role in Spanish justifications of the conquest—and therefore set much of the stage in which native actors lived and because they silenced Amerindians' knowledges and ultimately led to their repression. But they are also important because theology played a crucial role in Spanish discourses about Indians at large, regardless of whether they were religious or lay, whether they were sympathetic or unsympathetic to Indians, and the actual content of the discussions. As clergymen were often scholars, they had the capacity to make explicit the fundaments upon which common Spanish ideas about Indians rested—fundaments that are otherwise hard to grasp.

Studies of the religious dynamics in colonial Latin America often distinguish what are called the first and the second evangelization (e.g., Alberro 1994; Estenssoro 2003; MacCormack 1985; Rabassa 1993). Members of the so-called first evangelization are commonly characterized as arguing for a humanistic approach to the conversion of the Indigenous population and seen as sympathetic to Indians. Behind the religious beliefs and practices that preexisted the Spanish arrival, they saw expressions of man's universal search for God. They therefore considered Indian-Christian similarities as positive elements on which to build the Christian project. Often associated with the school of Salamanca, its most vocal and fullest theological and political expression is to be found in the prolific and widely influential work of the Dominican Bartolomé de Las Casas. This conception of the conversion process, scholars argue, contrasted with the more intolerant spirit of a second evangelization that saw the hand of the devil behind native religious practices and beliefs. This group was therefore extremely suspicious of any Christian-Indian similarities and actively sought to identify and extirpate—often by resorting to institutionalized violence—any traces of the old in the new. An important figure of this second theological and political current is the Jesuit José de Acosta, author of two highly influential books, *De procuranda Indorum salute* (How to provide for the salvation of the Indians) (1588) and the *Historia natural y moral de las Indias* (*Natural and Moral History of the Indies*) (1590).

While the terminology used to distinguish both schools of thinking about conversion suggests a temporal sequence, this is misleading. On the one hand, expressions of both ways of thinking coexisted during the entire colonial period; on the other, their preponderance fluctuated historically and geographically. In the Mexican case, scholars argue that a political shift from the first set of ideas about conversion to the second took place quite early, in the first years after the Spanish arrival; in the Andes, scholars suggest the process took longer and was more gradual. Some see early manifestations of the second evangelization in the 1567 Second Ecclesiastical Council of Lima archbishopric, some thirty-five years after the conquest. Most agree that the second evangelization got the upper hand toward 1583, when the influential Third Ecclesiastical Council of Lima fully adjusted local church doctrine to the resolutions of the Council of Trent (1545–63).

Distinguishing the first and second evangelization corrects simplistic understandings of the Spanish conversion project—it was far more complex than burning idols and repressing Indigenous religious ideas. However, the distinction can also hide their fundamental coincidences. There was something all Spanish colonial thinkers shared—regardless of the affiliation of their theological and/or political agendas, first and second evangelization included—which in turn was central to Indigenous understandings of the colonial order of things. It was an agreement on how to think about Indians, how they thought, and why. This way of conceiving Indians was expressed most often in terms of vision or sight. Since vision (a synonym of how one interprets reality) could not be accessed by a third person, Spaniards relied on language as proxy—what a person could say allowed access to what they could see and therefore know about the world. The key questions in the Spaniards' cognitive map about Indians were how reality was conceived, who could see what, and why. In all cases, it was clearly known that Spaniards both had a more sophisticated understanding of reality than Indians had and could see more of its complexities than Indians could for reasons having to do with theology and history.

This way of thinking about Indians worked on colonial relations like a two-headed monster. One head anchored meanings—it determined the meaning of what was there to be seen in reality. The other head hid meanings—it shrouded other ways of making sense of what existed or what was there to be seen. While Spaniards were aware of the works of the first head—and in fact were proud of them since they proved the superiority of their senses and mind over those of Indians—they were largely in denial about those of the second. And this was only logical given that, according to Spaniards, there was nothing to hide—what Spaniards were able to see was all there was to see.[2] What Indians saw was a defective, distorted image of what was there to be seen. Acknowledging the hiding would have implied that things existed that Spaniards could not see but others could, unsettling colonial hierarchies to the core.

As I will show down the road, this largely unspoken, double-sided, and denied agreement was a central concern as much to Indigenous thinkers like Garcilaso de la Vega and Guaman Poma de Ayala as it was to ordinary Indigenous actors. They all felt the discrimination that grounded this agreement and at the same time found in it a critical means with which to figuratively jump over the maze that the different Spanish feelings toward and political programs for Indians produced—the simplicity of abstraction. I begin my task by examining the questions of vision and abstraction in three paradigmatic texts penned by clergymen: Santo Tomás's 1560 *Grammatica o arte de la lengua general de los indios de los reynos del Peru*, Bartolomé Alvarez's 1588 *De las costumbres y conversión de los indios del Perú*, and José de Acosta's 1590 *Historia natural y moral de las Indias*. These texts showcase the range of colonialist theological and political views of Indians: the first two represent its extremes while the last one attempts to strike a balance, borrowing and mixing elements from both poles.

THE FRIENDS OF THE INDIANS: THE INDIAN AS A CHILD

Santo Tomás authored two important colonial books published in Valladolid in 1560: the *Lexicon o Vocabulario de la lengua general del Peru* and the *Grammatica o arte de la lengua general de los indios de los reynos del Peru*—respectively, the first bilingual dictionary and the first grammatical study of colonial Quechua, the language of the Inca imperial administration. Some scholars have seen in these landmark works valuable sources to study both the first attempts at finding equivalences between Spanish and Indigenous ideas and a variety of Quechua that no longer exists.[3] Other scholars have been interested in these texts for reasons more removed from their purely linguistic value—they see them as examples of the first evangelization in the Andes. The *Lexicon* and the *Grammatica* show that Santo Tomás argued for building the Spanish colony on Indigenous institutions and in particular for using Indigenous religious beliefs and practices to further the conversion of the Indigenous population (MacCormack 1985). In fact, he actively supported Andean ethnic lords' political struggle against conquerors.[4] According to this way of casting the texts, Santo Tomás's political position looks certainly more positive than that of those who saw in the same beliefs and practices the devil's hand and advocated for their elimination.

Santo Tomás stated the goal of his *Grammatica* in its oft-quoted prologue—there he tells the king that he has written the book "so that through it you see *very clearly and manifestly* how false it is what many have tried to persuade you about, that the naturals of those kingdoms of Peru are barbarians" ("para que por él *veáis muy clara y manifiestamente* quán falso es lo que muchos os han querido persuadir ser los naturales de los reynos del Perú bárbaros") ([*1560*] 1995, fol. 5, 8; emphasis mine). He would show that not only were Peruvians not so but instead were people with much *policia* (urban civility) and *orden* (order)—classic first evangelization ideas. To prove this, he reduced colonial Quechua to its principles and showed that they conformed closely to those of Latin and Spanish. This would enable the king to "see very clearly and manifestly" that native peoples were not barbarians because, if a language had police and order, so did the people who spoke it: "Since, according to the philosopher, in many places no other thing shows better man's ingenuity than the word and language he uses, which is the delivery of the concepts of understanding" (Santo Tomás [*1560*] 1995, fol. 6, 9).[5] The first part of the quote referred to a passage from Aristotle's *Politics* in which "the philosopher" identifies speech as the characteristic that sets man apart from animals and was therefore proof of the fact that man is by nature a "political animal" whose final end is social—a goal toward which peoples evolve as their social complexity increases through time.[6] The second part of the quote refers to an idea well established at the time the *Grammatica* was written: that words followed concepts. That is why they are the latter's *parto* (delivery)—which refers both to the product of the delivery and to the situation when concepts come to light—conveying that what is previously inaccessible, in the dark or hidden, ceases to be so. (In Spanish, "to give birth" is *dar a luz,* or literally "to bring to light.")

In other words, Santo Tomás argued that language (words and grammar) could be used as a proxy (a tangible reflection of the intangible) for what people think exists, or what they are able to see, in the world around them. In particular, words would tell of the concepts or lack thereof among a given people while grammar would tell of the rational order of the relations between those concepts. This explains why the Spanish king would be able "to see" how Andean Indians truly were by learning about the vocabulary and principles of their language.

Today these ideas would be part of the philosophy of language; in sixteenth-century Spain, they belonged to a scholarly province of certain thinkers called *modistae* (speculative grammarians). Their theories were the result of a long tradition of Greek, Roman, and scholastic ideas that shaped Spanish understandings of their interactions with Indians, regardless of whether linguistic or not. The concepts/word binary, including the stated primacy of concepts over words, were part of a larger binary conception with major philosophical and theological history and significance—it distinguished the really real (the unchanging, essential, and universal reality that responds to the absolute order of the *logos*, accessible only to the intellect) from the accidentally real (all changing, superficial, and particular realities, readily accessible to the senses and always different from the absolute). Plato's "ideas," Aristotle's "absolute categories," Augustine's "inner language," and Aquinas'"mental language" distinguished and privileged the intellectual over sensory experience and implied a relationship between the structure of reality, known to the mind first, with its best or worst reflection in particular tongues (Breva Claramonte 2008a, 2008b; Law 2003).

The ideal relation would be one of absolute correspondence—a one-to-one match between the really real and the accidentally real. In turn, the perfect tongue would be the one whose rationality and expressivity would best reflect or mimic the true order of things. That was, according to some thinkers, what had characterized the Adamic or natural language. Due to man's troubled history, that language had been lost and with it the one-to-one relationship between the human order of things and the really real one; however, not all (post-Fall) languages were equal. Some were deemed more rational and expressive than others. Following Aristotle, the most perfect language had to be spoken by the most socially and intellectually advanced peoples—those who could see most of what existed in reality and could express it best. In the sixteenth century, the honor went to Christians and Latin and to some extent to Spaniards and Spanish, which was thought to have retained much of Latin's excellence.[7]

The existence of a readily available version of the canon made it easy to tell whether other languages conformed to it—which allowed an intellectual like Santo Tomás to make an argument like the one just considered in his Prologue—and it also made it easy to tell when they did not. This point takes me to other parts of Santo Tomás's text. After having extensively laid out the regularity of Quechua and proved that it conformed to Latin—and thus having affirmed that Peru's native peoples were not barbarians but civilized peoples with much order—in chapter 23 of the *Grammatica*, Santo Tomás told that he thought it *a propósito* (convenient) to address in some detail some *términos particulares* (particular terms) that Indians used—terms that, due to the space constraints of a bilingual dictionary, he could not properly explain in his *Vocabulario*.[8] By calling them "particular," Santo Tomás signaled that these terms escaped the overall rule—they were not universal as Latin ones were. They therefore undermined his thesis that Quechua was equivalent to Spanish and consequently that Indians were not barbarians but civilized peoples. What was the function of a chapter highlighting the differences between Quechua, Latin, and Spanish in a book designed to stress their similarities? I suggest that it allowed the Dominican friar to both direct interpretive traffic by presenting his own explanation of the particular (how and why at times Quechua deviated from the universal canon) and make his political pitch. Both were in fact inextricably linked.

The first case of términos particulares—and the one treated in most detail—discusses how Indians swear. Santo Tomás stated that prior to the Spanish arrival, Indians swore with a *juramento execratorio* (like "a bad death shall I die" ["*mala muerte muera*"] or "shall the earth eat me" ["*cómame la tierra*"]) instead of invoking a witness like Christians do (with expressions like "I swear to God" ["*por dios*"] or "I swear to the Virgin" ["*por la virgen*"]). Such was the case because "since the Indians did not know the true God, nor the saints, they could not invoke them as witnesses" ("como los indios no conosçían al Dios verdadero, ni a los sanctos, no los podían traer por testigos") (Santo Tomás [*1560*] 1995, fol. 67v, 139). And the Dominican went on to note that Indians did not swear to their gods (idols) or to the devil because, although God was mad at Indians because they adored idols and even the devil, God still had his limits—he was not willing to allow "to invoke the father of all lies as witness of the truth" ("que truxessen al padre de mentiras por testigo de verdad") ([*1560*] 1995, fol. 67v, 139), which implies that God was not all that mad at Indians, something that will prove important down the road.

Things had changed some since the Spanish arrival, Santo Tomás continued. Some Indians had adopted the Christian way of swearing "and some even believe that to swear properly is to be a good Christian" ("y aún hay algunos que creen que jurar bien es ser buen christiano") (Santo Tomás [*1560*] 1995, fol. 68, 139). And he then gave an actual example of it (which I succinctly presented in the Introduction and will examine in detail now): "Asking once in a given province a cacique whether he was Christian, he told me: 'not yet, but I am beginning to.' And as I asked him what he knew of being Christian, he told me: 'I know to swear to God, and to play cards a little bit, and I am beginning to steal'" (Santo Tomás [*1560*] 1995, fol. 68, 140).[9] To this extraordinary exchange followed an also noteworthy explanation: "As I understood it, that sinner had to think that, in the same way that there was nothing else to being a tailor than what they see tailors do, which is to sew, and the same happens in other trades, he thus thought that there was nothing else to being Christian than what they had commonly seen Christians do" (Santo Tomás [*1560*] 1995, fol. 68, 140).[10] The dialogue and its explanation encapsulate much of what I want to address (and, I suggest, of what Guaman Poma and Garcilaso wanted to as well). I will first break down the passage, examining how Santo Tomás anchored its many meanings (or tried to) and then what he hid (or tried to) and conclude with a study of the cacique's response to both things.

To begin, before reading the dialogue and its explanation, readers already knew that the Indian's response would be an example of failure, of what Indians got wrong about being Christian (they believed that something that was not true was so). Readers also knew that to assess what Indians got wrong, the example would focus not on observable traits or what Indians did but on what they could think—more precisely, on what they were incapable of thinking.[11] That is, Santo Tomás's comment about the cacique's answer was not about its content but about what the latter told about what Indians could think. The friar reduced the dialogue to an example of Indian conceptual lack. Because they did not know that there was much more behind being Christian than there was behind being a tailor, Indians confused what they saw Christians *do* with what it *was* to be Christian. Their sight—which provided them with information from the sensory world—was constrained by their limited *conocimiento* (knowledge) of reality. That is why—unlike the Spanish king who, after having read Santo Tomás's *Grammatica* and *Vocabulario*, would have been able to "see very clearly and manifestly" Indians as they truly were—Indians could look but they could not actually see. And to make matters worse, they did not know that they could not know it.

By the same token, Santo Tomás's comment hid other possible meanings of the exchange. Although brief, the cacique's answer was quite complex—it involved a double move and worked at two levels. It is double because it addressed at once the substance of the question (knowledge about what it was to be Christian) and the politically loaded libidinal energies behind it—the request for a confirmation of Santo Tomás's position as knower and benevolent father. It worked at two levels because it played (masterfully, it seems to me) with the uncertainty between the literal and the ironic. In what concerns the substance, if taken literally—as Santo Tomás did—the cacique's answer was proof that Indians lacked the capacity to distinguish the example in front of their eyes from the system behind it because they did not know the latter. They therefore reached wrong conclusions—as if the cacique *had* actually been confused by the bad example. If read with a bit of irony (and very little was needed), the answer turned Santo Tomás's question about whether he *was* or *was not* Christian into a politically loaded comment about *what it was to be so*. The same holds true in what concerns the emotions behind the way in which the question was posed—it at once confirmed and dodged the assumption of ignorance implicit in the question (Indians cannot think well), upholding and rejecting the subject position the interpellation offered. If read literally, the answer lent itself to Santo Tomás's hailing act; if read ironically, the result was the exact opposite.

Vis-à-vis this ambivalence, more can be said about Santo Tomás's comment, its anchoring, and its hiding: it ensured that the cacique's answer functioned as a good example of what he was arguing at a political level. Proponents of the first evangelization cast Indians as meek and simple—innocent beings whose purity was ruined by the Spaniards nefarious influences. This demanded that Indians be two-dimensional fellows, people who could not think in abstract terms, either unrecognizing or disavowing their actual abstract thinking (choices that correspond to whiteness as "a state of mind" or "a moral choice"). In this case, irony, as a form of double-layered meaning (and therefore an exercise of abstraction), had to be flattened out. Had Santo Tomás considered an ironic reading, not only would Indians have ceased to be good material on which to build Christianity—they would have been an unstable, slippery quantity—but the heuristic model of correspondence at large would have failed with numerous consequences over how history in general and colonial superiority in particular were explained. It would have meant that there was more to be said about language and reality than Spaniards conceived or were willing to concede. The flattening was also necessary in emotional terms. Irony would have made plain the libidinal game that required of Indians a narrative confirming white superiority. It would have frustrated the friar's expectation of being seen as a benevolent and understanding father, exposing instead the true nature of the dialogue—a staged exchange in which two parties performed, although only one of them was aware of it.

Against what a pessimistic reading of the exchange between the friar and the cacique would suggest, it should be noted that the result of Santo Tomás's multilayered attempts to control meanings and emotions was very peculiar. On the one hand, the cacique's abstraction (his wit and quick conceptual moves) was ignored or remained unacknowledged. On the other hand, he could have a good laugh at the Christians' expense and despair at once because it was really the latter who looked but could not see—and did not know that they did not know it. This décalage was, in a nutshell, the organizing principle of colonial relations—and its complexities and embodiments the target of Guaman Poma's and Garcilaso's works.

The final part of Santo Tomás's analysis of the dialogue shows how he related Indian knowledge to awareness and agency. The Dominican offered the following coda to his take on the exchange: "I will not leave unmentioned here something to the great confusion of the bad Christians, and it is that to curse or blaspheme what they falsely held to be God . . . [the Indians] did not have terms, and not only did not have them, but it did not even cross their imagination such great irreverence and wickedness . . . but with much reverence and fear they put in their mouths the names of the things they held to be gods" (Santo Tomás [*1560*] 1995, fol. 68v, 140).[12] The goal of the passage was to shame Christians by highlighting precolonial Indian religiosity which, even if directed to the wrong target, exceeded that of Spaniards. Indians did not blaspheme, Christians did. The latter should be "confused" because, although Indians knew less and therefore saw less, they did the right thing and had the right attitude toward the divine.

The didactic point was consistent with the idea from the first evangelization that Spaniards could foster conversion by tapping into the potential for continuity by building on what preexisted. Unlike most Christians in the Andes, Indians already had faith and the proper attitude toward the divine—they just needed help redirecting their beliefs to the true object. This observation fit the usual portrayal of the first evangelization and so did the moral lesson to be learned from it. What I want to highlight, however, is that the moral lesson built on a definitive and *very* important distinction: *a "bad Christian" was so knowingly*. Unlike the cacique, a bad Christian did not mistake the wrongdoings of the tailor with what it was to be a tailor. He was aware of the true context of his existence, of the conceptual map of the world. A bad Christian knew what he ought to do and that he was deviating while an Indian did not. Like Adam and Eve before the apple, the latter did not know that he was naked. That is why a Spaniard could *be* a bad Christian while the question about an Indian was whether he *was* or *was not* a Christian—not if he was a good or a bad one (and also why throughout the text the ubiquitous opposition is Indians and Christians, not Indians and Spaniards). That is also why Spaniards' behavior (to be a good or bad example) was so important to thinkers of the first evangelization.

This analysis leads to four corollaries whose relevance to Guaman Poma and Garcilaso will be clear down the road. First, agency was dependent on knowledge and abstraction and vice versa. In the case of Christians, there was agency because they knew—they chose to be either bad or good. In the case of Indians, there was none—they just existed. The cacique did not choose to be anything—he just expressed what he was. If anything, his culture chose for him. There was no such thing as Indian abstraction or awareness. For him to be able to choose and thus to express agency, he would have had to know. Second, the fact that Spaniards could make the necessary distinctions, telling right from wrong, concrete from abstract, mattered more than whether they acted on that knowledge. The explicit didactic point, what Spaniards had to learn from the example, was that although Indians could not think well and knew much less than Spaniards did, they did not dare show irreverence—they neither blasphemed nor lied when they swore. The implicit assumption—that which went without saying—was that, at the end of the day, this difference did not alter the political hierarchy. The ultimate problem was knowing, not doing. Third, in Santo Tomás's texts (as in all cases of the detrimental defense), Indians were exculpated from their deficiencies at the very high price of being inferior, incomplete human beings. To be innocent, good material, and straight salvage- able, Indians had to be flat. Fourth, and last but not least, from an Indian's point of view, the colonial world was upside down—they had to talk to blind, ignorant men who, to make matters worse, thought that they were the ones who could really see while Indians could not. This double-blind was, I argue, what laid at the heart of coloniality, the principle organizing colonial relations.

In what other ways did Spaniards explain (away) the particularities that existed in the Andes during those years? I turn now to an exponent at the other end of the political and theological spectrum to start answering this question. This second paradigmatic example will make clear that first and second evan- gelization thinkers were entirely at odds and yet in total agreement—those on the opposite side, those who considered Indians the devil's children, shared the same ideas about what Indians could think.

THE FOES OF THE INDIANS: THE INDIAN AS DEVIL

Relatively little is known about Bartolomé Alvarez, *cura de indios* (priest of Indians) in the repartimiento of Aullagas (today's Bolivia), who in 1588 finished a memorial addressed to the Spanish king titled *De las costumbres y conversión de los indios del Perú: Memorial a Felipe II* (Of the costumes and conversion of Peru's Indians: Memorial to Philip II).[13] The text presents a negative view of Indians that went far beyond the second evangelization's reservations about the first evangelization's ideas. I will begin my analysis of the *Memorial* by fleshing out Alvarez's position, stressing his differences with Santo Tomás. I will then show that, in spite of their adversarial positions, Alvarez fished elements from the same pool as Santo Tomás (as we will see, Acosta, too) and, more importantly, shared the same underlying grammar of difference—at the end of the day, the Indian nature boiled down to the mental limitations of two-dimensional beings.

Alvarez's memorial presented a twofold scathing critique of the methods and state of the conversion enterprise in the Andes up to 1588. On the one hand, he criticized the institutions of the colonial church and vocally despised the work of the first evangelization. On the other, he stated that not only were Indians not Christians and ignorant of what it meant to be so (with which Santo Tomás would have concurred) but they were also essentially evil, deceitful people who faked their Christianness. Indians were not "poor ignorant things" ("pobrecitos ignorantes") (Alvarez [1588] 1998, 164) as pro-Indians had it—rather, they were "perverse and wicked" ("perversos y malignos") and "hypocrites, deceivers and liars by nature" ("de natural condición hipócritas, engañadores y mentirosos") (Alvarez [1588] 1998, 367); they said one thing and meant another, had neither faith nor the right attitude—definitely not Santo Tomás's territory.

Alvarez offered two reasons why Indians were the way they were (and would not change). To begin, there were historical reasons involving supernatural agents: Indians were as they were because of God's anger. Unlike Santo Tomás, Alvarez stated that God *aborrece* (abhors) Indians for their original sin and their repeated sins that followed and allowed them to grow ever more perverse so that "in them cannot be engrafted a sapling that would fructify" ("en ellos no se pueda injerir algún pimpollo que dé verdadero fruto") (Alvarez [1588] 1998, 73). God not only abhorred them but he also let the devil rule the Andes. The devil in turn had been a good master. He had taught Indians much—in particular his specialty: the art of deception. The consequence of this double problem (God's despising and the devil's rule) was twofold. First, Indians were inclined to do bad things and unable to do good ones—"the liveliness of their desire to do bad deeds persuades them, and to do good deeds, they are clumsier than the mole faced with the light" ("la viveza del deseo de lo hacer mal los inclina; y para el bien, son más torpes que el topo sacado a luz") (Alvarez [1588] 1998, 72). Second, no matter how hard missionaries tried, Indians did not want to learn.

The situation was unlikely to change by extraordinary means, Alvarez argued, because Indians were not faithful to anything. They erred not on the basis of honest belief, like Paul did, but because of malice and stubbornness; thus, God would not intervene to make them change their minds as he had done with Paul's (Alvarez [1588] 1998, 73).

While Alvarez's aforementioned reasons for why Indians were as they were and would not change were clearly at odds with those of Santo Tomás's, that was not the case when it came to the secular reasons he gave. First, he remarked on the insufficiency of Indian languages. Because Indians had no terms to talk about things related to the faith (e.g., *fe, esperanza, creer, alma* [faith, hope, to believe, soul]), they not could signify those things and were therefore incapable of understanding them (Alvarez [1588] 1998, 144).[14] Second, Alvarez noted their lack of *ciencia* (science) about any matter, be it human, moral, or natural. Indians neither could provide explanations for anything they did (they acted mechanically) nor were they interested in knowledge (they did not inquire, show curiosity, or desire to think). To make matters worse, *los antiguos* (their ancestors) mandated "that they always do what they have seen them do" ("que hiciesen siempre las cosas que les habían visto hacer") (Alvarez [1588] 1998, 144). Third and last, the little that they did know was "so material that it does not lift one bit from the dust of the earth" ("tan material que no se levanta un punto del polvo de la tierra") (Alvarez [1588] 1998, 144). For instance, they knew the moon, the sun, and the stars "because they saw them, and adored them as things capable of doing something" ("porque los veían, y los adoraban como cosas que podían algo") (Alvarez [1588] 1998, 147), but they knew nothing about these celestial bodies' movement, matter, essence, or creation, and even less about the number of skies these bodies inhabited. In short, among Indians there was neither the capacity nor the will for abstraction. These reasons kept Indians in their *perse-verante dureza* (persevering steadfastness)—"specially, with their visible huacas' material example, because seeing them and deluding each other . . . and neither believing nor having science or intelligence but about things they can see, they cannot come to know the truth through the terms and doctrine used to teach them. Because their entire signification is of intelligible spiritual things, and it is a tough job to persuade them to believe it, because their intelligence is fully material" (Alvarez [1588] 1998, 148).[15]

For Alvarez as much as for Santo Tomás, the Indians' world was two-dimensional. It consisted only of what was readily visible. Their sight could not elevate or detach itself from the concrete or transcend what was in front of their eyes. Also, like the Dominican friar, Alvarez gave a rich ethnographic example of the Indians' incapacity to see beyond the material, adding angles of their colonial predicament: "A soldier, traveling the sea in a raft two Indians were rowing, asked them, saying: 'At sundown, tell me, where does the sun go?' They said: 'it goes where God is, to complain in our name, because you treat us badly.' And the Spaniard asked: 'well, where is God?' They said: 'there, where you come from, don't you say that God is there? Well, he goes there, to tell that the English should come and kill you all, so that you will leave as alone and not treat us badly'" (Alvarez [1588] 1998, 148).[16] The soldier's goal was didactic—to face Indians with the limits of their own thinking (if there was any with which to begin), cracking an opening into a more complex conception of the world. His first question was about geography, astronomy, and probably theology. He intended to confront the rowers of his boat with the idea that the sun was a star that circled the earth, an object in space with no agency or will of its own. In turn, Alvarez's goal in retelling the story was to illustrate how helpless (and vain) the soldier's intention had been—there was no cracking. For the many reasons he had stated all along, Indians did not change, and on top of that, they focused their energies on deceiving or mocking. Their master had taught them well.

As in the case of Santo Tomás's dialogue, Alvarez's proposed reading of the dialogue anchored as much as it hid. And as in the previous case, the Indians' response could have two readings—it could confirm the Spaniards' expectations or it could challenge them entirely. The first reading would conclude that Indians could not think abstractly—they pretended to engage and answer the soldier's question but really did not. The second reading would turn the question about geographic theological abstraction into one of geographic political abstraction: 'We know what the sun does at night; it goes to the other side of the world and presents God with our grievances.' The answer was clearly full of irony, but on top of that, it was anything but the result of someone who was not interested in science or knowledge. For one thing, the sun had an intercessory role—exactly what Christians said in general about creatures that were superior to men and inferior to God. Also, it implied an answer to the question of why one could not see the sun at night: it was on the other side of the world. Quite abstract. Then, it is worth noting that the Indians' answer showed not pretending but "honest beliefs" like Paul's. It revealed that the deeper problem at hand was that Indigenous beliefs escaped the Spaniard's frame—the rowers' answer was not a belief about, or a faithfulness to, a being or beings but a belief about a social condition and a faithfulness to a practice, about coloniality and undoing it by proposing an honest conversation without masks or scripts. Finally, as in the case of Santo Tomás's curaca, the soldier's rowers tackled the libidinal energies behind the exchange. The setting could not have been more colonial: the white man asking the native rowers questions while they are rowing and he is—it would fit well—smoking a pipe. The expectation was that their answer would confirm intellectually what was already known—they were inferior; that is why they were rowing and he was pondering. As in the case of the curaca, the answer accepted two readings. If read literally, it confirmed the expectations—Indians were hopeless fools; if read with a bit of irony, it flipped them upside down.

The soldier's second question tried to reinstate the theological-political frame, probably because the rowers' answer did not deliver an acknowledgment of ignorance. Instead, it implied something that was not in the question's conceptual horizon—that it made sense to say that God was somewhere in particular. Thus, "And where is God?" intended to face the Indians (while they continued to row) with the nonsense of their first answer and thus have them realize their folly. However, the rowers' answer doubled the bid and faced the Spanish soldier with the limits of his own imagination: 'God is where you come from, in Castile, that is what you say all the time—he has abandoned us because he hates us for our sins, and the devil runs amok here.' Once it is clear why the location of God was knowable, the icing on the cake was to explain why the sun went to him every night—to ask God to send the English (who are with God) to come and kill the Spaniards.[17] Politics and theology went hand in hand. Quite abstract, again. And yet, like in Santo Tomás's case, the dialogue was presented as an example of Indians' lack of knowledge, abstraction, engagement, self-awareness, and reflexivity—and an abundance of material intelligence.

If there were clear coincidences between both poles of the spectrum in what concerned the Indians' nature, something similar can be said when it came to assessing the effect of the Spanish arrival. Indians had not changed—they could and had no will to—but the Spanish presence had had bad results: Spaniards terminated Inca order, which had kept Indians' sins in check, and had given them liberty, which had only helped deteriorate further their already wicked nature (Alvarez [1588] 1998, 243–45). To make matters worse, since ecclesiastic sympathizers of the "poor Indians" tended to side with the latter whenever they complained against priests, undermining the latter's dignity, they fed the Indians' dismissive attitude toward God (Alvarez [1588] 1998, 239). That is why, Alvarez summed up, the Spanish presence had turned the world al revés (upside down)—before, order and authority prevailed; now, sins and licentiousness, supported by the powers that be, fed Indian decay (Alvarez [1588] 1998, 239). The only way forward, if it could be called so, was to give priests the power to punish Indians and prevent them from doing *hacer el mal* (bad deeds). *Hacer el bien* (to do good deeds) was not on Alvarez's table—Indians did not know what a good deed was and had no interest in knowing it, and as theology dictated, doing good deeds was a matter of knowledge and will.

In summary, according to both Alvarez and Santo Tomás, Indians were unable to think—being creatures that lived close to the ground, they were incapable of abstraction. Likewise, while Indians in Alvarez's memorial may seem to be a bit more agentive than in Santo Tomás's portrayal—at least they could lie—they still had no real agency; in both cases they did what they did because it was the only thing they knew, not because they knew that different options existed and chose which course of action to take. Accordingly, any attempt by Indians to refute Spanish ideas about them went unnoticed or unacknowledged and was even presented as an example of Indian limitation. The only real difference in these two bitter enemies' presentation of Indians was the value they assigned to Indian nature: for Santo Tomás it was good while for Alvarez it was bad. The fact that the coincidences far outweighed the differences suggests that it should not have been difficult to strike a balance, to somehow meet both positions halfway. That was, in fact, the plan of the second evangelization's main figure, the Jesuit José de Acosta.

THE COMPROMISE: THE INDIAN AS HALF-DEVIL AND HALF-CHILD

Scholars often see José de Acosta as a key to understanding the shift from the first to the second evangelization that took place in Peru around the 1580s. Acosta was the main figure behind the 1583 Third Ecclesiastical Council of Lima and also penned two very influential books in the following years: one published in Latin for experts, the *De procuranda Indorum salute* (1588), and one published in Spanish for the general public, the *Historia natural y moral de las Indias* (1590). While it may be true that Acosta was the main figure, it is also clear that Santo Tomás and Acosta were not on the opposite poles of the theological and political arc as it is often implicitly suggested. Rather, the influential Jesuit was in the center of the arc, halfway between Santo Tomás and Alvarez. His texts tried to reach a compromise, taking elements from both positions and mixing them in original ways. The combination is relevant because of Acosta's influence and is therefore indispensable for understanding Garcilaso's and Guaman Poma's works. It is also revealing because, at the end of the day, it relied on the same assumptions the *Grammatica* and the *Memorial* did.

In his widely read *Historia natural y moral de las Indias*, published in Seville in 1590, Acosta struck a balance when describing the Americas before the Spanish arrival: Indians had been ruled by the devil and had engaged in all sorts of idolatrous acts and yet Inca rule had been in accordance with natural reason and in fact had given Indians the best kind of order they could have. In what concerns pre-Columbian Amerindian religions (the object of book V), the exposition followed a pattern that systematically undermined the first evangelization's idea of continuity. As he examined Indian religious practices and beliefs, Acosta pointed out the similarity with Christian ones and attributed the resemblances to the devil's agency. The idea was supported by a specific distribution of supernatural agents—the Americas had been the devil's land, his "final refuge" ("último refugio") after having been kicked out of "the largest and most noble part of the world" ("de la mayor y más noble parte del mundo") (Acosta [*1590*] 2002, bk. V, chap. 1, 300). True to his modus operandi, the devil had imitated God, mocking him in all possible ways, and had tricked Indians into all sorts of idolatries. Indians, particularly deceivable because of their lack of knowledge ("in addition to the supernatural light they lacked philosophy and natural doctrine" ["fuera de la luz sobrenatural, les faltó también la filosofía y doctrina natural"] [Acosta [*1590*] 2002, bk V, chap. 1, 300]) were thus rendered *ciegos* (blind). When it came to social and moral matters, however, Acosta presented Inca rule as having been good for Indians—in fact, it had been ideal considering their nature—and devoted several chapters of book VI to describe it in detail.

While so far Acosta's ideas largely align with Alvarez's and counter Santo Tomás's, there is a discrepancy that tilts the scales: Acosta saw behind Inca rule the strength of *luz natural* (natural light)—a key concept for thinkers of the first evangelization. Thus, unlike the Aullagas' priest, he concluded that Indians "have the natural capacity to be well taught, and they even are ahead of many of our republics" ("tienen natural capacidad para ser bien enseñados, y aún en gran parte hacen ventaja a muchas de nuestras repúblicas") (Acosta [*1590*] 2002, bk. VI, chap. 1, 373). They were perfectly capable of receiving the truth and their errors were not unchangeable expressions of their obstinate resistance to Christianity but instead *niñerías* (childish follies)—wild ideas that could be turned into pedagogic opportunities. If the devil *engaña* (tricks) Indians, then Christians should *desengañar* (un-trick) them. The method was simple: use reason because "it is something to ponder how subject they are to who makes them listen to reason" ("es cosa de ponderar cuán sujetos está a quien los pone en razón") (Acosta [*1590*] 2002, bk. VI, chap. 1, 373).

To drive the point home, the Jesuit friar presented an ethnographic example that brings out other angles of colonial relations in which Indians were asked to satisfy Spanish ideas about Indians. A captain "and good Christian," Acosta told, employed the following argument to persuade a cacique that the sun was not God but its servant. He asked the cacique for an Indian to carry a letter. As the cacique provided the messenger, the captain asked the cacique who was master, the Indian or the cacique, to which the latter responded, "Me, without any doubt, because he does not do but what I tell him to" ("Yo, sin ninguna duda, porque aquél no hace más de lo que yo le mando"). The captain then pointed out that the same happened "between that sun that we see, and the Creator of everything . . . You will thus see how it is contrary to reason and false to honor the sun when it is the Creator and lord of everything who should be honored" ("entre ese sol que vemos, y el Creador de todo . . . Así veréis cómo es sin razón y engaño dar al sol la honra que se le debe a su Creador y señor de todo"). All Indians present assented to the reasoning and "said the cacique and the Indians . . . that it was a great truth and that they had taken much pleasure from learning it" ("dijo el cacique y los indios . . . que era gran verdad, y que se habían holgado mucho de entenderla") (Acosta [*1590*] 2002, bk. V, chap. 5, 309). Acosta closed the anecdote: "And if with gentle reasons and that can be perceived, their falsehood and blindness are made clear to them, they admirably are persuaded and surrender to the truth" ("Y si con razones suaves y que se dejen percibir, les declaran a los indios sus engaños y cegueras, admirablemente se convencen y rinden a la verdad") (Acosta, [*1590*] 2002, bk. V, chap. 5, 310).

As in the two previous cases, those offered by Alvarez and Santo Tomás, the proposed reading of the ethnographic dialogue anchored as much as it hid. The anchoring turned the anecdote into an example of the argument: the Indians' limited rational capacity and lack of agency and abstraction were not obstacles for the ultimate triumph of natural light. All that was needed was a good, simple explanation and a good master. Indians could not see for themselves what they should; because of this, they stuck to the visible (the sun) and did not go higher. To go beyond the visible, they needed a helping hand like children. That is why having good masters who could teach Indians well and lead them with their good example was the central argument of Acosta's extensive Latin treatise on Indian conversion, *De procuranda Indorum salute*.

The reading also hid. As in the two previous cases, the Indians' response could have two interpretations—it could confirm the Spaniards' expectations or it could challenge them entirely. The first reading would conclude that the Indians were indeed mesmerized when the truth was revealed to them. Since there was no other argument being made, Spanish logic was confirmed as universal and self-evident. Grateful for being enlightened, the Indians took much pleasure from the explanation. The second reading, which as usual needed a bit of irony to oil the axes, would suggest that Acosta's Indians had learned the lesson of Santo Tomás's curaca and Alvarez's soldier's rowers: there was no use in talking to Spaniards so one may as well just go with the flow. In other words, because they knew it was hopeless to try to explain to Spaniards that things were not the way they imagined them to be, the Indians decided to play Indian—they were ready to assent and be dazzled by the colorful mirrors (they had been so, presumably, since they had met Columbus).[18]

Acosta suggested by no means that the teaching would be easy—in fact, it would require sustained evangelical effort due to the extent to which blindness had become ingrained in the Indians' nature. But the elements grounding his diagnostics were those at play in the first evangelization—natural light was, like with all men, at work among Indians. No one could resist reason and the truth and, consequently, there was no need for divine intervention (as Alvarez claimed) for a change to occur. At the same time, a good example and good teaching were essential, as Santo Tomás argued. Indian nature had been affected by the devil but it could be fixed. To support his idea, Acosta struck a balance between opposing versions of Andean history before the Spanish arrival. On the one hand, God was angry with the Indians because of their sins and this is why he let the devil rule—and justly so (Acosta [1590] 2002, bk. V, chap. 7, 312). However, like in Santo Tomás's writing, God's anger had its limits and was not without a plan. For instance, divine providence explained the favorable timing of the Spanish arrival: Spaniards had arrived once the Incas had conquered all the people of the Andes and thus had established the most effective environment for Spanish colonization—as it happened with the Romans, there was a common language that all could understand and most important of all Indians were used to obeying (Acosta [1590] 2002, bk. VII, chap. 28, 481). Thus, although it may have looked like God had forgotten them, he had not (Acosta [1590] 2002, bk. VII, chap. 28, 482).

While constantly intending to find a middle ground that neither suggested a naïve or direct path (as in the first evangelization) nor an impossible and negative one (as in Alvarez's memorial), Acosta shared with both authors the overall image of the Indians' condition: incapacity to think. For instance, Acosta argued that until the time when "the light and radiance of the Holy Gospel" ("la luz y resplandor del santo Evangelio") finally arrived ([*1590*] 2002, bk. V, 299), Indians had been unable to reach the right conclusions by observing nature and could go no higher than the material world. They adored low creatures believing them to be gods (Acosta [*1590*] 2002, bk. V, chap. 4, 306) and believed in temporal rewards only and in the resurrection of bodies but not of souls. Their language also reflected their mental shortcoming—Indians somehow knew intuitively that a supreme god existed but had no name for him, not even a generic one. The lack of a word, like in Santo Tomás's and Alvarez's texts, was taken to convey the rustic nature of the concept as it existed in the Indians' minds, which was in turn a reflection of the limited development of their mental capacities. Also, like Santo Tomás and Alvarez, Acosta stated the key distinction between knowing and doing—with the aforementioned relevance in terms of agency—and held the former in the highest esteem. For example, after praising the fact that Indians had no greed and lived a frugal life, he commented that for that reason they could be compared to ancient monks but quickly pointed out that Indians did what they did not by choice but by ignorance: "it is true that, if their life style were the result of their choice and not of their nature, we could say that it was a life of great perfection" ("que cierto, si su linaje de vida se tomara por elección y no por costumbre y naturaleza, dijéramos que era vida de gran perfección") ([*1590*] 2002, bk. V, chap. 17, 398).

While not as positive as Santo Tomás and not as negative as Alvarez, the end result of Acosta's text is similar to that of both of them: Indians neither had capacity for abstraction nor agency. If they thought/saw ridiculous things, it was because the devil was behind them; if they thought/saw reasonable things, it was because a good Christian was behind them. By themselves, they did not think/see much. The little good there was in them, like frugality, was there not because they knew otherwise and chose to be good but because that is all they knew—malleable material with which to work but painfully close to the ground.

MATERIAL INTELLIGENCE FROM A TEMPORAL POINT OF VIEW

History played an important role when it came to explaining Indians' *naturaleza* (nature): what they could think—their limited abstraction, lack of reflexivity, and agency—was a result of their past. Equally important, history also informed how Spaniards understood their relations to Indians. Although not explicitly stated in these terms, to all colonialist thinkers it was clear that Indians and Spaniards coexisted but were not coetaneous. Indians were in the Spaniards' past while Spaniards were in the Indians' future—a particular case of what Johannes Fabian (1983) calls a "denial of coevalness."[19] This colonial organization of the temporal continuum underlying Spanish imaginings about Indians made the latter an "absent presence" (Vizenor 1999). To Spaniards, Indians were there but not in any relevant way.

The Christian historical sequence resembled the trajectory of a boomerang— the two key ideas were what had been lost and what had been retrieved. With minor differences, European books that attempted to include Indians in the universal history presented a narrative that included the same events. After man's perfect creation in paradise and his Fall, his nature was damaged. The exact way in which this loss was conceived was an object of theological debate but the loss itself was not. Further events of transgression and decadence resulted in an increasingly diminished nature and a progressive estrangement from, and forgetting about, God. This falling away from the true order of things made deduction difficult as the premises became necessarily blurrier. From the landing of the ark and multiplication of Noah's children followed a long process of dispersal in different directions. This process involved time, and more time meant, according to most scholars, more trouble—progressive decadence, loss of knowledge about God, and increasingly frequent sins that produced only further deterioration. It was a downward spiral, a vicious circle that, if left unchecked, would continually worsen man's weakened nature.

At the same time, because Christian history was teleological, the Fall was not all that mattered. God had created man so that man could fulfill his *fin natural* (natural end), which was to adore God, and therefore gave man the means to do so. Chiefly, God bestowed upon man the natural light of reason, which set him apart from animals. It was reason that allowed man to learn (see/ think) about God through his work—enabling man to access the readability of nature. Thus, for example, the Franciscan Juan de Torquemada explained in his 1615 *Monarquía indiana*, by observing the *mundo visible* (visible world), man can *inferir* (infer), *sospechar* (suspect), and *concebir* (conceive) that which cannot be seen ([*1615*] 1986, vol. II, bk. VI, chap. 2, 4–6). In other words, man should be able to use his vision to go (conceptually) from the tailor to the laws to which the tailor is subjected, moving from seen particulars to the abstract general principles behind them. This upward trend opened the door for asking how much had been regained and how much of the forgotten premises had been rediscovered through observation and deduction.

It was commonly accepted that while a few could actually follow the right reasoning, most people erred (another result of the Fall). This explained, according to some theologians, the origin of idolatry: a failed attempt to go higher (I will return to this problem in chapter 2). And, while there was much disagreement about the details and the implications of this process, it was widely accepted that there were limits to how much man could know about God on his own. Las Casas and Acosta called this knowledge *conocimiento confuso* (vague, imprecise knowledge). It was a conceptual blurriness that conditioned the vision of the object, as Torquemada explained, "in the same way that knowing a person is coming from afar is not the same as knowing that it is Pedro, even if he is the one coming" ("de la misma manera, que conocer a una persona que viene de lejos, no es conocer que sera Pedro, aunque sea el mismo el que viene") ([*1615*] 1986, vol. II, bk. VI, chap. 1, 3b).

Explanations were intrinsically developmental: the one looking can see more of Pedro the closer he gets to him; to get closer, he needs time to walk; and (equally important) as he walks, he changes. Take, for instance, the origin of sacrifices. When man wants to communicate something, Torquemada explained, it is natural for him to use "signals perceptible to the senses . . . because it is natural to him to begin by them" ("señales sensibles . . . por serle cosa natural comenzar por ellas") ([*1615*] 1986, vol. II, bk. VI, chap. 1, 3b). Man's drive toward God is always in battle with the limiting effects of the Fall—Noah's children were "rude and ignorant . . . not reaching their considerations beyond what their exterior senses showed them, they only paid attention to those things that were beautiful, happy . . . and there they stopped" ("rudos e ignorantes . . . no alcançando más su consideración de aquello que los sentidos exteriores les mostraban, solamente los ponían en aquellas cosas que eran hermosas, alegres . . . y en estas pararon") (Torquemada [*1615*] 1986, vol. II, bk. VI, chap. 12, 26b). They thus adored planets, the sun, or the moon but did not go higher.[20] Failing to do so (to go higher through *recta razón*) had been an almost universal error. Egyptians had done it, Greeks had done it, Romans had done it—and Indians, examples of the past and present at once, did it, too.

A precise metaphor for man's incremental knowledge was that of distance— the closer to the truth, the more he could see, and the more he could see, the more he could know (and the closer to being, again, complete). This movement, presented metaphorically as physical proximity, was in fact temporal—if one is looking at Pedro from a distance, one is looking from the past. Christians knew it was Pedro while Indians only knew there was someone there. And more important yet, Christians knew that they knew and Indians did not while the latter did not.

This developmental process was at once universal and particular—universal because it was common to all men and particular because it went hand in hand with God's developmental revelation, which affected directly only those inhabiting the Middle East. When Torquemada explained the history of religious celebrations, he told that—as it happened with man's knowledge of nature, which went from the simple to the perfect—God revealed to man first the simplest and then slowly proceeded to the more complex ([*1615*] 1986, vol. II, bk. X, chap. 7, 243b–244a). Thus, under natural law, Saturday was reserved for God *naturalmente* ("naturally"). However, under the written law, it was explicitly stated, and under the law of grace, it was transferred to Sunday, when the sacrificial lamb of the Jews was replaced by the "true lamb." It was a two-way developmental process—as man progressed, God made things progressively clearer, "bringing to light, and making clearly manifest, what was prefigured" ("sacando a luz, y a clara manifestación la cosa figurada") (Torquemada [*1615*] 1986, vol. II, bk. X, chap. 7, 244a–244b). The fact that there was no easy shortcut, only a long mental process ahead, explained Acosta's and Santo Tomás's tribulations.

When it came to Indians, Spaniards mixed and matched these ideas to diagnose their condition—how much they had lost of that primordial state of goodness and how much they had regained from what had been lost. To some, Indians were doomed. Not only had Indians lost all the good in themselves and gained nothing back but they had also continued to degenerate. This was Alvarez's position and also that of widely read, influential political thinkers like the well-known defender of the Spanish right to conquest and colonize the Americas, Juan Ginés de Sepúlveda.[21] Indian human material or *naturaleza* (part of what centuries-later Western thinkers would call "race") was irreparably damaged. As Alvarez stated, all that could be hoped for was to prevent them from *hacer el mal* so as to prevent them from further decline, angering God. In fact, when debating with Las Casas, Sepúlveda stated that thwarting their degeneration was as much a *derecho* (right) as a *deber* (duty) to the golden rule to treat others as one would like to be treated ([1551] 1975, 67). To others, Indians were good because as they were primitive—primitiveness here expressed the original, good nature of man—they had not been corrupted as much as Spaniards (and other Europeans) had been. Thus, Santo Tomás's example of the cacique was meant to confuse bad Christians precisely because of its boomerang-like paradox: Indians were in the past and yet in some regards were more advanced than Christians—their faith was stronger and they neither lied nor blasphemed.

That is, to explain Indians' present social customs, Spaniards resorted to ethnographic images from histories about "the" past—the Western past, taken to be that of man (universal). As difference was rendered into time and time was linear, coetaneous Indians were seen as remnants of the past in the present, examples of bygone, simpler elsewheres.[22] Language was also seen in direct relation with social evolution. When explaining the third kind of términos particulares, Santo Tomás told that while Spaniards switched from formal to informal ways of address when they greeted each other (e.g., use of "vos" or "usted"), Indians "do not care for ceremonies or talk in plural instead of in singular . . . but they plainly treat each other" ("no curan de muchas cerimonias ni hablar en plural por singular . . . sino que llanamente se tratan") ([*1560*] 1995, fol. 69v, 142). I stress the *llanamente* (plainly, simply)—in terms of visual metaphor, simplicity expressed the shortness of words or gestures connatural to primitive, initial attempts at something (not unlike the idea behind Emile Durkheim's *Elementary Forms*). This *llaneza* (simplicity, plainness), which conveyed in yet another way the material flatness characterizing Indians, also prevented Indians from naming in different ways the sounds different animals make—the last term about which Santo Tomás found an extended explanation necessary. While Spaniards *metaphóricamente* (metaphorically) would say *bramar* (roar) for the lion, *relinchar* (neigh) for the horse, and so on, "it seems to Indians that brute animals and birds cannot properly sing or feel . . . because they see that none of them has intellect to know or tongue/language to speak" ("a los indios no les paresce que propiamente los animales brutos y aves pueden cantar ni tener otros afectos . . . porque veen que ninguno de todos ellos tiene conoscimiento para conoscer ni lengua para hablar") (Santo Tomás [*1560*] 1995, fols. 71–71v, 144–45). In other words, Indians were less metaphorical *because* they were primitive people, not the other way around.

While Santo Tomás saw in the Indian present traces of a good future and Alvarez signs of a bad past, other saw in it stasis—Indians were suspended in a state of arrested development. This stasis accounted for even the most mundane aspect of Indian behavior, like dressing, painting, or loving. Consider, for example, Diego D'Avalos y Figueroa's *Miscelánea austral* (Austral miscellanea). Printed in Lima in 1602 and organized as an extended dialogue between Cilena (the wife) and Delios (the husband), the book is a miscellaneous compendium of several matters related largely to marriage, love, and poetry. It touches upon Indians but only here and there—a sign of the changing times, of a moment in which Creoles allowed themselves to think that civilization and the arts could gain center stage and colonialism could linger on the margins.

Perhaps precisely because of this desire, the margins were consistently in another time-space. Colloquium 28, for instance, centered on the etymologies of names different peoples at different times and in different places of the world gave to kingdoms and cities. Its purpose was to explain the ways in which names result from, or express something about, particular historical events. Toward the end of the chapter, Cilena asked Delios if that could also be said of Indian names—if they also "have some etymology or reason" ("tienen alguna ethimología o razón"). Delios answered that "some have it, although of little interest and complexity; as with everything else, they show their obscure and limited inventiveness" ("en algunas la tienen aunque de poca curiosidad, y artificio; como en todo lo muestran sus obscuros y limitados ingenios") (D'Avalos y Figeroa 1602, 124).[23] To exemplify this limitation and obscurity, Delios remarked that Indians "call their mother mom" ("llaman a su madre mama"). What made this an example was that "mama" was common to many other languages because it was easy to pronounce for a child who was beginning to speak, "and since these Indians remain always in the innocence of children, they stay with the same style" ("y como estos indios siempre se están en la innocencia de la infancia, quedanse con el mesmo estilo") (D'Avalos y Figeroa 1602, 124). Indians were not coeval with their colonizers but eternal children (a trope inaugurated by Columbus and extensively disseminated by Las Casas). They were *cortos* (short) in their imagination, as all children were, since they lacked words/concepts with which to imagine. That is why Delios pointed out (like Santo Tomás, Alvarez, and Acosta did years before) that their languages lacked terms for key, advanced Christian notions like "forgiveness and to forgive" ("perdon y perdonar") (D'Avalos y Figeroa 1602, 125) or "charity" ("caridad") (D'Avalos y Figeroa 1602, 150).

This childlike stasis that explained Indians' limited grasp of reality went, logically, hand in hand with their incapacity to represent reality adequately. After several pages in which the case is made that Indians had not built any of Peru's magnificent pre-Hispanic buildings (they did not have the capacity to do so, instead giants who predated them had built them), a counterfactual question arises: if such were the case, Cilena asked, why are there no portraits of these giants? The answer is simple: "This is contradicted by their insufficiency when it comes to painting and how poorly they get to form in painting human faces, which is something they never get right, because although animals they paint with great imperfection, that is much worse, and thus it is something that it is not known that they did"[24] (D'Avalos y Figeroa 1602, 147v). In other words, there were no portraits because there could not be—Indians had not developed the capacity to paint human faces.[25]

The lack of linguistic, social, and visual coevalness also explained things very distant from abstraction or religion, like Indians' sex life in ways reminiscent of early twentieth-century Andean experts.[26] Indians largely do not feel love, Delios stated, and in those rare occasions in which they do, it is not a love "elevated and subtle" ("levantado y sutil") but one of a very low kind "because it cannot be believed that they are wounded by such lovely arrow with any difference from beasts . . . but according to their intellect, which never rises up from the ground, or their thought from the earth" (D'Avalos y Figeroa 1602, 154v)[27]—an iteration of Alvarez's materiality but on the sexual terrain.

Logically, and more important yet, the Indians' childishness affected their capacity to abstract themselves from the present. Children's and brutes' material flatness, their proximity to the ground, also made them care about "only that which is exterior and present, and to lack any kind of prudence" ("solo lo exterior y presente, y carescer de todo genero de prudencia"). Unlike other human beings, for whom it was natural, Indians could not grasp "the memory of past things, governance of present things, and providence for future things, and through reason, to understand how things are, to make distinctions, to arrive to conclusions, to persuade and to inquire"[28] (D'Avalos y Figeroa 1602, 155). Indian stasis was due not just to their ancestors asking them not to change, to their lack of interest in knowledge, or to their being too close to the ground—Alvarez's arguments—but also to their lack of temporal reflexivity and critical attention to the past, which were what allowed men to improve. That is why—also anticipating twentieth-century scholarly arguments about Indian socialism—Indians (each and all) knew how to do everything necessary for human life but not more. They repeated all things the way they had been invented by the one who had come up with them—be it making huts, shoes, or plowing—but never went a step forward or higher (D'Avalos y Figeroa 1602, 155).[29] They were thus present but, to all relevant accounts, they were absent.

FROM IMAGININGS TO ROYAL
AND ECCLESIASTIC POLICIES

All these ideas about Indians held by clergymen and laymen alike were echoed by official state and ecclesiastic documents and policies. By the end of the sixteenth century, colonial legislation defined Indians as a particular kind of legal minors: *miserables*. Like children or women, Indians were unable to handle the complexities of life without help from adult (white) males. According to Peru's tenth viceroy, the Marqués of Montesclaros, this was because they were of a very limited mental capacity, one that hardly measured up to reason ([ca. 1615] 1990, 122). Used in political and ecclesiastic treatises and royal documents a bit contradictorily and erratically during early decades of the conquest and colonization of the Americas, Indian *miserabilidad* (miserability, wretchedness) was solidly established by the time Garcilaso and Guaman Poma wrote their texts (Castañeda Delgado 1971; Cunil 2011; López Díaz-Valentín 2012; Sánchez-Concha Barros 1996). The legal characterization codified precise limitations to what Indians could do and also guaranteed the Spaniards' role as tutors. And, tutors not only helped children do what they could not do by themselves, like helping them achieve their goals, but also forced children to do what they did not want to do but was good for them—like working.

Not by chance, the establishment of the keystone of the colonial economic system in the Andes in the 1570s—the compulsory work of Indians in mines—went hand in hand with the idea, solidly established by the late 1500s, that freedom was bad for Indians. If not forced to work, the argument went, Indians would lose themselves by indulging in vices. The facts that Indigenous communities were economically successful to the point that the Crown and colonial officers used communal funds for their own benefit, that Spaniards were known for refusing to do any kind of hard work, and that the debates about the fall of the population subject to the compulsory mining work exposed a good share of Spanish abuses against Indigenous laborers, did not change the argument. Indians felt *repugnancia* (revulsion) toward work "because of their natural inclination to an immoral and easy life" ("por su natural inclinación a vida viciosa y descansada"), stated the important *real cédula* (royal decree) of May 1609 that regulated Indian forced labor across the viceroyalty.[30]

In what concerned conversion, the Indians' special condition led to two different but mutually reinforcing ideas. On the one hand, Indian inferiority was put to work to adjust the scales of salvation. Thus, the Third Ecclesiastical Council of Lima produced a number of different *confesionarios* (books that taught how to confess) that went from extremely simple to quite complex, each adapted to the mental capacity of the one confessing—from the lowest for common Indians to the highest for educated Spaniards. In his *Symbolo cathólico indiano* (Indian Catholic symbol), published in Lima in 1598, the Franciscan Luis Jerónimo de Oré stated in plain language the idea behind the Concilio's gradation: "God gives them heaven cheaper than he gives it to others, according to the little talent of the intellect with which they learn about it, because that sovereign kingdom of heaven is worth as much as each person has" ("les da Dios el cielo más barato que a otros, según el poco talento de su entendimiento con que lo adquieren, pues aquel soberano reyno del cielo tanto vale como cada vno tiene") ([*1598*] 1992, fol. 45, 167).[31] On the other hand, the Indians' condition required that they be constantly tutored to ensure that they would be good Christians. The official decision to proceed by eliminating any traits of native religious practices had been in place since the 1583 Third Ecclesiastical Council of Lima. As this doctrinal shift was progressively put into practice, the infamous campaigns to extirpate Indian idolatry began.[32] By the end of the 1500s, extirpators were crisscrossing the Andes and what initially were individual enterprises in certain districts turned into full-fledged, extensive campaigns in the early 1600s.[33]

The most comprehensive and influential manual for extirpators, José de Arriaga's *La extirpación de la idolatría en el Pirú* (*The extirpation of idolatry in Peru*) explained the need to these inquisitional-style campaigns through differences between Spaniards' and Indians' mental capacity—what each could see and why.[34] Although devoted largely to Indians—their idolatric practices, their origin and manifestations, and what to do with them—the manual began by praising one of Arriaga's predecessors, Francisco de Avila, for having opened the path to extirpation when few believed in the existence of Indian idolatry. In spite of this incredulity, Avila "went on, little by little, continuing with his quest, until he *brought to light the truth and uncovered* the lie . . . so that it became clear how *al dente* idolatry was" ("fue poco a poco prosiguiendo en su demanda hasta que *aclaró la verdad y descubrió* . . . la mentira, de suerte que se vino a entender cuán en su punto estaba entre los indios la idolatría") (Arriaga [*1621*] 1999, chap. 1, 14). The climax of the uncovering took place in Lima in December 1609 when, in a grand auto-de-fé, Avila burned more than six hundred idols and punished a renowned "master of idolatry."[35] All political and ecclesiastic Spanish authorities in attendance were finally "persuaded" that there was idolatry among Indians (Arriaga [*1621*] 1999, chap. 1, 15). Soon after, other discoveries piled up throughout the Andes. In other words, the object existed—both as a concept in the Spaniards' minds and as an Indian practice—although *cubierto* (covered). Avila's contribution was to *descubrir* (uncover) the latter in its material manifestation, making it visible—but the object preexisted conceptually. That is why, once Indian idolatry was exposed, Spaniards sprang into action.

Arriaga's visual/conceptual economy was different when it came to Indians. Like many others, Arriaga stated that Indians were material beings who adored low things, like stones, rivers, etc., and only cared about "temporal and visible [happiness], because the spiritual and eternal ones . . . they neither expect them nor ask for them" ("temporal y visible [felicidad], porque de la espiritual y eterna . . . ni la esperan ni lo piden") (Arriaga [*1621*] 1999, chap. 1, 14). The way forward was therefore to retrain their eyes: "since they cannot be removed from before their eyes [the huacas], because they are fixed and immobile, [the extirpators] try to . . . remove them from their heart, teaching them the truth and disabusing them of the falsehood" (Arriaga [*1621*] 1999, chap. 2, 30).[36] Since rivers, surging waters, clouds, rain, etc., could not be eliminated or destroyed (like other idols), Indians had to be taught to see them differently (and for what they really were)—to see them as natural phenomena, things that had no trace of the supernatural in them.

This difference between Indians and Spaniards had an impact on humor. When explaining the obstacles to teaching Indians the complexities of the faith, Arriaga argued that, even if some managed to learn something, it was not actual learning, just mindless memorizing. He then gave an ethnographic example that showed, once again, as much Spanish expectations about Indians as the latter's use of them: "even in this case, when they say it right, it is like parrots, with no understanding of what they say" ("aún de esta manera, cuando bien la dicen, es como papagayos, sin entender lo que dicen") (Arriaga [*1621*] 1999, chap. 7, 72).[37] The best an Indian could be according to him was a *papagayo* (parrot). He memorized and played back without comprehending because of his material thinking—true in general, more so for matters of faith, the highest and most complex form of knowledge.[38] Even those well trained by good masters made playback mistakes without noticing it. When Christianized Indigenous helpers taught doctrine to other Indians, Arriaga continued, they did it poorly with many "errors, altering or changing some words or letters, through which they produce very diverse meanings, such as in the creed, instead of saying *Hucllachacuininta*, which means the communion or gathering of saints, to say *Pucllachacuininta*, which means the mockery of or joking about the saints" ([*1621*] 1999, chap. 7, 72).[39]

As it happened to Santo Tomás and Alvarez, Arriaga's Indians refused to conform and confirm. The result was also similar—other ways of making sense of playback discrepancies were lost on the Spaniards, the native agency behind unacknowledged or disavowed. Irony and laughter could not be part of a parrot's repertoire. Their existence would be inconsistent with the characterization of Indians as lacking awareness about the larger conditions in which they existed, incapable of reflexivity, unaware of meanings other than literal ones, capable only of expressing what crossed their minds with neither filters nor subtleties, and lacking agency.

THE "INDIAN" DILEMMA: WHAT TO DO IN A WORLD UPSIDE DOWN?

The Spanish ideas fleshed out in this chapter capture the entire colonial ideological and social spectrum, from those belonging to the so-called *partido de los indios* (Indian party) to those opposing it, from those who defended ideas of the first evangelization to those who were leading figures of the second, from those writing legal reports or ecclesiastic treatises to those writing about poetry or extirpating idolatries or regulating Indian labor. Each had different goals and felt differently about Indians and yet, at the end of the day, they all agreed on what Indians ultimately were, what they could do, and what they could not do—Indians were material, two-dimensional creatures incapable of abstraction, a condition proper of their evolutionary stage. Present but absent, Indians could not think beyond the visible and lacked knowledge of the larger map. Because they did not know and did not know that they did not, there was no such thing as Indian agency. Whatever they said or did was either the mechanical expression of what was natural to them or the mechanical (and defective) copying of someone else's words or acts. They lived in the past and had no ideas about the future, no humor, and no elevated love or art. Personal or individual variation among Indians did not exist, "because, as the viceroy don Martín Enríquez very well put it: 'Indians are not only ones, but one'" ("pues como decía muy bien el señor virrey don Martín Enríquez: 'todos los indios no solamente son unos, sino uno'") (Arriaga [*1621*] 1999, chap. 7, 25).[40]

In all relevant accounts, Spaniards considered themselves to be airily superior. Their field of vision was more advanced because they knew the larger map and could make sense of the world accordingly. The fact that Christians had the terms to express all that existed proved it. As a consequence, Spaniards could easily examine and diagnose Indians to better discuss their future. And, in fact, they did. Far from being innocuous ethnographic comments, the charges that Indians deviated from correspondence, were blind to things of the faith, were unable to conceptualize them (and to conceptualize in general), had a material intelligence close to the ground, and were largely stuck in a static developmental stage, legitimized Spanish rule and ascendancy at large, making Indians absolute others and absolute inferiors. In particular, they influenced the set of institutional practices that affected Indians the most during these years, such as the enforcement of the *mita minera* in the context of population loss and the campaigns of extirpation of idolatries that crisscrossed much of the Andean landscape in the early 1600s.

The fact that the native thinkers involved in the very same everyday exchanges Spaniards quoted as examples of Indian limitation—like those presented by Alvarez, Acosta, Santo Tomás, or Arriaga (and the list could go on)—contradicted and challenged the Spaniards' ideas about Indians tells that denial was central to colonial relations. Indigenous actors not only had to put up with exploitation but they also had to live in a world upside down, a twisted contraption in which interactions were limited by Spanish imaginings about Indians. It was something "so blindingly obvious that only . . . extraordinarily clever and sophisticated persons fail[ed] to grasp it" (Samuels 2016).

These Spanish imaginings and emotions begged a number of questions. On the one hand, how could one effectively communicate with someone who failed to see and hear and who did not know that he had visual and hearing impediments? How could an honest conversation ever take place? Could there be true understanding? On the other hand, did all natives see the situation in the same way? Or were there some who believed what white people said about them or found some of their simulations attractive? Did some wear *White Masks* ([1952] 2008)? How could alternatives to the options Spanish colonialism offered be made available if Spaniards censored all texts?

PART II

GUAMAN POMA DE AYALA'S *NUEVA CORÓNICA Y BUEN GOBIERNO*

I know they will not hear these words, but I want to tell them that I know how bad they are doing . . . but I want them to know that they are on the side of justice.

—NADIA MURAD, *EL MUNDO*, 25 MAY, 2017

2

HISTORY, RACE, AND GRACE FOR PEOPLE WHO SEE THE WORLD THROUGH WHITENESS

THE *NCBG*, a 1,189-page Andean manuscript likely finished around 1614, lay dormant until it was found in the Royal Library in Copenhagen in 1908. With the shifting of Latin American colonial studies away from Spanish-centric interests toward those of Indigenous actors, the text has assumed a central position in this field. Scholars generally agree about the text's outline: it highlights Andean peoples' precolonial social, religious, and cultural achievements, criticizes the unjust changes triggered by the Spanish conquest of the Inca Empire, and demands colonial reforms. The colonial order—or rather disorder—is commonly presented as one in which native actors suffer the abuses of Spanish officers and clergymen, a *mundo al reués* (world upside down) that only the Spanish king, the text's alleged primary reader, can remedy. The remedies the text proposes go from a radical request for the restitution of lands and authorities to Indigenous peoples with the Spanish king as distant leader to a more mainstream request for colonial reform that touches every aspect of the system.

The ways the *NCBG* sustains its cross-cultural critique and its effectiveness in demanding reform are matters of varied opinions. While some scholars stress Guaman Poma's use of the polemical historical discourse and of the sermon's effective persuasion, others highlight the presence of Indigenous elements, mainly found in the text's 398 images, that expressed the "cultural" or "episte-mological" clash of colliding "mental structures" or "orders."[1] When it comes to assessing the text's success, some scholars find the scaffolding of Guaman Poma's writing falters toward the end as he is overwhelmed by the colonial chaos and loses hope of actual change or effective communication; others see the text as a partial success insofar as the request for reform expresses a belief in the power of writing to spring the king into action.

I argue, first and foremost, that readers were invited to approach the text through the lenses of race and coloniality as much as those of cultural differences. Guaman Poma's problem was not only how to make Spaniards understand Andean culture, correcting the record, but more importantly how to make people who saw the world through whiteness realize they did this when words and concepts like "racism" and "whiteness" did not yet exist. His main goal was to teach readers to see the colonial world anew—to have them recognize the color line, see its arbitrariness—and thus turn readers into instruments of change. He did this through a unique, decolonial use of theological ideas common in Spain but never heard of in the Andes. He used the distinction between knowing and doing seen in chapter 1 to blur colonial racial taxonomies. When it came to the idea of being Christian, everyone knew. Therefore, everyone was equal. But when it came to doing, not everyone did—and for different reasons. In some cases, he pointed out that man (unmarked) needed God's grace and focused the question on how to access it, which was a theologically orthodox path, just one that had never been mentioned when it came to Indians. In other cases, he reinserted the question of knowledge but gave it a decolonial twist: those who saw the world through whiteness were blind to their ignorance. They did not know and did not know that they did not know. As a result, for them to do the right thing, they had to be taught first to recognize discrimination, and privilege. The readers who had to be taught were plural—all sorts of Spaniards, all sorts of Indians, and to a lesser extent blacks. The king was just one more of them. In all cases, the problem was neither in peoples' skin color or origin but in their eyes.[2]

Second, I suggest that the text's main means to alter reality were neither polemical nor moral but rather pedagogical. To teach its readers to see the world anew, the *NCBG* recurrently faced them with riddles—seeming incoherences, blatant historical impossibilities, puzzling challenges to the colonial common sense—which could be solved only if readers questioned the assumptions that make them look so to begin with. In other words, it asked readers to relearn the art of making sense. By making sense, I mean to critically examine both the discourses about the colonial order of things and what went without saying, the embodied senses of order that deserved no comment—the "colonial normal" (Lamana 2008). The text, then, was as much a manual about unlearning as a catalyst—a narrative that helped the coalescence of until-then fragmented ideas, feelings, and subjectivities. It was neither a political chart for reform (as in restitution or *arbitrismo*) nor a political manifesto for a revolution (as in the *Eighteenth Brumaire* or a return to a culturally specific past) but the enunciation of a new form of seeing the world that hoped to change it, one pair of eyes at a time.

Third, I bring to light the fact that Guaman Poma showed that the colonial world was wrong in a specific way: it was extraordinary in that it did not follow reason—a reversal of Spanish colonial discourse. And reason was as much Andean as it was European; they were, in a last instance, local expressions of one and the same thing. The ordinary, the colonies as state of exception, implied the everyday currency of a world turned upside down. Feeling upside down triggered a subject position of inadequacy—one is wrong, not the world. And the only solution is accommodation: one has to flip himself upside down and act as if everything were all right, pretending not to notice. The text faced readers with a rich conceptual ethnography of the many incarnations of this nonsense, aiming for a reboot—a metanoia.

That the text was primarily pedagogical—and its intended readers included Spaniards—is revealing in terms of Guaman Poma's view of the racial problem: it tells that he believed that people who thought of themselves as white could be taught, that they were not hopeless. At the same time, while being an optimist by the simple fact that he gave it a very serious and complex try, Guaman Poma did not delude himself. As he stated with good doses of humor at the very end of the *NCBG*, after reading it "some will cry, some will laugh, some will curse, some will commend me to God, others will get rid of it driven by pure anger, others will want to have this book and chronicle handy to restrain their soul, conscience and heart" ("unos llorarán, otros se rreyrá, otros maldirá, otros encomendarme a Dios, otros de puro enojo se deshará, otros querrá tener en las manos este libro y corónica para enfrenar su ánima y consencia y corasón") ([ca. 1614] 1987, fol. [1178]1168, 1244).

THE READERSHIP AND THE COLOR LINE: AN UNEXPECTED "CRISTIANO LECTOR"

There is something that must have been striking about the way the *NCBG*'s opening pages identified its intended readership:

The said book . . . is very useful and beneficial and it is good for the rectification
of lives for the Christians and the infidels, and for [the] said Indians to confess
themselves and amend their ways and wrongdoings, idolaters, and for the said
priests to know [how] to confess the said Indians, and for the correction of the
said *encomenderos* of Indians and the *corregidores* and friars and priests of the said
doctrinas, and of the said miners and of the said principal caciques and of the rest
of the Indian *mandoncillos*, of common Indians and of other Spaniards and other
persons. (Guaman Poma [ca. 1614] 1987, fol. [1]1, 2)[3]

This quote began the text on several uncommon notes. First, the "book" (the
word he used to describe it, not a "letter," as at times scholars call it) had plural
addressees—from the lowest Indians to priests, from caciques to corregidores,
from miners to Indian men and "other persons." In fact, the text addressed not
just these but many more colonial actors, each in a specific chapter. It was clearly
not directed to the king—or at least not to the king alone, as often stated. Second, the list of readers mixed all kinds of peoples in no specific order: Spaniards,
Indians, blacks, men, women, commoners, noblemen, caciques, priests, corregidores, etc. Third, this heterogeneity and mixing were quickly reduced under one
label. Guaman Poma asked God, the Virgin, and the Holy Spirit for help so
that his book was good "for . . . all Christians" ("para . . . todos los cristianos")
([ca. 1614] 1987, fol. 3, 2). In fact, throughout the book, cristiano lector was the
recurrent and prevalent way in which he addressed the readers.

The way Guaman Poma conceived and addressed his readership was not
common in texts produced in colonial Peru. The large majority did not identify specific readers and the very few that did—for example the doctrinaire
religious texts produced by the Third Ecclesiastical Council of Lima, material
Guaman Poma knew well—clearly distinguished and grouped the addressees:
(Spanish) priests on the one hand, Indians on the other.[4] But to understand the
signification of the contrast between Guaman Poma's way of conceiving and
addressing readers and the manner in which most colonial texts did this, readers
had to consider its second striking characteristic: the cristiano lector. Like the
heterogeneous reader list, this way of addressing the reader did not appear in
any other Andean colonial text; however, it was not Guaman Poma's invention. While cristiano lector was not used in colonial texts, it was not unusual
in peninsular religious literature. In particular, it was the Dominican Luis de
Granada's favorite way of addressing readers in his well-known *Memorial de la
vida cristiana* (*Memorial of a Christian Life*)—a text with which Guaman Poma

was very familiar. Where lay the novelty then? To understand it, readers had to compare the manner in which each way of addressing readers functioned in its own geographical and political context—what each way of address assumed and what each accomplished.

In the peninsular context, Fray Luis used cristiano lector to address Spaniards (and other Europeans) who, it went without saying, were Christian. His goal, as he repeatedly stated, was to help Christians live a good life—what he called *vivir bien* or *el bien vivir* (to live well or the good living)—to which end he highlighted the importance of spirituality in a post-Trent, post-Reformation era.[5] Fray Luis was then not *teaching* his readers things unknown to them—he was *reminding* them of a number of things that were important to them. Cristiano lector intended to guide the reader to think of himself primarily as Christian and to move him to act accordingly because, when it came to the two key elements (to know and to do), Granada focused not on knowing—everybody knew—but on doing: "Of these two parts that are necessary to live well, the second is much more necessary and excellent than the first . . . since we all know and recognize what is good, but not all of us dare to do it, because of the difficulty it entails" ([1565] 1994–95, vol. 15–16).[6]

Guaman Poma in contrast addressed (among others) those about whom it could have hardly been said that their status as Christians went without saying. They could not therefore be simply *reminded*. The 1583 Third Ecclesiastical Council of Lima and the 1600s extirpation campaigns and texts were conducted and written, respectively, on precisely the opposite presumption. If the texts they produced at no point used as their mode of address "cristiano lector," it was because they could not—doing so would have meant an insurmountable contradiction since their raison d'être was that Indians were not Christians. Thus, Indians were repeatedly labeled "people new in the faith" ("gente nueva en la fe") or people "of short and tender understanding" ("de cortos y tiernos entendimientos") ("Tercero catecismo" [*1585*] 1990, 625). Christianization of Indians required teaching them only the ABCs of the complex things of the faith, using uncomplicated examples in a simple language (like feeding little children baby food) and also much patience and much repetition ("Tercero catecismo" [*1585*] 1990, 628).[7]

All these statements about Indians from Spanish colonial texts implied a geopolitical claim of privilege: knowledge and historical consciousness flowed from Spaniards, who knew, toward Indians, who did not—doing was not even in the picture. Thus, when doctrinaire texts addressed Indians as *hijos míos* (my children), the paternalistic relationship that always characterized this kind of text (even when addressed to Europeans) acquired a special colonial significance—Indians (aka children) were being taught by Spaniards (aka fathers). In this colonial context, while not as shocking as addressing the reader as *hermano* (brother)—as Granada sometimes did—addressing any reader as cristiano lector from the get-go, as Guaman Poma did, had disruptive effects..

First, it implied a specific kind of equality: there was nothing the ones being addressed did not know—Indians (as a much as Spaniards) were being *reminded*, they were all Christians. Therefore, the superiority and distinctiveness upon which colonial rule rested—and which all Andean colonial theological texts stated as fact—were implicitly called into question.

The second, important difference that cristiano lector made was that it reconfigured the "geopolitics of knowledge" (Mignolo 2000) central to the colonial project. Unlike in colonial doctrinaire texts or juridical-political documents like *El requerimiento*, according to the *NCBG*, knowledge and history did not flow from Spaniards to Indians. While Spanish texts assumed that Indians not only did not know but did not know that they did not know, Guaman Poma flipped the frame upside down—Indians knew and it was Spaniards who did not know that they did not know and thought they did (I will return to it).

Third, once the pressing colonialist questions of knowing and the historical narrative had been redressed, then the key question shifted from *knowing* to *doing*—a drastic departure from Santo Tomás's, Alvarez's, or Acosta's texts, all who discussed Indians' capacity to know (not do). Guaman Poma thus aligned himself with Luis de Granada and a couple of times called his text "Primer y nueua corónica y uien vivir de los cristianos" ("First and new chronicle and good living of the Christians") ([ca. 1614] 1987, fol. [11]11, 9, fol. [15]15, 12). He asserted that its goal was to have them *mudar* (transform) their lives. As I will show, far from a simple matter of will, this change in doing involved seeing in a new light well-known complex theological issues (such as natural reason, grace, and divine intervention) and learning about new complex issues (such as coloniality and whiteness).

In short, by choosing this specific way of conceiving and addressing his readership, Guaman Poma undid the (alleged but enforced) colonial order of things and the historically grounded claim of privilege upon which it rested. But, this was just one side of the coin. The other side, equally important or more, was that he destabilized beliefs and unspoken colonial understandings about people in general. That is, he questioned other things that went without saying, that needed not be stated. As is known, conquerors' accounts and chronicles of the conquest of the Inca Empire used "Christian" or "Spaniard" interchangeably to identify their main actors or protagonists (the others were "Indians") (Lamana 2008, 223). In semiological terms, Spaniard and Christian were two interchangeable parts of the same sign. Either could work as signifier or signified because each referred to the other. The implicit assumption was that Spaniards were what Indians were not—and since Indians were not Christians, identifying Spaniards as Christians was not problematic.

That this had been the case in early colonial Spanish accounts describing the events of the conquest was not remarkable. However, that it continued to be the case thirty, fifty, or eighty years later should have been so; and yet, it was not. In contrast, by calling disparate actors "cristiano lector," the *NCBG* exposed and removed from the realm of the tacit the arbitrariness of the pervasive Spaniard/ Christian sign, which underlaid even the pro-Indian critical work of thinkers like Las Casas.[8]

From the get-go, the text confronted its readers (whether Indigenous, African, or European) with this initial uncertainty and forced them to figure out who was being addressed. Guaman Poma used this pedagogical strategy extensively throughout the *NCBG*. As readers advanced through its pages, they had to repeatedly put together pieces to eventually see a coherent image. In this case, since many of the intended readers were Indians, they clearly could not be Spaniards but from that, it did not follow that they could not be Christian. The outcome was a new setup of colonial relations with transgressive and equalizing effects: if all readers were Christian readers, then there was no privilege and, equally important down the road, expectations were the same for everyone. Here, too, the question was doing, not knowing.

Cristiano lector thus challenged deep-seated relations of authority and hierarchy and lumped together in uncomfortable proximity what was supposed to be separate. Not only was there no color line but the many equivalences that sprang from the Spanish/Indian opposition—and which formed the fabric that made colonial relations look normal—were also cast as contrived. This was not something Spaniards in Peru took lightly. Toward 1544, conquerors had recriminated Viceroy Blanco Núñez Vela for something analogous: he not only had made Spaniards in Peru start paying Indians for things for which they did not used to pay but he also had thrown them into the same jail where Indians were, which Spaniards considered "something that could not be suffered" ("cosa que no se podía sufrir") (Lamana 2008, 223).[9] Such actions were insufferable because they called into question colonial statuses, the expectations that went with them, and all that supposedly went without saying.

The repeated juxtaposition of apparently discordant ideas, leaving puzzles for the readers to solve, showed that Guaman Poma's primary goal was to teach—more precisely, to teach readers to see reality anew. His was a pedagogical text: he intended to flesh out a different visibility and have others partake of it—an ironic mimicry of theological texts' goals and modus operandi—but one that aimed at whiteness and coloniality as truths, not at God. As I will show, as the text progressed, Guaman Poma added other teaching strategies, like rewriting passages from well-known works or showing the many ways in which what in the colonies passed as normal was not and vice versa (that what should have gone without saying did not). In other words, he showed that the colonial world was al reués. Without excluding other sources of cross-polinization that informed this oft-quoted expression (such as Inca dynastic history [Imbelloni 1939; Ossio 1977; MacCormack 1988; Mignolo 2011, 156–58] and popular medieval literature and early-modern political thinking [Hill 1972; Van de Guche 1992]), I suggest that in the *NCBG* the world upside down resonated with a notion and claim fundamental to Christian thinking, specifically to the apostolic: the first Christians were seen as turning the (then usual) order of things upside down (Rowe 2010). As usual, the text gave this idea a decolonial twist.

UNEXPECTED HISTORIES 1: PRECOLONIAL HISTORICAL NARRATIVES

The disruptive effects implicit in Guaman Poma's innovative way of addressing readers became explicit—and their implications multiplied—in his extraordinary historical narrative and in the way he presented the colonial disorder in the Andes at the turn of the century. I begin with an examination of the former. Of the two parts of what is commonly considered the historical narrative of the *NCBG*, Andean peoples' pre-Hispanic history and that of the conquest of Peru, the latter is by far the most thoroughly studied. With the exception of those works that discuss the ways in which Andean and European elements coexist in the *NCBG*'s pages about pre-Hispanic history (e.g., Barnes 1995; Duviols 1980; González Díaz 2012; Flemming 1994; Husson 1995; Ossio 1977; 2008; Plas 1986; Szemiński 1983; Wachtel 1973), scholars only briefly mention them as prelude to the (seemingly) key and radical critique he makes of the histories of the conquest Spaniards penned, critique that sustained his claim of restitution of land and authority to Indigenous peoples (e.g., Adorno 1989, 2000).

According to Guaman Poma, it is often mentioned that prior to the Spanish arrival, Andean peoples had acquired knowledge of God through their use of natural reason or natural light—elements he borrowed from the conceptual frame of thinkers like Luis de Granada or Bartolomé de Las Casas—and a primitive evangelization had taken place, carried out by Saint Bartolomé (Adorno 1987; Adorno 2000, xxvi–xvii, 27, 143; Farías 2008, 203–6). These elements, the argument goes, undermined one of the pillars sustaining the rights Spaniards granted themselves: they had brought the light of Christianity to the Andes.

However, calling into question the right Spaniards arrogated to themselves and asking for restitution was not as radical as it may seem. It was largely a variation of what Las Casas and others in the so-called party of the Indians had done during much of the sixteenth century. On the other hand, Guaman Poma's historical narrative of the pre-Hispanic past was radical in its own right and its primary goal was not to question the validity of the conquest and to ask for restitution but instead to produce in the reader a new way of seeing the world. Because the past, both European and Andean, played such a fundamental role in Spanish explanations of the colonial present, Guaman Poma chose to rewrite them. But, it was a means to an end.

Fundamental to understanding his rewriting was the distinction between the history of the world (what I will call "global history") and the history of man (what I will call "universal history"). The difference between these histories was theological in nature. Something could be global because it happened everywhere but that did not mean that it made a difference in terms of man's history from the lows of the Fall to salvation. The Western expansion could be a case in point. In turn, what made a difference in the aforementioned sense was universal but it may or may not be global. Christ's life in the Middle East could be an example of it. This distinction explained why the historical elements of the narrative of the precolonial past in the *NCBG* were subordinated to the theological ones—chiefly among them natural light and divine intervention. The striking differences between Spanish historical narratives and Guaman Poma's narrative forced readers to reconfigure their ways of making sense.

NATURAL LIGHT AND GOD'S SHADOW

To understand the role ideas like natural reason or natural light had in sixteenth-century Spanish accounts, it is important to note that Granada and Las Casas were not the only possible sources of these concepts in the *NCBG*. These ideas were widely available in sixteenth-century Spain and were also important theological concepts for thinkers of the so-called second evangelization, regardless of whether friends or foes of Las Casas, like José de Acosta, Cabello Valboa, or Jerónimo de Oré—authors whose work Guaman Poma also knew well. There were, however, important differences in the ways each of these Spanish authors used these concepts and how their employment of them diverged from Guaman Poma's. These differences were inextricable from the ways in which each author related his historical narrative of the pre-Hispanic past to the history of humanity at large. In particular, the differences had a lot to do with the way in which their respective historical narratives were organized which, in turn, had concrete political consequences since they also explained the Indians' present and future. That is, the Indians' past in these texts laid the groundwork to explain both the future of what the authors narrated (the present time in each narration) and the future (the way forward).

In his widely read and influential 1583 *Introducción al símbolo de la fe* (Introduction to the symbol of the faith), Granada presented natural light as a means for people to understand God's existence and oeuvre on their own. Following Thomist ideas, Granada explained that there were two books in which God's divine knowledge could be read: that of nature and that of revelation. While the latter could only be read by those who have access to it through Christ, the former could be accessed by anyone. Granada gave many examples of God's readability—the general principle organizing them was that from effects, causes can be deduced. Be it looking at the sky, animals, or the human body, man could perceive an extremely complex order, and if there was order, there had to be someone producing it.

These explanations about creation, about what was in it to be observed, went hand in hand with man's built-in characteristics that drove him to inquire. If all peoples understood that there was a true god, even if they did not exactly know which one it was, it was because, "In the same manner that he imprinted in men's hearts the natural inclination to love and to revere their parents, the Creator also imprinted in them a similar inclination to love and to revere God as universal father of all things and sustainer and governor of them" (Granada [*1583*] 1989, chap. 3, 156).[10] While Granada did not write specifically about Indians—their origin and history or if/how they could know God—other authors who did often followed a very similar path.

Among the most influential was Las Casas. As seen in the previous chapter, in the *Apologética historia sumaria* (Brief apologetic history), he used two of Granada's main elements, the equipment (natural light) and man's innate drive to seek. A key question for Las Casas (and for most thinkers of the Salamanca school) was how much man could know by his own means—that is, without external help provided either by God (grace) or men (doctrine). Las Casas's answer was some but not much: "Through this light we can know no more than that there is god, to whom men are obliged to adore and serve as true lord and creator. But be it one or many, through natural reason one cannot easily ascertain it, since it exceeds the capacity of our understanding to an infinite extent. . . . That is why we say that that knowledge we attain through natural light is very vague" ([ca. 1550-56] 1992, chap. 71, 634).[11] To go beyond this basic idea, Las Casas declared more than once both in the *Apologética historia* and in *El único camino* (*The Only Way*) that man needed grace and doctrine. Accordingly, in precolonial times, Andean peoples had adored for generations all kinds of creatures, even the most absurd, a situation that had continued, albeit improved, under Inca rule. Thus, while the Inca king Pachacutec had reached knowledge of God's existence by his own means, this knowledge was *confuso* (vague) and *parcial* (partial) and in fact he had continued adoring the sun and other deities (Las Casas [ca. 1550-56] 1992, chap. 126, 891–93).

This restrictive position about what man could know about God by himself was likely concerned with the political consequences of the theological exposition: the more man could know by his own means, the more could be asked of Indians. Other influential sixteenth-century theologians had developed the idea and given it political import. Francisco de Vitoria, for instance, emphasized the fact that Indians could not be held accountable for not knowing due to their *ignorancia invencible* (invincible ignorance)—a twist on the fact that they did not know that they did not know.[12] This explains why, regardless of the numerous coincidences, Las Casas was less generous than Granada, who in the *Introducción* declared that to know that God was only one was not only possible but reasonable ([1583] 1989, chap. 3, 167–68). Granada therefore had a harsher view of idolatry than Las Casas.

José de Acosta, often cast as the central figure of the second evangelization in the Andes and therefore Las Casas's adversary, also gave lumbre natural importance and surprisingly deviated little from Las Casas's position. In his influential 1590 *Historia natural y moral de las indias* (*Natural and Moral History of the Indies*), for instance, Acosta stated that "although the darkness of infidelity have obscured the understanding of those nations, but in many things the light of the truth and reason do no cease to work in them to some extent, and thus commonly, they feel and confess that there is a Supreme lord and maker of everything" ([*1590*] 2000, bk. V, chap. 3, 302).[13] And yet, this "some extent" was rather limited. Like Las Casas, Acosta declared that, on his own, an Indian could only know so much—not that he was the only one, the first mover or primary cause—and that, to know more, he would need (as Las Casas argued) external help. In fact, in his 1588 *De procuranda Indorum salute* (How to provide for the salvation of the Indians), Acosta argued that the Indians' lack of good masters was one of the key reasons behind their lousy Christianity.

What was the difference between Las Casas and Acosta, then? To explain it and better situate what made the *NCBG* unique, one has to examine the historical narratives, universal, global, and local, in which each of these authors inserted (or not) the notions of natural light and the will to search for God, the last of which Acosta entirely left out of his theology.

Indigenous and colonialist intellectuals who penned histories of the Andes had to write them in ways that made them compatible with the Western histories of the world available around 1492. Schematically, the indispensable events and elements that had to be present, one way or another, included creation and paradise, the Fall and its consequences, the deluge and the ark, the progressive repeopling of the world, idolatry, the multiplications of tongues, and Christ's birth and the dissemination of his message. This schema set important limitations, affecting the way in which other key elements of the narrative fell into place.

First, all hypotheses about the repeopling of the world after the deluge, the Americas included, involved time. This meant progressive degeneration—loss of knowledge about God followed by ever increasingly frequent sins that further diminished man's already damaged nature—and sooner or later idolatry. It was a vicious circle, a downward spiral that, if left to its own devices, would continually weaken man's already weakened nature. Second, all hypotheses involved supernatural events and the existence of a chosen people who had a privileged relationship with God. Biblical history at large testified to it and the New Testament in particular was the result of the event that opened the door to step out of the circle (Christ's birth). As a result, universal history was so in a very specific manner: it had a central plot that made it universal—that is, it was relevant to all men, wherever they were and independently of whether they were or not aware of it—and took place in a privileged location and orientation; it happened in the Old World and from there flowed to the peripheries. As a result, Amerindian history, in whichever way it was explained, was both subsequent (important things happened elsewhere before) and derivative (what happened in America was a corollary of what had happened first elsewhere). As a result, the Spaniards' role (bringing Christ's message to the Americas) was providential.

What did colonialist thinkers do with these key elements? Las Casas's position was complex. On the one hand, the *Historia de las Indias* (*History of the Indies*) made Indians fit into the providential map—for reasons incognizable to man, God decided that certain peoples receive the light before others do, and in the case of the Americas, Spain was God's chosen agent and Columbus his instrument ([ca. 1561] 1994, chaps. 1–2, 353–61). On the other hand, in the *Apologética historia sumaria* (Brief apologetic history), the global historical process had two stages, each with a particular location and agency. The first stage was universal because it was human and pluricentric: as a result of his innate impulse, man, anywhere he happened to be, tended to search for God. For reasons having to do with his diminished nature, man often took the wrong path while searching and offered to creatures that which belonged to God alone— the origin of idolatry (Las Casas [ca. 1550–56] 1992, chaps. 73–74, 640–50). As a consequence, idolatry was something natural, a largely universal error that made man take *apariencias* (appearances), *vestigios* (traces), and *semejanzas* (resemblances) of the truth for the truth itself. The second stage was also universal but for an entirely different reason that made it global—because of Christ's birth and the dissemination of his message, which reached Indians with the conquest. It had therefore a unique setting, a privileged orientation, a temporal causality, and a supernatural agent.

Acosta's version of Andean history combined the same variables in a more straightforward manner. Like Las Casas, Acosta divided history into two. The first stage, as in Las Casas, went up to Christ's birth and included the beginning of idolatry, but he explained it in a radically different manner: it was not man's quasi-universal mistake but instead the result of the devil's work (Acosta [*1590*] 2002, bk. V, chaps. 1 and 4, 300, 306). In addition to including this supernatural agency, which had a negligible role in the work of Las Casas (and most thinkers of the Salamanca school), Acosta gave idolatry a precise origin: the portraits of the gentiles narrated in "the book of wisdom" ([*1590*] 2002, bk. V, chap. 6, 310).[14] Universal history overlapped with the global and had, then, a privileged orientation from the get go: Indians brought idolatry with them from the Old World and as a result the pre-Columbian Americas were—unlike in Las Casas's depictions—the devil's territory, a place where he ruled a land of "blind men" until the arrival of "the light and radiance of the Holy Gospel" ("la luz y resplandor del santo Evangelio") (Acosta [*1590*] 2002, bk. V, chap. 1, 299) delivered by the Spaniards. In this blindness, hereditary and very hard to fight, resided "the entire Indian problem" ("todo el problema indiano") (Acosta [*1588*] 1987, bk. I, chap. 5, 125). Finally, Acosta's history had, like in Las Casas's, a providential frame but, unlike in Las Casas's, it was cognoscible, "deserving their sins [of the Indians] that the almighty God leaves them under the power of his enemy, whom they chose for their god and shelter" ("mereciendo sus pecados [de los indios] que les deje el altísimo Dios en poder de su enemigo, a quien escogieron por dios y amparo suyo") ([*1590*] 2002, bk. V, chap. 10, 321). Indians had it coming.

At the time the *NCBG* was being written, Acosta's version of global and universal history had won the day. Campaigns to uproot Indian idolatry traversed the Andean landscape, and even late defenders of the lumbre natural in the Andes influenced by Granada, like the Franciscan Jerónimo de Oré, described Indians as "uneducated people of the hidden world, by dark fog until now besieged and in the deep sea inundated by the satanic choleric kingdom" ("inculta gente del oculto mundo, de niebla oscura hasta aquí cercada y en el piélago anegada del sathánico reyno furibundo") and called on them to "wake up already from such deep sleep" ("despierta ya de sueño tan profundo") ([*1598*] 1992, fol. 6v, 74). Indians were sleepyheads, present but absent—unaware remnants of the past.

UNIVERSAL, GLOBAL, AND LOCAL HISTORY, ACCORDING TO GUAMAN POMA

Guaman Poma's version of Andean precolonial history connected with the universal history in ways that differed from those just examined. The same elements were present—sixteenth-century readers would have recognized them and would not find them odd—but the ways in which he weaved them together defied all usual ways, unsettling all expectations. And yet, there were no heterodoxy or foreign elements in the pattern: everything was theologically sound and legitimately open to speculation since there was no record of Amerindian history in Western texts. In other words, the unusual aspects of Guaman Poma's history only made clear the rules of the game: all versions of Andean history were inventions that connected a few facts and as such conjectural. There was therefore no reason why alternative connections could be off-handedly dismissed.

The *NCBG* began with the very beginning: the question of origin. Spaniards had debated at large the way in which Indians had arrived in the Americas and from whom exactly they had descended.[15] Although there were numerous hypotheses, all framed the arrival as part of the long process of repeopling of the world that followed the deluge, with the aforementioned consequences. In contrast, in the *NCBG* not only was there no drifting away and errancy but there was also supernatural agency—although not of the kind imagined by Acosta or Alvarez and of a kind largely denied by Las Casas. It was God who had brought Indians straight from the Old World to the Americas: "Ordered God to leave this land [Ararat], spill and multiply over all the world of the sons of Noah; of these said sons of Noah, one of them brought God to the Indies; others say that he descended of Adam himself. The said Indians multiplied, that God knows all and as powerful he can have aside this people of Indians" (Guaman Poma [ca. 1614] 1987, fol. [25]25, 22).[16]

If miracles of this sort had happened in the Old World according to the Old Testament, why could they not have had happened in the New World? No one could prove or disprove the idea. Far from being a minor quirk, this unusual version of the origin of Andean people was the stepping stone of what proved to be a very coherent tale. By having Indians transported directly from Ararat to the Americas, Guaman Poma did two important things at once: he eliminated the passing of time and man's drifting and errancy, with its aforementioned consequences in terms of decadence, and he weaved the key elements of the theory of degeneration into a different heterodox narrative, laying the groundwork for Indian exceptionalism, one of his important claims.

As is known, according to Guaman Poma, in pre-Hispanic times Indians knew that God existed, addressed their prayers to him, and behaved in all regards like good Christians. What is not commonly pointed out is that, unlike any other colonial author, to explain this knowledge, the *NCBG* talked repeatedly about the *sombrilla* (little shadow) or *sombra* (shadow) of God—not about lumbre natural.[17] It referred not to the innate light that illuminated the darkness of the scholastic tradition but to the remains of what at some point had been something clear—the shadow or *huella* (trace) of what had once been present.

Guaman Poma took the shadow image from a text he knew well: Cabello Valboa's 1586 *Miscelánea antártica* (Antartic miscelanea). Cabello used the image of shadow to explain the outcome of a failed pre-Hispanic predication done by disciples of Saint Tomas who had arrived in the Andes from India. What was left of that early evangelic episode was shadow and not light because it had failed because Indians had not been ready (in Christian evolutionary terms) to receive the truth (Cabello [1586] 2011, bk. hs, 298, 303, 321). Guaman Poma took Cabello's image but rejected resolutely the Indians' incapacity mentioned by all colonialist authors, foes and friends of Indians alike. That is why he explained the knowledge of God in a different manner—in fact, in an obvious way: unlike all other peoples of the world who had wandered away from Ararat, walking from one place to another generation after generation (reaching eventually India) and on their way progressively losing their memories of God and degenerating, Indians had made it to the Americas instantly. Their memories were fresh and were therefore their most important tool in what concerned their knowledge about God. This explanation was absolutely unthinkable to any European author—Indians, they all agreed, entered global history too late to be able to recall anything, were too far away to have heard the good news, and (to some) had been the devil's deluded victims for centuries.

But by presenting this version of the origin, Guaman Poma did not simply eliminate the theory of degeneration altogether—instead, aware of its political capital, he used it to further propel his claim about Indian exceptionalism. He took the theory's ineludible elements and milestones, meeting the readers' expectations, and weaved them into an unexpected narrative that was orthodox and heterodox at once. For instance, while Indians eventually forgot some things about God and "they missed the path of glory" ("perdi[eron] el camino de la gloria"), this was due to the fact that they "did not know how to read or write" ("no supieron leer ni escriuir") (Guaman Poma [ca. 1614] 1987, fol. [60]60, 56). Guaman Poma constantly highlighted that, in spite of it, they did not deviate an inch from the practice of el bien vivir, of being a good Christian, implicitly denying that degeneration had occurred. Likewise, he included in his Andean history the multiplication of languages: "in this entire kingdom many kinds of castes and Indian languages came up" ("en todo este reyno salieron de muchas maneras de castas y lenguages de yndios") ([ca. 1614] 1987, fol. [61]61, 57), making plain that it had had no consequence whatsoever.

Unlike their peers in the Old World, Indians' nature had not only not worsened but it had actually improved and in fact they had gone way beyond what

the best and worst friends of the Indians considered possible. Thus, when Guaman Poma described the Andean peoples of the third age, he pointed out to the
Christian reader: "Look, Christian readers, look at this people, the third man,
who went further with his law and ancient ordinances of knowledge of the God
and creator. Although they were not taught, they had the Ten Commandments
and good deeds of mercy and alms and charity" ([ca. 1614] 1987, fol. [62]62, 58).[18]
In other words, Guaman Poma asked readers to note that, by their own means,
Indians had discovered not only what scholastics called primary truths (such
as God's existence) but also secondary ones (like the virtue of charity, the most
important of all, whose alleged lack figured prominently in Spanish colonialist
texts) and even those that, in other temporal and geographic contexts—and
not in any but in the one that was taken for *the* context: the Middle East of
biblical history—had been accessible to man only through direct supernatural
intervention, like the Ten Commandments ([ca. 1614] 1987, fol. [62]62, 58).[19]

Second, as it happened with the theory of degeneration, which was present in
unusual ways, the emphasis Guaman Poma gave to the Indians' natural capacity
to know God did not preclude the manifestation of the divine in the precolonial Andes. Guaman Poma's way of weaving the supernatural into the text
diverged again from that of any other colonial author. In the *NCBG*, there was
divine intervention and there was direct contact with the supernatural but they
followed a very specific rule: they were manifest only when truly necessary—
which was, as usual, orthodox and consistent with good scholastic theology.
Thus, on the one hand, God punished those who did not behave well—most
importantly, as is well known, the Incas. On the other hand, the lack of manifest divine intervention that characterized by and large Andean pre-Hispanic
history did not have to do with the fact that God looked away, disgusted by
the Indians' sins, or was simply elsewhere where true action was happening
while the devil ruled the Andes—it had to do with a very reasonable reason:
God looked at Indians constantly, even sent them disguised friars to test their
charity, and always found out that Indians behaved well and "they did not cease
to worship the God of the sky and kept the good commandment they had and
the good deeds of mercy" ("no dexauan de adorar a Dios del cielo y guardauan
el mandamiento que tenían y las buenas obras de misericordia") (Guaman Poma
[ca. 1614] 1987, fol. [78]78, 71–72).

Likewise, when he told that Indians discovered the Ten Commandments
and other important concepts on their own, what Guaman Poma implicitly
said was that to go beyond the allegedly universal *conocimiento confuso* (vague

knowledge), Indians needed neither grace nor doctrine, as both Las Casas and Acosta stated. Likewise, when he stated that the multiplication of the languages that occurred in the Andes was due to its vertical terrain—"the reason is the land, because it is so twisted and broken, they twisted the words and thus there are many dresses and ayllus" ["es por la causa de la tierra, porque está tan doblado y quebradas, torcieron las palabras y ancí ay muchos trages y ayllo"] ([ca. 1614] 1987, fol. [61]61, 57)—not to Babel and the following dispersal, what he implicitly said was that there had been no challenge to God and therefore there had been no punishment.[20] In fact, God liked what he saw. The fact that Indians multiplied abundantly in precolonial times proved it. This contrasted with both the biblical plagues of the Old World and the colonial plague . . . Spaniards were to Indians ([ca. 1614] 1987, fol. [95]95, 89)—humor was never too far in the text.[21]

In all cases, there was a subtext, however implicit, that must have been clear to any sixteenth-century reader: Indians achieved all this, *unlike* what happened to Old World peoples. That is, Guaman Poma not only told that universal history was (and is, as I will show) pluricentric but also that to all relevant extents Indians were superior to all other peoples in the world—which, for lack of a better phrase, I call Indian exceptionalism. Accordingly, all these examples also expressed a rejection of the detrimental defense proposed by the school of Salamanca. The latter's solution was to lower the bar, capping what could be asked of Indians as much as possible, and to largely exclude the supernatural.[22] The Yarovilca intellectual did the exact opposite: he went for the full package, engaging Spaniards in their own terrain, no disclaimers needed, no paternalist goodwill or enunciations of victimhood accepted.

From all this follows, thirdly, that there had been no privileged peoples who (they and only they) had enjoyed a personal relationship with God. Israel was just one more nation in the world map and what had happened in different parts of the world up to the moment of contact had followed separate, independent paths. This version of history implicitly challenged the crux of biblical history: there was neither a privileged place where *the* history occurred nor was there *a* people who knew the truth first and then shared it with the rest. Guaman Poma's history *was* global and universal but not in the way that the histories of Acosta, Las Casas, or Cabello Valboa were. It followed from this drastic reconfiguration of the spatial and temporal map that Indians had not been in a land outside time and space until the Spaniards arrived, as Oré put it. History neither had arrived in a (Spanish) boat—like *El requerimiento*, Acosta, and Oré declared—nor was Amerindian history subsequent and derivative, as Las Casas stated. It is as if Guaman Poma had said to Western readers, 'You generalize from your own mistakes and flaws and you never learn.' In fact, he pointed out, "consider that the Spanish nation was Jewish . . . and they had Moses's law and commandment. Which the Indians did not have, neither his law, or dressing, or face, or writing" ("conzedera que la nación de español fue judío . . . y tubieron ley de Muyzén y mandamiento. Lo qual no las tubieron los yndios su ley ni áuito ni rrostro ni letra") ([ca. 1614] 1987, fol. [954] 940, 1036). Spaniards did not know that they did not know.

Fourth, and for the same reason, history was truly simultaneous in the *NCBG*. Although focused in the Andes, it constantly sprinkled references to characters of and events that took place in the Old World. I can discern two functions of this sprinkling. On the one hand, it situated local history in the global sequence. Thus, for instance, the names of popes or Spanish kings, including the years and dates when they ruled, helped the reader have a synchronic view of the entire world—there was no arrested time like Oré declared. On the other hand, the sprinkling also disrupted the order of things of Western histories. Thus, for instance, Christ's birth or the arrival of Saint Bartolomé were mentioned in the flux of Andean events—they neither ordered the plot nor worked as watersheds, as was the case in Eurocentric narratives; instead, they were subordinated to the Indigenous plot. And yet, Indians in the *NCBG* were not cast as unaware while the narrator was omniscient—an option no colonialist account considered.

The result of this simultaneity was clearly different from Las Casas's first stage because it did not imply that the same process happened in each and all places and was different from Cabello's history because there was no single direction or Indian lag. These differences effected a redistribution of historical consciousness. Colonialist texts either assigned Spaniards a global consciousness prior to the conquest that turned them into the only active party (that is why Europe "discovered" the Americas and not the other way round) or suggested the Old World had known about the Americas' existence prior to its official "discovery."[23] Either way, Indians had no idea what was happening or that it was happening to them. Their position in the global history was of passive reception followed by after-the-fact hectic catching up. Guaman Poma inverted the distribution of historical awareness: Indians knew about Christ and Europe but Europeans did not know about Indians and the Americas. He stated explicitly that Indians knew about Europe through their "philosophers" ([ca. 1614] 1987, fol. [72]72, 67) and implicitly that they were not ignorant of Christ's birth. In his rewriting of the story of that event, as in all history books, the wise men paid homage to Christ when he was born; unlike in those other texts, in the *NCBG*, Balthasar was a Spaniard, Caspar was a black man, and Melchior was an Indian ([ca. 1614] 1987, fol. [91]91, 84).

Another important characteristic of the *NCBG*'s unique way of linking universal and Andean history was that it at no point suggested the existence of a pre-Hispanic evangelization. The issue was important: if Indians had known the truth, then they were not only idolaters but also apostates (Duviols 1977, 56). Las Casas dodged the problem entirely by declaring God's designs incognizable and stopping short of including external help. Cabello Valboa solved it poorly by saying that while the evangelization had reached Indians, they had not been ready for it. The *NCBG* solved the problem through chronology: both events—Christ's birth and the arrival of Saint Bartholomew—had happened when the Andes were under Inca rule, and according to Guaman Poma's historical narrative, the Inca had partnered with the devil and took Andean peoples down the idolatry drain.

In sum, the text's unbiblical yet Christian Orthodox rendering of precolonial Andean history was extraordinary and in fact unthinkable on several accounts. First, Guaman Poma made the case that Andean peoples, unlike any other, had managed through their own means alone to know God's existence, had acted according to what he had mandated, and had learned more about him as time passed by—contra what any theologian would accept. Second, he entailed a historical plurality cast in the language of Spanish radical texts but taken well beyond the limits of the Spaniards' thinking and summed it up in an unthinkable notion: "nuestra cristiandad" ("our Christianity") ([ca. 1614] 1987, fol. [679]665, 714). Third, of all the *cristiandades* (Christianities)—a theologically impossible plural—the Amerindian one had been the best. Indians had always behaved better than any other Christians, be they Chinese, Spanish, French, or Mexican ([ca. 1614]19 87, fol. [890]876, 956). They had no stain of Judaism or Moorish blood and therefore should be considered "old Christians" ("cristianos viejos") "of good blood and lineage" ("de sangre y linaje"). Finally, while Inca rule had negative effects in what concerned religious practices, Guaman Poma also made plain that these effects were rather superficial.[24] Thus, because they had never forgotten how things really were, Andean peoples continued to live according to the virtues of charity, compassion, and love under Inca rule.

UNEXPECTED HISTORIES 2:
NARRATIVES OF THE CONQUEST

The most unique and challenging version of the precolonial past just examined would have gotten readers to wonder if and how the events that took place during the conquest could acquire new meaning. The narrative of the conquest, the second part of the *NCBG's* devoted to retelling history, seems to be the most straightforward of the text. As scholars point out, these pages ground two central claims of the book: the negation of a just war having taken place in Peru and the acid critique of the Spaniards' Christianity. These assertions play a key role, the explanation goes, because they change the way in which the Spanish presence was to be understood. First, it was not the result of a legitimate act of war, as conquerors claimed. Guaman Poma repeatedly stated they "did not defend himself and there was no conquest" ("no se defendió y no ubo conquista"); therefore, the rights of people to their own government could not be overridden, Andean lords' authority had been unfairly removed, and it had to be restituted. Second, since the conquerors behaved as anything but good Christians and had not brought Christianity to Andean peoples, their claim to moral superiority and civilizing tasks was null and restitution was in order (e.g., Adorno 2000, 13–35, 59–61).

While many elements in the narrative of the conquest support this reading, I want to consider others that have not received equal attention with the hope that they broaden the frame of intelligibility. After all, restoration was not such a polemical idea—it was also part of Las Casas's political frame and pretty much along the just-mentioned lines.[25] I will analyze instead narrative strategies oriented not toward political polemics but toward decolonial pedagogy. To that end, I will focus on elements that seem to be either blatantly false, therefore absurd, or contradictory, therefore incoherent. For instance, a reader with some knowledge of the events in question would not have failed to wonder why an Inca ambassador was allegedly sent to meet people never heard of before. Conversely, an attentive reader would have wondered why, if the conquerors were cast as looters, thieves, and rapists, their bosses were dignified and called "ambassadors." Finally, any Christian reader would have had trouble reconciling the fact that the hand of God—manifest in the overall providential character of the conquest and in particular in the occurrence of miracles—was at work with the fact that its ultimate effect was the end of el buen orden (the good order) and the beginning of el mundo al reués ([ca. 1614] 1987, fol. [411]409, 416).

I argue that these seeming instances of blatant historical absurdity or argumentative incoherence had a purpose: they aimed to alter how the readers saw the world, how they made sense of it. Puzzling oddities were present to make them wonder, hesitate, and finally realize that it was the premises they held about the world that made these elements look odd, absurd, or incoherent, not the elements themselves. That is, the puzzles were key parts of a pedagogic strategy with specific decolonial aims.

WHY "GOVERNORS" AND NOT "AMBASSADORS": COLONIALITY MADE PLAIN

I begin fleshing out the oddities by examining the meeting of Inca and Spanish "ambassadors" in Túmbez, an alleged first-contact political scene. The fact that, according to Guaman Poma, an Inca ambassador welcomed the Spaniards in Túmbez was one more element that set the *NCBG* apart. While the presence of some sort of Indigenous spy was mentioned in passing by some sixteenth-century Spanish authors, none called him an "ambassador." Even fewer staged a solemn encounter accordingly, as Guaman Poma did.[26]

Scholars signal three rhetorical purposes that the (fictitious) presence of a greeting native ambassador may have served: it boasted Guaman Poma's pedigree since the ambassador happened to be his father, Don Martín de Ayala; it answered well-intended but demeaning representations of Amerindians as lacking the means and capacity to act politically; and it supported the no-resistance, no-just-war claim (Adorno 2000, 29–30).

While these are reasonable arguments, they do not help explain some inevitably odd things about the meeting. To begin, why was someone sent to welcome the Spaniards if no one knew who they were or even that they were coming? On a different but equally puzzling note, why did Guaman Poma call him "ambassador," given that he was going to meet conquerors, not diplomats? Likewise, if addressing the native actor as "ambassador" could make some sense for the aforementioned reasons, why were Pizarro and Almagro also called "ambassadors" (e.g., [ca. 1614] 1987, fol. [382]380, 386), especially when the conquerors were cast as sexual predators and looters, men overcome by greed to the point of sleeplessness? Why the dignifying misnomer?

I propose the bizarre meeting worked as one more element that supported Guaman Poma's goal of effecting a profound conceptual reconfiguration of the geopolitical map: it redressed the unequal distribution of historical awareness

FIGURE 1 "They made peace, the king emperor of Castilla and the king of this realm of Peru Uascar Ynga, legitimate. In his place went his second person and his viceroy Ayala." ("Se dieron pas el rrey enperador de Castilla y el rrey de la tierra deste rreyno del Piru *Uascar Ynga*, lextimo. En su lugar fue su segunda persona y su bizorrey Ayala.") (Guaman Poma [ca. 1614] 1987, fol. [377]375, 383)

and it signaled to the attentive reader that absurdity and incoherence lay not in the *NCBG* but in the world as it was commonly seen. This suggested, in turn, that the text should not necessarily be read as a way to claim historical truth, morals, or political rhetorics but instead as a way to undo settled ways of sense-making. Blatant historical falsity was not a disingenuous use of the historical genre in an attempt to sell something to the reader but an ingenious means to face him with a riddle.

The blatant fallacy in question had two components that are important to distinguish. The first one, the presence of an Inca ambassador, concerned a factual historical impossibility; the second one, the fact that Guaman Poma called Pizarro and Almagro "ambassadors," pointed to a conceptual impossibility. In addition to responding to demeaning representations of Amerindians as lacking the means and capacity to act politically, the presence of an Inca ambassador was coherent with Guaman Poma's narration in preconquest chapters of a related but separate global history in which Andean peoples were self-aware parties. In the same way that Christ's birth was known to Incas but had not changed things so was the Incas' understanding of the Old World and the Spaniards in particular.[27] The Inca ambassador redressed the asymmetry implicit or explicit in Spanish narratives in which Amerindians did not know about the Spaniards and the Old World while Spaniards knew about Indians and therefore were the only agents. That is, the meeting of the ambassadors undid the one-sidedness of global history. There was no gap—be it historical, political, or theological—separating Spanish and Indigenous peoples. This was the way nations related to each other. The result was that time became coeval, equal yet different at once. This rejection was one with and followed the same logic as the rejection of the Spanish/Christian sign, which was a direct result of the former.

But readers who were able to make sense of the presence of an Inca ambassador would have been left pondering the other piece of the puzzle: the presence of Spanish ambassadors. This second blatant fallacy also questioned established ways of making sense of the world although in a different manner—it hinged not on historical impossibilities but on conceptual ones. Guaman Poma labeled the conquerors' deeds and presence in Peru as illegal and repeatedly cast them as driven primarily by their thirst for riches and lust. And yet, he called the heads of the conquest enterprise "ambassadors." Why so? It would seem that something along the lines of looters, thieves, rapists, or murderers would have been more fitting. It is contradictory to denigrate them as madmen while dignifying them as ambassadors, to cast them as actors who followed their pulsations to subdue and steal but who also upheld the international right of peoples to their land and self-government.

The discrepancy was intentional. Its function was to effect change—it pushed the reader to look for a solution. In this case, the discrepancy pointed to a double problem: one part had to do with the local scene, the other with the center of power. In what concerned the first, if readers pondered how Spaniards had *behaved*, what they had done, the answer was clear: they (largely) stole and raped, like crooked Christians. If one asked how they *should* have behaved, what they should have done, the answer was equally clear: they should have acted as good Christians and with the dignity of ambassadors. The solution to the apparent puzzle was rooted, as it often was, in sixteenth-century theology: one thing was what people *should do* but what people actually *did* was another. And, the difference did not have to do with knowing—to know, everybody knew—but with acting accordingly. In other words, Guaman Poma's decolonial twist, based on Granada's theology, worked not only at the level of content but also at that of the narrative frame.

The second part of the problem, the discrepancies between how things had been in the center of power and how they should have been, signaled incoherence not by the conquerors in Peru but by the highest political players at court—what, from a Spanish point of view, was the center of the global/universal picture. To point out that conquerors acted poorly was not a very controversial or original thing to do—it was part of the pro-Indian repertoire, as Las Casas's *Brevísima* (1552) abundantly made plain. But to implicitly point out that the king had sent conquerors or governors and not ambassadors *was* indeed controversial and original. It went to the core of coloniality and told that Guaman Poma saw it as permeating Spanish colonialism from its lowest members (conquerors) to its most dignified head (king).

As a result of these two discrepancies between how things had been and how they should have been, every time the *NCBG* called Pizarro or Almagro "ambassadors," the incongruence screamed. Vis-à-vis this cognitive dissonance, readers had two choices: either to agree that such should have been the case although it was impossible (a Vitoria/Las Casas-inspired position of regret that they themselves largely allayed by Indian incapacity) or to smirk, thinking that such an idea was a ridiculous proposition. Behind the denial or the smirk would have been the problem Guaman Poma wanted a European-minded reader to see and confront: his belief in the (allegedly) self-evident abysmal difference between the parties' standing. Clearly, the Incas were not the French or the

British; therefore, to talk about sending ambassadors instead of conquerors or governors was ludicrous—as ludicrous as it would have been to send conquerors to Paris or London, giving them the title of governor or adelantado.

The *NCBG* tried to make visible the colonial (dis)order of things—the assumptions and narrative plots that went without saying and that made the aforementioned reactions to the meeting of ambassadors appear reasonable. To that end, it repeatedly confronted readers with discrepancies between the way things were and the way they really were. At the end of the day, the meeting contraposed two different kinds of impossible. The fictitious presence of an Inca ambassador was the representation of a *factual, historical impossible*: Incas could not know, that is why there had been none. The fictitious presence of a Spanish ambassador was the representation of a *conceptual impossible*: Spaniards knew, that is why there had been none. The joke was on them—and the laugh on anyone who could see.

THE OTHER HAND OF GOD

After solving this riddle, readers of the *NCBG* had to face, without respite, another apparent incoherence in the narrative of the history of the conquest. On the one hand, there had been no just war, as Guaman Poma repeatedly stated, and the aftermath of that injustice had been chaos and misery. On the other hand, the Incas had been defeated with divine help. The conundrum of an unjust outcome helped by the hand of God triggered the question of why. And, it fed two very popular Spanish ideas: Spaniards had carried out God's will (they were his chosen agents) so the outcome had to be celebrated (this was the conquerors' take), or the Indians had had it all coming (it was their fault) so the outcome, as bad as it may have been, was morally right (this was often clergymen's take). Either way, it justified the Spanish presence and actions. In what follows, I argue, as it happened with the first apparent historical incoherence (the meeting of ambassadors), the solution to the second apparent incoherence lay in a decolonial use of theology that defied racial lines as they were commonly imagined.

The expression "the hand of God" is commonly used to convey divine intervention, and while Spaniards did not often use it, it would have fit their accounts well. I employ the phrase "the other hand of God" to indicate that Guaman Poma's ways of making sense of divine intervention differed from the common ones at work in the colonies. The crucial element of his take was grace: who deserved it and why—matters the detrimental defense entirely sidelined.

To answer these questions in ways no one in the colonial Andes considered allowed him to provide an alternative interpretation of why the Incas had been defeated with divine help that in turn forced readers to reconsider their place in the world.

Guaman Poma began the story of the conquest by explicitly adopting the providential frame present in all Spanish narratives. He explained the timing of the arrival as follows: "And it was God's venture and permission that, in so much battle and bloodshed and loss of the people of this kingdom, came the Christians. God was served and the Virgin Mary adored and all the saints and sacred angels called that the conquest should happen in so much disorder of Uascar [and] Atagualpa Incas" ([ca. 1614] 1987, fol. [380]378, 384).[28] That is, divine providence had the Spaniards arrive when the Inca armies and energies were focused on the war of succession. Later on, miracles at key moments of the conquest further undermined Inca resistance.

These references to a hands-on master whose goals and means were cognoscible fit a particular version of divine intervention defended by Spanish conquerors—they were his agents, the executors of the divine will. Cristóbal Colón inaugurated the providential frame in the diary of his first trip, making of himself God's chosen agent (e.g., 1989, 127, 134), while in the official report of the discovery—the letter to Luis de Santangel—he explained the success of his enterprise as being a result of the intervention of God, who helped the king and the queen, as he always does to all who "walk his path" (1989, 145). The idea was picked up and developed ever after. Thus, for instance, in his first letter to the king, Hernán Cortés explicitly mentioned at least three acts of divine intervention: the hand of God prevented the Spanish fleet from leaving the island of Cozumel, allowing Jerónimo de Aguilar to rejoin the Spaniards ([1519] 2002, 58); it also helped the 400-strong Spanish force defeat 40,000 Indians in the battle of Veracruz; and to sum it all up, it allowed the discovery and conquest of the Aztec Empire to happen so that the Indians could be saved ([1519] 2002, 72). The same overarching frame was present in several accounts of the conquest of Peru, including its most well known: Xerez's *Verdadera relación* ([*1534*] 1985, 59, 113).

While conquerors used the trope largely to celebrate their deeds and to claim honor, rewards, and their right to rule, clergymen employed it with didactic ends, which also involved honor, deeds, and the right to rule, but over souls.[29] The twenty-fourth sermon of the *Tercero catecismo y exposición de la doctrina cristiana, por sermones* (Third catechism and exposition of the Christian doctrine through sermons) ("Tercero catecismo" [*1585*] 1990) stated that the conquest, and all the bad things that followed from it, happened because God wanted to punish the Indians for their precolonial and current sins. The sermon's theme was fornication and adultery—it began by explaining why, in spite of being forbidden acts, they happened and God did not punish the offenders. The answer was double. On the one hand, the explanation was individual: if God did not punish these sins right away it was only because he would deliver an even harsher punishment as sins piled up. On the other hand, the explanation was collective: while an offender may not be punished on the spot, his people as a whole may be. After presenting biblical examples of collective divine punishment, the point was driven home: "Know that the cause of why God has allowed the Indians to be so afflicted and hounded by other nations, is because of this vice [sodomy] that your ancestors had, and many of you still have. And know that I tell you on behalf of God that if you do not reform, all of your nation will perish. And God will finish you and scrape you from the earth" ("Tercero catecismo" [*1585*] 1990, 710).[30] Moreover, the sermon went on to say that even the sexual sins of Spaniards were the Indians' fault. For instance, it was because Indian women seduced (Spanish) priests that the latter had sex with them—a particularly reprehensible act, given that they were holy men.

In short, while not celebrative of Spanish deeds and outcomes like conquerors, clergymen still invoked the providential frame to explain the present: everything bad that happened and continued to happen to Indians was the Indians' fault—this followed, in essence, the same structure of *El requerimiento*. In other words, much of what Guaman Poma vehemently denounced, including sexual abuse of Indian women by Spaniards and the looming physical end of the Indians, was cast by the 1583 Third Ecclesiastical Council of Lima as being the Indians' fault—and their deplorable state as being part of God's plan. The council inverted moral standing and blame and presented the inversion as a description of the true order of things: the world upside down. In addition, in this and other cases in which the catechism used examples of the past to justify current and future ecclesiastic politics, it went without saying that correcting Indians and teaching them how to be good Christians was what was needed.

To understand Guaman Poma's way out of this predicament (to explain a bad outcome helped by God), the first element readers had to take into consideration was the fact that the Incas were evil.[31] Scholars explain it by saying that Guaman Poma's father's nation, the Yarovilcas, had been conquered by the Inca. While this may be true, it neither explains why he chose to not identify with his mother, who was of royal Inca lineage, nor considers the problems that result from it. After all, the portrayal of the Incas as taking native peoples down the idolatry drain seems to contradict the overall positive image of pre-Hispanic Andean peoples. I suggest that portraying the Incas as evil responded to the needs of the overall coherence of his historical narrative. It is a way to reconcile two facts: the first that Indians did not adore God when the Spaniards arrived and yet had been on the upward track and the second that Indians neither had lacked God's favor prior to it nor were *novatos* (novices or rookies) after it, as the Third Ecclesiastical Council of Lima stated.[32] The key elements he used in this part of the plot were the devil, miracles, and grace.

The devil was a necessary part of a solution. If, according to Guaman Poma, early Andean peoples had been proto-Christians (Christians avant la lettre) and, unlike Spaniards, had always been on an upward line of development that faced no limits or deviated from the right path, then the only way to introduce idolatry without contradicting Indian exceptionalism was to bring an outsider into the picture. To invoke the presence of the devil in the context of universal history was to some extent unproblematic. According to all Western stories, he had appeared everywhere, sooner or later, to all peoples—his presence did not necessarily signal God's anger or his looking the other way. But, the devil also played an important role in most Spanish justifications of the conquest, be they celebrative ones like Xerez's *Relación* or somewhat critical ones like Acosta's *Historia*. Regardless of how exactly his presence was explained, it helped cast conquerors and priests as bearers of the light and defeaters of the enemy. The question then was how to fit the Inca-devil partnership into an alternative providential narrative. Guaman Poma's answer was to turn the conquest into an event that helped Andean peoples for their own sake and on their own terms.

First of all, if readers considered the effects of Guaman Poma's presentation of the devil, they would realize that they were unlike those mentioned by any Spanish text. In the *NCBG*, the devil was linked to idolatry but idolatry equaled neither the Las Casean image of Indian "error" nor the Acostean image of the devil "tricking" easy-to-delude Indians. Instead, it only meant the oppression of the Indians' persistent true will, which continued to be revere God only. The fact that Indians had continued to adore the creator while forced to adore Inca *huacas* made plain both the persistence of their true will and the fact that they had not been tricked or fooled.[33] In short, even if ruled by idolaters, under Inca rule Indians had not turn into idolaters tout à coup.

The second element readers had to examine in order to understand the other hand of God was the occurrence of miracles during the conquest. The *NCBG's* conquest pages mentioned important miracles that took place during the 1536–37 year-long siege of Cuzco led by Manco Inca. These references were not accidental—Guaman Poma could have chosen to exclude them (not all Spanish accounts of the siege mentioned miracles).[34] In other words, he chose to include them. Why? A possible answer was that the occurrence of miracles answered explanations of Amerindians' failure to embrace Christianity when it was first presented to them, advanced by proponents of the detrimental defense—since miracles had not happened, Indians had not been persuaded. Another possible reason for their insertion was that Guaman Poma was writing against later theologians who had introduced a plot twist: they had argued that Indians were such low people that no miracles were needed to impress Spanish (Christian) superiority onto them, unlike what had happened with Greeks and Romans (Adorno 2000, 31). While it may well be true that the inclusion of miracles related to either of these arguments, the miracles would still serve critical or celebratory narratives' take on the hand of God—at the end of the day, God had helped the Spaniards. There was however an understudied clue in the *NCBG* that signaled elsewhere: miracles did not happen to make the Spaniards win; they happened to make the Incas lose so that Indians could win—which was not an option to any Spanish author, critical or celebrative.

When Santa María appeared during the siege, "from seeing her the Indians were frightened and it is said that she threw soil on the eyes of the infidel Indians. How God and his blessed mother performed a miracle to grant favor to the Spanish Christians" ("de uelle se espantaron los yndios y dizen que le echaua tierra en los ojos a los yndios ynfieles. Cómo Dios hizo milagro para hazelle merced y su madre bendita a los españoles cristianos") (Guaman Poma [ca. 1614] 1987, fol. [405]403, 410). So far, the quote supported traditional readings of the miracle and the hand of God. But, the sentence continued with a clarification: "or better said, the Mother of God rather meant to grant favor to the Indians so that they would be Christians and their souls would be saved" ("por mejor dezir que más quiso hazer merced la Madre de Dios a los yndios porque fuesen cristianos y saluasen las ánuimas de los indios") (Guaman Poma [ca. 1614] 1987, fol. [405]403, 410). Had the Incas won, Inca rule would have continued and, with it, idolatry.

In light of its particular way of casting Peru's Indigenous peoples' idolatry, it was only reasonable that the *NCBG*'s portrayals of divine intervention during the conquest primarily addressed the Indians, not the Spaniards. The former pleased God, who expressed his love by helping them. The latter were just military pawns with a function to eliminate the Incas, but completing this mission did not make them partakers of God's grace.[35] In fact, it could be argued, in what concerned the Spaniards, the miracles were meant to remind them of God so they behaved as good Christians—a point they had clearly missed.

Equally important, God's goal was not to help Spaniards convert Indians; it was to help Indians practice their Christianity—something that, once again, was not in the horizon of any Spanish text written in the Andes. That is why, sardonic and straight talk mixed, Guaman Poma's version of the Indian *Pater Noster* (Our Father) asked God's protection not only from the usual foes of man, like any other *Pater Noster*, but also from corregidores, priests, and other colonial "helpers" ([ca. 1614] 1987, fol. [850]836, 901). This solution also differed from a common position of Lascasean-influenced chroniclers: the messengers were unworthy but delivered the right message. In Guaman Poma's text, the Spaniards not only were unworthy of the message but they also did not deliver it. There was no contradiction, unlike the good-willed internal Spanish critique which, as critical as it might be, sustained privilege. In short, the conquest was the Indians' movie, not the Spaniards'. That is why Guaman Poma highlighted that, had the Spaniards arrived right before Inca rule began, Indians would have become saints ([ca. 1614] 1987, fol. [61]61, 67). Indians had known about God, had always had the best possible order, had lived in direct contact with him, and had continued to maintain a relationship with him despite all odds.

The third and final element that would have led readers to see the other hand of God was grace—which in the *NCBG* was bestowed to Indians alone. The Holy Spirit appeared in only three of the text's 398 images: it descended upon Martín de Ayala, Guaman Poma's brother and teacher ([ca. 1614] 1987, fol. [14]14, 13); it descended upon poor Indians praying in church ([ca. 1614] 1987, fol. [623] 609, 651); and it descended upon a lonely Indian woman praying before Christ's image ([ca. 1614] 1987, fol. [837]823, 883)—but never upon a Spaniard.

The significance of Indians being the recipients of God's gift in the only three instances it occurs cannot be understated. God's grace not only mattered as a punctual and extraordinary manifestation of the divine—this was true of the role of miracles as well—but it was also the key element of the general new regime of intelligibility, of which the text invited readers to partake. As mentioned, in his *Memorial de la vida cristiana*, Granada stressed repeatedly that of the two key elements that must be considered to the good living, which was the ultimate goal of a Christian, the most important was not *saber* (to know) but *poder hacer* (to be able to do) ([*1565*] 1994–95, vol. II, 15–16).[36] Granada asked, why

FIGURE 2 "Martin de Ayala, hermit / excellent sire, prince / lady Juana Curi Ocllo, coya [queen]/ in the city of Cuzco" ("Martin de Ayala, hermitaño / don Martin Ayala, excelentísimo señor, p[r]incipe / doña Juana *Curi Ocllo, coya* [reina] / en la ciudad del Cuzco").

FIGURE 3 "My children, I will announce the gospel, the sacred scripture. You should not serve the local gods. Before, your ancestors lived like that, but you right now have already been baptized, my children" ("Evangelista sagrada escritura *uillascayque, churicona. Uaca uilcataca manam* sermo *y quicho. Chaytaca naupa machoyque chi yacharca. Camca* bautisacca *nam canque, churi* Hijos míos, les voy a anunciar el evangelio, la sagrada escritura. No deben servir a las divinidades locales. Antes, sus antepasados vivieron así, pero ustedes ahora ya están bautizados, hijos").

FIGURE 4 "Cristiana"

does man do what is wrong if he knows it is so? Because he cannot help it. As a result of the Fall, no man can do the right thing all the time—it exceeds his natural power. To overcome this limitation, he needs a supernatural supplement: grace (Granada [*1565*] 1994–95, vol. II, 15–16).

The Granadine master devoted much of his *Memorial* to questions about grace. In which conditions may God grant or withdraw it? What are the means to access it? How do they work? As in previous cases, bringing up these theological views in a colonial discussion shifted entirely the terms of the local conversation. In Granada's text, not only was the question of knowing not an issue but his *Memorial* also did not make qualifications about race or origin—grace was a personal, individual matter. That is, all men were in the same predicament. In a peninsular context, such an idea was unproblematic; in a colonial context, it was highly controversial. It questioned the cornerstone of the colonial order: the difference between Spaniards and Indians. To omit it meant that when it came to explain what any given Indian did or did not do, the question ceased to be guided by the color line. Instead, it shifted to how any men (regardless of whether Indian, Spaniard, or black) could access grace.

With these three elements in mind, the specific puzzle about colonial history (how to reconcile the hand of God with the fact that Indians suffered and Spaniards went unpunished) ceased to be so. Guaman Poma alerted Christian readers not to jump to easy conclusions. Miracles, he said, were many different things: from checking the Indians' charity to earthquakes; from pests like smallpox and measles to extraordinary snow storms; from frozen harvests to mice and other plagues. Miracles even included, in another titillating mix of sarcastic and straight talk, "bad Christians to steal property from the poor and to take away their wives and their daughters and use them" ("malos critianos a rrobar hazienda de los pobres y quitalles sus mujeres y a sus hijas y seruirse de ellas") (Guaman Poma [ca. 1614] 1987, fol. [95]95, 89). Why? Because "with all this God reminds us and tells us to call on him, and in each man and in each house God sends his punishment to the world so that we call him and he gives us grace so that he may take us to his glory where the most holy Trinity lives" (Guaman Poma [ca. 1614] 1987, fol. [95]95, 89).[37] Calling on God was, according to Granada, the most efficient way of accessing grace, and Guaman Poma echoed this idea numerous times throughout the text. It was this theological line of thinking that opened up the reading of Cuzco's siege as an example of divine intervention favorable to Indians, as presented above. Miracles happened neither to move Indians to convert nor to help God's chosen ones (aka the Spaniards) as the reductionist and prevalent colonialist Spanish readings affirmed. Rather, they happened to help Indians get rid of the Incas and eventually to remind those who called themselves Christians (but did not behave accordingly) about what mattered—a position that neither friends nor foes of the Indians considered.

This alternative theological way of thinking about divine intervention also explained, in different terms than the Concilio, why God chose not to punish those who did bad deeds and not reward those who did good deeds. In the first case, he could let sinners lose themselves irretrievably so that their eternal punishment would be the harshest and most definitive. Granada explained: "The punishment these deserve is the one God gives them, which is the greatest that can be given, which is to let them do as they do all their life until death arrives, when it will happen to them what usually happens to those who never really did true penance" ([*1565*] 1994–95, vol. I, 65).[38] In the second case, God could let good doers suffer to test their faith, patience, and perseverance before adversity, wanting them to feel their *desamparo* (abandonment) and *olvido* (oblivion), pray to him for help, and then wait to be rewarded with the highest recompense (Granada [*1565*] 1994–95, vol. II, 51–55). While the twenty-fourth sermon mentioned the first possibility, it not only did not consider the second but it also read the Indians' present circumstances as evidence of past sins.

To these alternative theological ways of interpreting divine intervention, with their important consequences in terms of history, Guaman Poma added a couple more as the text progressed. In the "Conzideraciones" ("Considerations") section, he told Spanish readers in particular of another reason why there was no punishment: there were many effective prayers asking God for forgiveness and *misericordia* (mercy). "Saint Mary Peña of France prays to her son Lord Jesus Christ, and the he-saints and she-saints, angels of heaven, for the world and sinners" ("Santa María Peña de Francia ruega a su hijo señor Jesucristo, y los santos y santas, ángeles del cielo, por el mundo y por lo pecadores") (Guaman Poma [ca. 1614] 1987, fol. [946]932, 1026). Finally, there were the prayers of "those who are in the world, the holy priests, clergymen, friars and hermits, and others with no habits, holy men and holy women of the world" ("los questá en el mundo, de los santos saserdotes, clérigos, frayles y hermitaños y otros que no traen áuito, santos y santas señoras del mundo") (Guaman Poma [ca. 1614] 1987, fol. [947]933, 1028).

In short, things were not as Spaniards in the Andes made them look. Nothing in the past had been as they said it had been, and God's acts were not readable only in the ways colonialist authors ubiquitously and self-confidently stated they were. A theologically sound understanding of providential history and divine grace based on highly reputed Christian authorities told an entirely different story. From it, clear consequences for understanding the future followed. The Spaniards had done their job. They had removed the Incas. Now, it was time to start walking again the path of universal history—that which was really important to everyone. And, when it came down to it, Andean peoples had always been ahead of Spaniards. Therefore, the discussion toward 1614 should have not been about how to teach or to eradicate errors but about how to let be what should be. And yet, it was not. How did Guaman Poma explain the discrepancies between how things were and how they should be? And, equally if not more important, what did he think could be done about it?

3

THE COLONIAL PRESENT
EXPLAINED TO BLIND MEN
UPSIDE DOWN

ONCE THE unthinkable yet entirely reasonable historical narrative of the *NCBG* reached the present, the text switched to describing the way things were and argued for how they should be. This second part, often called "Buen Gobierno" ("Good Government"), has different sections. The first one examines each and every imaginable colonial social actor, telling each of these Christian readers what they do well, what they do not, and what they should do instead. The next two sections, which have specific addresses, are in line with the debate anchored around the 1601 and 1609 royal decrees about forced mining labor: the Considerations, a sort of recapitulation directed to Spanish readers, and a fictional dialogue with the king in which Guaman Poma listed problems and suggested changes. After a description of Peru's cities comes one of the text's most commented chapters, "The Author Walks" ("Camina el Autor"), which narrates Guaman Poma's experiences as he traveled toward Lima, where he intended to deliver the *NCBG* so that it would eventually reach the king. The book ends with a to-do list for colonial authorities to help Indians thrive.

In the most detailed study of the transition between the first and the second parts of the text, Rolena Adorno characterized it as a switch from history to sermon. This change in the method of delivery, she argues, testifies to both the failure of legal and political discourses as avenues for reform and Guaman

Poma's failure to make sense in a coherent way of what happened since the Spanish arrival. By adopting the sermon genre, he intended to use its emotional effectiveness to move readers, especially the king. However, even that attempt faltered. The text becomes tiresomely repetitive—there is no overall plot, just a number of starts and stops that end in despair. Thus, Adorno notes, as he neared Lima on foot, Guaman Poma cried, "World upside down, it is a sign that there is no God and no King, they are in Rome and Castile" ("Mundo al reués, es señal que no hay Dios y no hay Rey, está[n] en Roma y en Castilla") (Adorno 2002, 78–79, 140–42). Expanding the study of Guaman Poma's use of the sermon rhetoric to include apocalyptic prophetic discourses, Rocío Quispe-Agnoli also sees the shift as indicating Guaman Poma's incapacity to explain in a satisfactory manner the ills affecting native peoples in colonial times. However, highlighting the arbitrista elements of the text, she suggests that he still had faith that the king would address the situation once properly informed (Quispe-Agnoli 2006, 38–91, 88–89, 253–257). Juan Ossio takes a different path to explain the arbitrista goal of Guaman Poma's "letter to the king" (1977): it aimed to reconcile Andean and Western ideas of order and time. In this light, the Spanish king is the successor of the Inca, a mediator between human and divine orders, and as such the only one who can provide a solution to a world that the Spanish presence has turned upside down, a true "Pachacuti" (Ossio 2008, 25, 200–72).

In what follows, I present an alternative interpretation of the so-called second part of the text. I argue that—like the previous one—it was geared not toward remedying the present through direct action (a reform that a persuaded king would carry out) but toward teaching. Also, the solution was in the future but not because there was no one to effect political remedies in Peru. Rather, because the only way to fix the way things were was to change the way people saw the world. It was an internal change that required time and that no authority could effect. Making that change possible one reader at a time demanded constant challenges to the readers' common sense and plenty of repetition so, as the effect accumulated, the shift in vision became a new common sense. These challenges, which in the first part of the text were present in the form of puzzling historical accounts, in the second part were present as striking short stories that faced readers with the ways in which the colonial world was upside down.

While the stories worked at different levels simultaneously, for the sake of clarity, I focus each of the three following sections on different traits of the overall pedagogical project. The first section tackles repetition. It argues that what may look like the same thing retold over and over was in fact a collection of singular attempts to have readers recognize the different ways in which coloniality manifested itself in everyday life in order to question privilege. The next section focuses on Guaman Poma's walk. It argues that it did not matter where he was going or what he might achieve there but instead what he taught while he walked. Once seen through the lens of Guaman Poma's particular theological take, the walk revealed itself to teach not failure but success and validation. The final section focuses on ecclesiastic rhetorics. It argues that he used it not to move readers (prominently the king) to make reforms but to have all readers see the world anew. That would be the real game-changer. Until then, colonial administrators should lessen the damage, following the month-to-month suggestions with which the book ends.

AN ETHNOGRAPHY OF COLONIALITY AND PRIVILEGE

It has been suggested that the *NCBG*'s "ethnographic chapters" (the so-called "Buen Gobierno" part) are a strong indictment of Spanish colonialism. Like a reverse mirror of colonialist discourses, they repetitiously present Spaniards' abuses and sins and Indians' suffering and good deeds. While there is no shortage of examples to support this reading, this interpretive frame also faces some problems. For it to work, Spaniards would always have to be bad and Indians would always have to be good—and yet that is not so. In many cases, there are bad Indians, and in others, there are good Spaniards. Guaman Poma did not cast all Spaniards as bad and all Indians as good because that would have reproduced the divide constitutive of the Spanish race-thinking he questioned. That is why Las Casas's radical inversion, exemplified abundantly in the *Brevísima* (1552), was not attractive to him. He emphasized individual actions instead. Indians, like Spaniards or blacks, could act well or not. They could condemn themselves or not. Because they all answered to the way things really were (dictated by the order of the logos), they were all equal. At the same time, not everyone deviated from the way things really were in the same ways or for the same reasons. And equally importantly, not everyone was aware of it.

Addressing these differences required shifting the analysis from discussing the way things were to discussing the way people made sense of how things were. In other words, since the difference was between how some *thought* reality was (those who reaped most of the benefits of that way of thinking) and how reality *really* was, the central task was to undo the effects of the veil on those (be they Spaniard or Indian or black) who saw only the projection on the screen and took it for the real thing, finding in the movie either validation or damnation. To debunk the workings of race-thinking and coloniality, Guaman Poma exposed readers to the different ways in which these distinctions came into play in everyday colonial situations. The stories offered, in short, a conceptual ethnography. They confronted readers with discrepancies and anomalies and offered a solution only if readers let the premises they used—their usual ways of seeing the world—crash. A good place to begin fleshing out the text's complexities is a well-known passage of the Conzideraciones in which he called Spaniards *extranjeros* (*mitimacs* or foreigners):

> "You should consider that the entire world belongs to God, and thus Castile belongs to the Spaniards and the Indies belong to the Indians and Guinea to the Blacks. [And] that each of these are legitimate owners. . . . The law of Castile . . . , *which because of the Indians, it is referred to and they call it the law*, and they should call it [of the] foreigners [*sic*], and in the language of the Indians, mitmac, Castile manta samoc, that they came from Castile. (Guaman Poma [ca. 1614] 1987, fol. [929]915, 1004–1005; emphasis mine)[1]

To say that Castile's law was valid in Spain but in Peru Indian law should be the law fit the theological-juridical frame set by Las Casas in his 1565 *Doce dudas* (Adorno 2000, 25–26); and to say that Spaniards should be called mitmacs inserted local categories into Las Casas's map (Ossio 2008, 208–9). But to say *"which because of the Indians, it is referred to and they call it the law"* (*"que a razon de los yndios que se quenta y le dize por la ley"*), meant to stress that, at the end of the day, the problem was *why* the dominant narrative said what it said. It highlighted the abysmal difference between the parties' standing that existed in the Spaniards' mind. Spaniards thought Indians were a subspecies whose customs were okay when only those with special needs were involved (as in tournaments for children only, in which adult rules are modified or disregarded)—but when it came to the real thing and adults were involved, Spanish law was *the* law.

What was Guaman Poma's response to the fact that Spaniards acted as if Indians and Indian things were not just different but a substandard variety? It was not a rewriting that emphasized equality (as in the cristiano lector case) but a rewriting of difference that contrasted the colonial difference with the correspondence between earthly and divine orders. The colonial difference, as

Guaman Poma conceptualized it in this case, was backed by the Western narrative of global and universal history (two but one), with its (their) privileged orientation, causality, and agency—from Europe to the Indies, driven by Spaniards. The former was a particular past to be superseded by the latter's universal future. That is why Westerners' ways and laws were superior and Indians' were ignorable. Guaman Poma's historical narrative instead had no privileged orientation and different causality and agency: it was God's design to have Indians in the Andes, where they had developed their order—which was as close to the right one as it came. As a consequence, not only did it not go without saying that Castile law was *the* law but it also showed ignorance of a very special kind: Spaniards could not grasp the larger conceptual map, the true order that allowed people to make sense of the everyday experiences they faced. In other words, Spaniards often mistook their being in Peru for what they saw Spaniards in Peru doing, in the same way the cacique in Santo Tomás's example allegedly did with Christians and tailors (see chapter 1). And, they did not know that they did not know.

This difference, central to Guaman Poma throughout the text, did not necessarily entail any other difference—be it cultural or epistemological (as today's thinkers often call it) or national or historical (as sixteenth-century thinkers often did). Spaniards regularly deviated from, and were blind to, not other orders (in plural) but to *the* order that took a particular shape in Peru and another in Spain but remained the same—the plural cristiandades, an unthinkable idea to those who conflated the universal and themselves and one that made of Guaman Poma's an avant la lettre decolonial theology.[2]

While this first example of Guaman Poma's conceptual ethnography tackled coloniality by arguing that there were differences—although not of the kind most Spaniards were capable of imagining—others demonstrated the opposite: the same principles and laws should hold for anyone, regardless of where they were and who they were. And yet they did not, which in turn made following colonial law an assertion of privilege. A good, recurring example was that of taxation, which Guaman Poma entangled with questions of blood and status. In the "Buen Gobierno" chapters, he repeatedly called the readers' attention to the following nonsense: while Indians were called *tributarios*, Spaniards in the Andes were not called *pecheros*. Tributario referred in Peru to the social condition of any Indian (ethnic lords exempted) since they all had to pay a *tribute* (personal tax) for the simple fact of being Indian. And while used there to refer to taxes, in the Spanish peninsula it related to religious difference—it was the name of the payment Christians who did not convert had to make to Muslim authorities prior to the Reconquista (Seed 1995, 69–99; 2001, 73–81). Pechero, on the other hand, referred in Spain to the social condition of any Spaniard who had to fulfill the obligation of paying a *pecho* (personal tax). It distinguished commoners or plebeians from nobles, who were exempt. The terminological problem pointed to a larger, well-known attitude problem: Spaniards, from the moment they set foot in America, acted as if no one was their lord and they were lords of everything and everyone.

Because the legal terminology effected an unreasonable transformation, Guaman Poma argued that Spaniards in Peru "should pay His Majesty's personal tax, for it is Castile's law and they are children of commoners; even if they were conquistadors, they have to pay, and it is fair that they pay" (Guaman Poma [ca. 1614] 1987, fol. [471]467, 478).[3] In other words, it was who they were that determined peoples' statuses, not where they were, what they did, or how much money they might have. A pechero did not cease to be so in the Americas.[4] Note that the problem Guaman Poma signaled was not one of an Indigenous order being upset but of Indigenous *and* European orders being upset, in the colonies, because they were colonies. His solution was to have any and all Europeans carry a document "on their chests" that identified "if he is a commoner, a nobleman, a knight, a Jew or a Moor or a mestizo or a Mulato or a black" ("ci es pechero, ci es hidalgo, ci es cauallero, ci es judío o moro o mestizo o mulato o negro") (Guaman Poma [ca. 1614] 1987, fol. [546]532, 560).[5]

The statement, radical as it was from a racial and political point of view, was also meant as an intervention in the heated debate that surrounded the 1601 and 1609 *reales cédulas* (royal decrees) regulating Indian labor. The crux of the debate was triggered by the fall of the tax-paying Andean population of the late 1590s and early 1600s. And while there were many (Spanish) voices and opinions in the debate, they all revolved around how to better manage demands for Indian labor so that the Indigenous population would grow back to secure the survival of the system.[6] While many of the points Guaman Poma argued (mainly in the Conzideraziones and in his fictional dialogue with the king) echo those raised by other participants in the debate, his reclassification of all tax payers (regardless of who they were and where they came from) as pecheros was unique to him.[7] And, it meant nothing short of turning the world upside down: instead of having Indians be the problem, as Spaniards argued, he wrote Spaniards as the problem—both what they did and what they thought. He highlighted the contrived nature of the colonial everyday by pointing out, full of acid humor, that when an Indian woman gave birth to an Indian (therefore a taxpayer) instead of a mixed blood fathered by an abusive Spaniard, those in power in colonial Peru found it "scandalous" ([ca. 1614] 1987, fol. [984] 966, 1061).

And, there was even more to the argument. As for *tributo* (tribute)—since it was a word that related taxation to religious difference and Indians had always been and were Christian—as the *NCBG*'s historical narrative abundantly proved, "if someone were to say tribute or tax, he sins mortally, because he makes a slave out of a free man" ("quien digere tributo o taza peca mortalmente porque de libre le haze esclabo") because "that which God did not make no child of his can be" ("lo que Dios no hizo no puede hacello su criatura") (Guaman Poma [ca. 1614] 1987, fol. [902]888, 972). Therefore, "let us not call them tributaries but pecheros; the children of lords, excise-payers, and the common Indians, pecheros" ("que . . . no se llame tributario sino pecheros; alcaualeros, los hijos de los principales, y los uajos yndios, pecheros") (Guaman Poma [ca. 1614] 1987, fol. [995]977, 1072). In the same way that Spanish pecheros did not cease to be so in the Americas, Indian pecheros did not cease to be so once Spaniards arrived.

Besides (or precisely for that reason), he reminded the readers of the true order of things: "Because the Christians' law is all one, the governor and the justice must believe what the gospel and God's holy scripture say and keep the law of God and the King our lord" ("porque la ley de cristianos es todo una, el gouernador y la justicia a de creer lo que dize el euangelio y la sagrada escritura de Dios y guardar la ley de Dios y del rrey nuesto señor")—not to do this "is a lie and it cheats on obedience" ("es mentira y se engaña en ello obediencia") ([ca. 1614] 1987, fol. [471]467, 478). Note the word choices: to disbelieve what God mandated was not simply wrong, it was "a lie," and to not follow God's word and yet claim to be Christian, was to cheat on obedience—that is, to fake or to pretend to do or be what one was not. The word choice involved a reversal of another common Spanish idea about Indians: converted Indians pretended to be Christians. Clergymen and administrators in the Andes frequently stated that Indians faked it. Guaman Poma's reversal, as is often the case in the *NCBG*, connected what (in the colonies) were disparate phenomena (taxation and conversion), demanding abstraction from the reader—exactly the capacity Spaniards unanimously denied Indians had. In short, the example asked readers to do two related things: first, to visualize that the colonial social order was wrong and contrived, and second, to accept that Spaniards were less capable of abstract thinking than Indians since the former failed to see while the latter's eyes were quite sharp.

The previous example fleshed out the (colonial) problem of following the law as an assertion of privilege—after all, it was colonial law that allowed Spaniards to no longer be pecheros, that made of Indians' tributarios, and that stated that Castile law superseded native law.[8] The next examples of Guaman Poma's conceptual ethnography tackled its Janus sister: the practice of ignoring the law as an assertion of privilege—which made perfect sense because, after all, privilege was privilege. The first example addressed the usual colonial practice of disregarding colonial laws with the argument that the king had not been properly informed prior to issuing them and they were contrary to the common good. Shifting from the mode of logical argumentative exposition to that of personal experience, like Spanish chroniclers did when they wanted to illustrate a point they argued about Indians, Guaman Poma told the following anecdote. As he walked, he arrived in a town where a Spaniard told him that he was wasting his time, that he should have Indians work as much as the local Spanish authorities wanted. Guaman Poma responded that the work Indians were being asked to do exceeded what *ordenanzas* (colonial laws) stipulated; the Spaniard responded: "'Know that the ordinances . . . are good for Indians, not for Spaniards. That the ordinances and laws are in Castile of the Spaniards. We are free. And thus, I tell you not to tire. Knit, weave promptly. With that you will finish and they will be happy'" ([ca. 1614] 1987, fol. [1116]1106, 1183).[9]

There was no faking, no discourse of tough love, no invoking of the common good. He just told it like it was: there was privilege, and it was fine. In Castile, Spaniards were constricted by the rule of law, Castilian law. In Peru, they were not; they were "free." One could read the recommendation for Indians to not bother arguing about it as one more example of the fact that Guaman Poma believed that there was no solution. I think that while that reading is not necessarily wrong if one is thinking how the colonies actually worked, there is another layer of meaning in the same example and therefore another purpose: it made visible that, to Spaniards, privilege was constitutive of the colonial order of things, legal or not.

Guaman Poma thereby anticipated later scholarly discoveries about the West. First, he pointed out the causal link between colonialism and whiteness: while there were different kinds of people in Europe, once in the Americas they all became white. And being white had, in a last instance, nothing to do with skin color or place or origin—natives could be as white as Spaniards could.

Second, he highlighted that the colonies were different, that they were in a permanent "state of exception" (Agamben 2005). Peru was a place in which the exception was the norm which resulted in deeply embodied senses of hierarchy and humiliation, a "colonial normal" (Lamana 2008, 14). But unlike in Agamben's formulation, Guaman Poma's exception resulted as much from the state's legal frame as from everyday practice. There was no real exception in the state's law—it was just a manifestation of a larger structure which was colonial and racial in nature.

The pedagogy of the next example reversed that of the previous ones, although it had the same target. To expose coloniality, Guaman Poma brought what went for ordinary behavior in a Spanish setting to bear on Peru. The result of this contextual shift was that the ordinary became immediately extraordinary and even unthinkable. Readers were once again in the context of personal experience, which made the switch more effective. As he continued to walk, Guaman Poma ran into a group of Spanish men and women leaving a *tambo* (Inca inn or way station) with no Indians carrying their stuff—which was the practice of the land. Surprised, Guaman Poma asked them why they did not, to which they answered "that they would rather go loaded than load the poor Indians, that in the Christians' law and in Castile, Christians are not loaded, but horses, animals. That for that God gave him animals, that in Castile neither mitayos [Indians serving their *mitas*] nor guides are given. And thus, I fear God" ([ca. 1614] 1987, fol. [1132]1122, 1195).[10]

Note that the argument was not that colonial laws banned the use of Indians as loaders (which they did). It was that in Castile, Christians were not used as loaders; it was not fair according to the *ley de cristiano* (law of Christian). The story thereby equated Indians and Spaniards (they were all Christians) and made what was normal in Spain be normal in Peru. As a result, what collided were not cultures but embodied senses of order, bringing coloniality to the fore. The problem this story signals was not the chaos that resulted from the clash between a perfect Indigenous moral order and one that was not (Ossio 2008, 201–40), but the fact that *the* order (the ley de cristiano) worked in Spain but not in the Andes. In addition, there was in this example a pedagogy that worked though sarcasm and the impossible. The exchange was blatantly false and in fact almost hilarious—Spaniards never carried their own stuff in the Andes. This, however, did not make it any less poignant. On the contrary, as it happened when Guaman Poma called Pizarro and Almagro "ambassadors," it confronted readers with the nonsense of colonial practice.

The paradox that could not be missed by any colonial reader was that no such Spaniards existed—and yet that worked toward the colonizers' further condemnation, not to their advantage.

The next example of Guaman Poma's stunning conceptual analysis and pedagogy I can discern worked by further reversing the move he made in the two previous ones. To make sure that Western readers could not evade the discrepancy between how things were (the colonial order of things) and how they *really* were and ought to be (the true order of things of the logos), he transported the extraordinariness of the local setting to the ordinariness of a Spanish village. The result was a different kind of unthinkable. With an uncomplicated example in simple language—that is, exactly as priests recommended that things be explained to Indians—he drove the point home and asked:

> If you [were] in your land, [and] an Indian from here went there and loaded you like a horse, and spurred you on with a whip like a beast, and called you a horse, a dog, a pig, an asshole, a demon, and on top of it took away your wife and daughters, and [your] estates, and [your] lands, and [your] farms and cattle ranches, with little fear of God and [of the] law, consider, what would you Christians say of these evils? It seems to me that you would eat him alive, and [even that] would not satisfy you. ([ca. 1614] 1987, fol. [964]950, 1046)[11]

In other words, what would Spaniards have done if Indians had behaved in Spain the way Spaniards often behaved in Peru? They would have eaten them alive. The argument, straightforward and simple, involved irony. By forcing the extraordinariness of the colonial quotidian onto Spanish readers, Guaman Poma mirrored religious pedagogy and once again gave it a decolonial twist: clergymen intended to make Indians realize the extraordinariness of their ordinary ways, how they deviated from reason.

One can argue that Guaman Poma aptly summarized this contrived, racially organized state of exception with the well-known expression el mundo al reués. However, this oft-quoted expression functioned in different ways at different times that are relevant to fully grasp their meanings. In specialized scholarship about the *NCBG*, the most commonly cited quote is: "world upside down, it is a sign that there is no God and no king, they are in Rome and Castile" ("el mundo al reués. Es señal que no ay Dios y no ay rrey, está en Roma y Castilla") ([ca. 1614] 1987, fol. [1136]1126, 1197). But in fact it continued: "for the poor and to punish them, there is justice; for the rich, there is no justice" ("para los pobres y castigallo, ay justicia; y para los rricos, no ay justicia") ([ca. 1614] 1987, fol. [1136]1126, 1197). Read in the context of the text, it was directed to bad Christians (no skin color or place of origin attached) and "the world" referred to its theological meaning. He was complaining about those who were more interested in greed than in compassion and who pretended to administer justice but only served their own interests. In this case, this well-known expression signaled not despair (the impossibility of ever achieving justice), as it is often understood, but a conceptually informed, ethnographically grounded description of what there was: the world was upside down because priorities and ways of accounting for it were upside down.

That is why the opposition was not Indians versus Spaniards (as it would be according to a reading of the text along cultural clash lines) but instead the poor versus the rich. When it came to punishing the poor (largely but not only Indians), justice was readily available; when it came to punishing the rich (Indian or Spaniard), it was not. On the other hand, God and the king were in Castile not because they did not care about Peru—as Spaniards explicitly or implicitly alleged—but because they were there in the same way that the laws restricting Spaniards were in Castile and so was the Christian moral order. The metropolis was where supposedly things were as they were meant to be. (At least, that is what Spaniards told and seemed to believe.) The colonies were where that which was upside down, that which did not follow reason, was the norm. And to make matters worse, those who saw the world through whiteness and coloniality were incapable of recognizing and/or accepting it—as Baldwin would have it, "they don't know it and do not want to know it" (1993, 5). Like the rowers that Bartolomé Alvarez's soldier wanted to prove wrong (see chapter 1), who had told him that God was in Castile and added, with much irony, that the sun went there every night to inform him about all things Spaniards did wrong to Indians (see chapter 1), Guaman Poma ironically said he was going to inform the king about it all, although he knew well that the king was part of the problem, not its solution.

The second occurrence of the world upside down, quoted less often than the first one, happens two pages later. Already in Lima at the end of his journey, Guaman Poma reported seeing the city packed with "absent Indians and Cimarrons turned yanaconas, skilled workers being mitayos, low Indians and tributaries, [who] put on collar and dressed like a Spaniard and donned a sword, and others [who] shaved their hair so as to not pay tribute or work in the mines. See here the world upside down" ([ca. 1614] 1987, fol. [1138]1128, 1198).[12] This time the world was the actual world, not the material as opposed to the divine. And, it was upside down in two related ways. First, Indians did all those things to avoid having to pay tribute and work in the mines while Spaniards did not. If all contributed, there would have been no incentive to cease to be Indian. Second, while the conversation should have been about why Spanish pecheros avoided paying tribute and working in the mines, it was about why Indians did it. The world upside down because all of this, which was clear as water, was not held to be obvious. As a result, Indians were forced to live contrived lives, pretend that the world was right, and accept being made the problem (a four-hundred-year old precedent of the *problema del indio* [problem of the Indian]) whenever the colonial machine did not crank as desired. In other words, they had to live upside down so that reality fit them well, like a poorly tailored camel hair suit, and pretend that it all made sense.[13]

WAY TO GO: *CAMINAR* AS VINDICATION AND SUCCESS

Although the actual end of the book is an annualized to-do list for colonial authorities, the stories about the colonial disorder end with a section called "Camina el Autor." The section is particular because Guaman Poma becomes its main character (the one who walks) and also because of the constant hardships surrounding his trip. As he walked "naked," poor, and with little food, he faced time and time again unjust situations; each time he denounced the injustice, argued for the right thing to take place, and failed—the bad ones won, the good ones lost.

This arduous, pitiful walk and the repeated failure receive different interpretations. To some scholars, the chapter reveals that the *NCBG*'s overall scaffold falls apart. There is no God, no justice, no hero, and no hope—Guaman Poma's plan for reform to redress the world upside down comes undone, the coherence of the text falters, and readers are left with pointless iteration and despair (Adorno 2000, 78–79, 140–43). Others propose a slightly more optimist reading: the chapter shows Andean peoples' faith in the power of writing. While there is clearly no remedy in Peru and Guaman Poma grew increasingly pessimistic as he walked, he still hoped that once he delivered his text to the king, the latter would remedy the chaos (Quispe-Agnoli 2006, 252–57).[14]

I suggest that, as important as it may seem, the point was not what he might achieve at the end of the journey (the deliverance of the text to the king) but what he taught readers along the way—a pedagogical goal. The key to this interpretation lies in seeing the walk in light of Guaman Poma's theological take. Seeing his walk as failure (regardless of whether he delivered the text or not) would follow the same principle as seeing the conquest as favoring the Spaniards and punishing the Indians—it would imply accepting the rendering of human action grounded on the particular reading of theology colonial thinkers upheld and Guaman Poma rejected. If readers adopted instead his particular theological take, the walk taught about success, not failure, about validation, not damnation, and about how to see reality anew.

An important place to begin reading the final pages of the text in such a way is to examine the title of the chapter, "Camina el Autor." *Camino* (path) and *caminar* (to walk) were words heavily loaded with Christian meanings. There was the *camino de las virtudes* (path of virtues) and the *camino de rosas y flores* (path of roses and flowers), according to Saint Crisóstomo; the *camino de la virtud* (path of virtue) and the *camino del vicio* (path of vice), according to Saint Jerónimo; and the *camino de los buenos* (path of the good ones), *camino del cielo* (path of heaven), *camino de los malos* (path of the bad ones), and *camino del mundo* (path of the world), as labeled by Granada. All these labels boiled down to or were expressions of a well-known biblical passage: "Enter through the small gate. Because the road that leads to perdition is wide and espatious, and those who go through it are many. Because the gate is small, and narrow is the road that leads to life, and few are those who find it" ("Entrad por la puerta estrecha. Porque el camino que lleua a perdicion es ancho y espacioso, y los que van por el son muchos. Porque la puerta es estrecha, y angosto el camino que lleua a la vida, y pocos son los que lo hallan") (Matt. 7:13–14). Seen this way, Guaman Poma's and the poor Indians' predicament acquired new meaning. As he stated, he returned to "the world" to walk among the poor, where he faced all sorts of difficulties, injustices, and temptations—it followed that he was walking not any path but the narrow path of the righteous. The same could be said about the poor Indians he encountered. Clearly, the path they metaphorically walked was not a camino de rosas y flores.

In this light, the most common reading of his walk would have been upside down. Hardship was not a sign of damnation, of God's anger and abandonment—and the easy life was not a sign of God's favor and vindication. Rather, it was the other way around: the narrow path led to life, the wide one to destruction. Furthermore, the easy life was itself a punishment, since by adding sins to sins men further condemned themselves. Guaman Poma and poor Indians walked the former, other Indians and most Spaniards walked the latter. And while the former knew it, the latter did not. Moreover, those on the easy path deluded themselves, thinking that they were the chosen ones and that those who struggled were the damned. They either outright celebrated having the upper hand or lamented it—either way, they considered it God's call to punish Indians. In other words, the hard walk was the one of victory over "the world"—in Spain, in its theological sense only, while in the Andes, in its theological and colonial senses.

Further elements that turned the chapter into victory and validation came into focus if readers considered other meanings of caminos and caminar. The question was not simply to know which path was worth walking—the answer was plain—but how to actually be able to walk the hard and narrow path. There were, Granada explained in his *Memorial de la vida cristiana*, two ways to achieve el buen vivir. There was the *vía escolástica* (scholastic way) or exterior, that of industry and doctrine (clearly the one preferred and in fact the only one considered by all colonialist authors, from Las Casas to Alvarez, including Santo Tomás and Acosta). And, there was the *vía mística* (mystic way) or interior, that of grace, prayer, and devotion (Granada [*1565*] 1994–95, vol. II, 345). The latter, which was Guaman Poma's and Granada's choice, involved much interior work, true and sincere faith, and determination. The former, which was Guaman Poma's and Granada's least favored option, required adhering to the right practices and knowing the letter of the book but not necessarily grasping and nurturing its spirit. That is why it was the less secure path and it could lead to empty gestures—like the false expressions of charity in the world Guaman Poma walked through.

As Granada's and Guaman Poma's theology stressed, doing the right thing was not something that men could do on their own—it required a supernatural supplement, grace. And, the best way to get God's attention was to observe the exact practice followed by both Guaman Poma as he walked in the world and poor Indians in the only three images in which grace was present: to pray to God with profound sentiment. But, this was not a simple or straightforward thing to do either. Granada described in detail the six conditions a prayer must meet for God to hear and respond: spirit and attention, humility, faith and confidence, good deeds and good living, to ask for spiritual goods, and patience and perseverance ([*1565*] 1994–95, vol. II, 37–55).[15] And even if these conditions were met, God's answer might not come right away. That did not express God's abandonment or anger—rather, as the Granadine master explained, it might express God's favor: "To test our faith, to see if because it is delayed [the answer] we undertake to search for the remedy through illegal or bad paths, or so that we recognize our need more, or to light in us greater praying fervor with this delay" ([*1565*] 1994–95, vol. II, 52).[16] In this light, Guaman Poma's often-quoted calls to God with no answer—e.g., "And thus, my God, where are you?" ("Y ancí, Dios mío, ¿adónde estás?") ([ca. 1614] 1987, fol. [1114]1104, 1182) and "Where are you, God of the heavens?" ("¿Adónde estás, Dios del cielo?") ([ca. 1614] 1987, fol. [1121]1111, 1187)—were further evidence not of despair and failure but of righteousness. Until a prayer was answered, Granada continued, the recommended course of action was to be patient and to persevere, keeping the faith. And as it happened with the sun going to Spain to inform the king about Spanish abuses, the matter of praying was not dead serious—although it absolutely was. When detailing the things that good Indians should do, Guaman Poma devoted several pages to write down long prayers Indians must pray each day ([ca. 1614] 1987, fols. [846]832–[851]837, 894–905). While they largely resemble prayers, Granada included in his *Memorial* asking God, Christ, or Mary for protection; Guaman Poma's versions—written in Quechua—added to the well-known threats of the "world" dangers that were pointedly colonial in nature. For example, one prayer pleaded, "Protect us from the justices, the corregidor, sheriff, judges, inquisitors, fathers, encomenderos, notaries, majordomos, lieutenant, Spaniards of the tambo, robbers of men and thieves" (Guaman Poma [ca. 1614] 1987, fol. [850]836, 901).[17]

Guaman Poma's and the poor Indians' walk coalesced then in a structure that, far from teaching failure, taught validation. Poor Indians persevered, kept their faith, and did not try illicit means. And, they did so despite the incredible hardships of walking the narrow path—the innumerous injustices they faced day after day, the corruption Spaniards relentlessly effected on them, and the actual attempts to twist their faith by well-known extirpators of idolatry.[18] They were the just—Christ's chosen ones. Not by chance, Guaman Poma called them repeatedly "the poor of Jesus Christ" ("los pobres de Jesucristo"). The rich and proud misread poor Indians' hardship and dismissed it, "seeming to them that where there is the poor there is no God and no justice" ("pareciéndole que adonde está el pobre no está aý Dios y la justicia") (Guaman Poma [ca. 1614] 1987, fol. [917]903, 989). But regardless of whether earthly justice was in Castile or not, he pointed out, "it should be known clearly through the faith that where there is the poor there is Jesus Christ himself, where God is, there is justice" ("a de sauerse claramente con la fe que adonde está el pobre está el mismo Jesucristo, adonde está Dios, está la justicia") ([ca. 1614] 1987, fol. [917]903, 989). It was an effect of the dominant colonial narratives to make it seem otherwise and of the blindness of those who thought of themselves as white not to notice.

The double implications of the Indians' metaphorical walk could not be clearer. On the one hand, it exposed the discourse of the campaigns to extirpate idolatries—which were running amok in the Andes during these years—as contrived. It flipped it upside down. Indians did not hold onto their idolatry but to their faith—and they did not resist Christianity but the innumerous challenges to it. At the same time, it told that most Spaniards—which at best looked for the external matching of the "scholastic way"—missed it all, deluded by their projections on the veil. In fact, the projections worked not only as a false image of what Indians were but also as a good (although dangerous) tool to build the colonizers' vision of their own selves: the Indians (alleged) sins both compensated for the Spaniards' own faults and blinded them to their own blindness.

The implications of Guaman Poma's walk must have been clear since his description of the world resonated closely with Paul's in the Second Epistle to Timothy:

> This I hope you know: that in the last days perilous times shall come. For men shall be lovers of their own selves, miser, covetous, boasters, proud, blasphemers, disobedient to parents, unthankful, unholy. Without natural affection, perfidious, false accusers, incontinent, fierce, with no meekness, with no goodness . . . lovers of pleasures rather than God. Having a form of mercy, but denying the power thereof: from such turn away. For of this sort are they which creep into houses and lead captive silly women laden with sins . . . men who always learn and can never really reach knowledge of the truth. (2 Tim. 3:1–7)[19]

Readers could not miss that the quote fit, almost word for word, Guaman Poma's descriptions of bad Christians—most often Spaniards but not only so. They loved themselves and had no love for others; they were proud; they were cruel; they corrupted women; and they appeared to show compassion but did not, like a "wooden Christian" ("cristiano de palo") (Guaman Poma [ca. 1614] 1987, fol. [1121]1111, 1194). Furthermore, their *entendimiento* (comprehension) was faulty—they saw but failed to make proper sense of their vision, which at once reversed Santo Tomás's and Alvarez's diagnoses (Indians could see, Spaniards could not) and flipped the roles (the Indians were the ones telling the truth and being misunderstood). While, like Guaman Poma and the poor Indians, the righteous ones found themselves in calamitous situations and faced evil people and fake Christians, Paul stated that this was no reason to change course: "But you should persist in what you have learned and has been asked of you, knowing from whom you have learned . . . I urge you . . . that you should preach the word, that you urge in time and out of time; reprove, rebuke, reprehend harshly, exhort with all patience and doctrine . . . Be temperate in everything, endure afflictions, work as an evangelist, fulfill your ministry" (2 Tim. 3:14; 4:1–2, 5).[20]

And so Guaman Poma did. Following Paul's command, he never tired to denounce injustice, to speak the truth, and to argue, never losing his faith— not even in the face of extraordinary personal adversity, like when his own son deserted him and his close servant stole from him.[21] In this light, the fact that Guaman Poma was the main character of a story acquired a different meaning: he walked the walk and talked the talk, like the apostles did, and wrote about it, like an evangelist would—something that could hardly be said about most Spaniards in the Andes.

While this could have been seen as some form of eschatology, I suggest that Guaman Poma was not asking those who could see colonial injustice for what it was and who suffered it to endure it until the second coming or the afterlife. He was telling them that they were not upside down and getting what they deserved, as Spanish official discourses stated, but were right on their feet and suffering injustice from blind men. Most Indians were an active presence, most Spaniards an absent one. To those who could not see the injustice and inflicted the pain, Guaman Poma urged them to make sense of the present differently: it was not a free pass—a reward to most Spaniards and a punishment to most Indians. They were upside down. From this pedagogical point of view, the repetition also acquired a distinctive meaning: according to ecclesiastic rhetoric, teaching complex things required repetition so that the new concepts, which initially exceeded the rational capacity of the reader, became second nature. Even if the results were not forthcoming, the right choice was to persevere, his walk made plain. After all, God's chosen ones were meek and patient, but never tired of speaking truth to power.[22]

SEEING, NOT MOVING (*VER*, NOT *MOVER*)

Scholars have suggested that the "Buen Gobierno" section followed the logic of the sermon: it revolved around archetypes and its main goal was to move readers to repent and mend their ways. To that end, Guaman Poma often resorted to the rhetorics of *amenaza* (threat). However, scholars also point out, the project failed. As he walked, he either entirely gave up his hope of moving readers or hoped only that at least the king would be moved (Adorno 2000, 140–43; Quispe-Agnoli 2006, 253–57, respectively). The similarities with the genre of the sermon are clear but I think that Guaman Poma's money was not on moving readers but on helping them see. This is coherent with his overall take: true agency was doing the right thing willingly, not because one was forced, even if that forcing was due to shaming. First came knowing, then came choosing—an ironic reminder of Acosta's comments.

Toward the end of his apostolic journey (which was also the end of the book's stories), as he got closer to Lima and the roads got crowded, Guaman Poma crossed paths with many Spaniards and Indians, all of whom failed to understand why he was walking in such a miserable condition—old, poor, naked, and alone. Trying to make sense of it, they asked him whom he was serving, to which he replied:

> [He] was coming in the service of a great man named Christ-opher, instead of saying Christ, he added "opher," even though [he] said Christopher of the Cross. The men asked him who this so-called Christopher of the Cross was, if he owned mines or [if he was] rich. He responded that his lord had been a great miner and [that] he is now rich and powerful. They asked him: "Will not we see this man?" [And] the author responded: "He is right behind me. That is where you will find him if you look for him." (Guaman Poma [ca. 1614] 1987, fols. [1119]1109–[1120]1110, 1186)[23]

Why were the travelers unable to understand Guaman Poma—his condition, what he did, and what he told them? A concise answer would be that they had lost the capacity to recognize things as they really were. A poor, powerless Indian walking alone through rough terrain made no sense to them unless someone powerful had ordered him to do it. And, the powerful was only so if wealth was involved. When trying to make sense of Guaman Poma, they forgot that the apostles were poor and powerless and that Christianity and wealth were at odds. That is why they could not see Guaman Poma for who he was. In contrast, poor Indians, the poor of Jesus Christ, never failed to recognize him for who he was: someone who, like the apostles, did good deeds and cared about the poor—not about riches and power; someone who never tired of stating the truth; and someone who never strayed from the narrow path, like Saint Paul recommended in Timothy's Epistle, not even in the face of renewed adversity. They understood what he did, whom he was serving, and why, and like him, they could see reality as it really was, recognizing justice and injustice (e.g., Guaman Poma [ca. 1614] 1987, fol. [1119]1109, 1186). In short, unlike most Spaniards and high-rank Indians, poor Indians could see the truth.

This reversal was meaningful in at least two ways. First, it was meaningful in light of the importance that being able to see reality as it really was had for colonialist thinkers. As seen in chapter 1, ideas such as natural light and natural law played key roles in most justifications of the conquest and colonization of the Americas. Spaniards argued that there was a natural order of things and that they could recognize it while Indians could not—proof of it was that the latter did not know and deviated from what nature itself dictated. Spaniards believed Indians were either blinded by their material intelligence or by the devil and idolatry. However, my impression is that this example offered a more lapidary reversal yet. It was not simply that most Spaniards (and many Indians) could not see the true order of things, as anyone endowed with natural reason should; it is that they could not see the *cristo minero* (miner Christ), the one who descended to rescue the souls from purgatory and came back up, and that is why they could only think and talk about he whom Guaman Poma served as a *minero rico* (rich miner).

The critique, fine and profound, also distinguished Guaman Poma from (Spanish) friends and foes of the Indians. While they disagreed on much, friends and foes concurred that of the two books in which man could apprehend God's order (the logos), the book of nature was accessible to everyone, while the book of revelation was so to Christians alone. In Guaman Poma's example, what the travelers failed to read was the written book, the one of revelation, while poor Indians did it with no mistake. While the latter had a privileged role in the Bible as the poor of Jesus Christ, for the former, scripture left only two damning possibilities: those who refused to see (like the Jews who denied Christ) and those who had been blinded by the devil (and could not see Christ)—both popular images in colonialist texts with which the *NCBG* dialogued.

The second way in which the reversal was meaningful had to do with the role blindness played in Granada's thinking. Unlike colonialist thinkers, who associated blindness with Indianness, he associated it with the love of the world as opposed to the love of God. While those who loved the latter could see, the former could not—and did not know it:

What greater blindness than, knowing so well that we must die, and that at that time it will be forever determined what our lives will be, we live so carelessly, as if we were going to live forever. . . . What greater blindness than, for the relish of desire, to lose Heaven? To be so careful about estate, and so little about conscience? Of these blindnesses you will find as many in the world that it will seem to you that men are enchanted and bewitched, so that, *having eyes, they do not see, and having ears, they do not listen, and having a sight sharper than that of a lynx to see the things of the world, they have that of moles to see the things of heaven.* (Granada [*1565*] 1994–95, bk. 1, chap. 28, 868; emphasis mine)[24]

In other words, those who walked el camino del mundo had their eyes open but could not see. They were blind like the mole—probably not by chance, the same image Alvarez chose (see chapter 1).

So, was Guaman Poma simply mimicking Granada? Not quite. Not only did he take a theology developed for Westerners in the West to bear in a colonial context, which made it politically significant, but he also gave it a decolonial twist: his goal was not to move readers but to change their eyes. For one thing, not once in the *NCBG*'s innumerable examples in which Guaman Poma tells wrongdoers about their wrongs did a change of heart follow. And, this made sense: there could be no change of heart leading to action until the blind could see what they did for what it was. Guaman Poma's money was on a change of vision, because to qualify a point I have made many times, when it came to things that were commonly accepted, that had a name, the important thing was not knowing—to know, everybody knew—but doing. But when it came to things that were not understood, that had no name yet, like coloniality or whiteness, Spaniards did not know and had to be taught.

As in the case of the walk and Paul's letter, Guaman Poma used textual parallels as pedagogical means in this case, too. His example of the miner Christ was a rewriting of a Granadian story. In chapter 12 of his 1574 *Meditaciones muy devotas* (Very devout meditations), Granada asked the reader to ponder Christ's life at a moment when he stopped to drink water:

And it is of no less consideration . . . that fatigue of Christ, who was . . . alone, tired, utterly weary, exhausted from the hard path and the hunger and the thirst, just as any other poor and skinny man. Who would be so happy in this occasion to pass by that place and, considering the paths and fatigue of this lord, would humbly approach him and ask him: "Sir, *what life is this one that you live? . . . What are*

*you looking for through so many roads and journeys? What kind of life is this laborious
one that you have, walking from place to place . . . without letting the exhaustion of the
paths or the contradiction of the world deviate you from that goal?* You never take a
break, never stop for an hour of rest; during the day, you walk through different
places; at night, through the hills, praying. So, *what kind of treasure is this that you
search for with so much travail?*" ([*1574*] 1788, 479a–b; emphasis mine)[25]

Like Christ, Guaman Poma walked unceasingly, prayed when he was not walking, and never rested, regardless of how tired he was or how many contradictions
of the world he faced. Like Christ, Guaman Poma met others who could not
make sense of who he was and why he was doing what he was doing. And when
others tried to make sense of it, both Christ and Guaman Poma got asked for
what kind of treasure they were looking, as if only man's thirst for worldly riches
could explain their special kind of behavior. And, the answer was similar, too:
"What could be responded is that, like a good shepherd, he was looking for his
lost sheep. It hurt him much it having gone astray and lost itself; and because
of it there was no path or travail he would not undertake to bring them back to
the fold" (Granada [*1574*] 1788, 479b).[26]

While the similarities were clear, the key difference entailed distinguishing
two kinds of impossible, like in the case of the ambassadors.[27] When the imagined person who met Christ asked those questions, he could not make sense
of him because of a historical impossibility: there had been no Christ before.
Therefore, he had a hard time understanding what Christ did, like anyone would
when meeting a new kind of being for the first time. The impossibility was factual. The people who met Guaman Poma were in a totally different situation:
they knew Christ and knew how those who served him behaved and should
behave. Therefore, their incapacity to see him ("Will not we see that man?")
spoke of a conceptual impossibility, not a factual one. In other words, Guaman
Poma's primary concern was not so much the *ceguera del mundo* (blindness of
the world) as was in Granada's case but the *ceguera de la colonialidad* (blindness
of coloniality). People who saw the world through whiteness failed to grasp the
conceptual map and in consequence gave reality the wrong meaning. And no
example in the text could have had Guaman Poma cure such blindness—he
was no superhero. But as was the case for the apostles, even if the results were
not easily achievable, the right choice was to persevere and speak the truth to
both, reassure those who inhabited the world in a disadvantaged position that
they were on the side of justice, and produce a change that had to be internal,

altering the way people saw the world one vision-impaired reader at a time. This was no naiveté. As he stated in the closing pages of the *NCBG*, some readers might laugh, others curse, others be grateful. If the persistence of racism and coloniality in the twenty-first century tells something, it is that changing how people see the world does indeed take time.

PART III

GARCILASO DE LA VEGA'S *COMENTARIOS REALES DE LOS INCAS*

"When I use a word," Humpty Dumpty said, in rather a scornful tone, "it means just what I choose it to mean—neither more nor less."
"The question is," said Alice, "whether you can make words mean so many different things."
"The question is," said Humpty Dumpty, "which is to be master—that's all."

—LEWIS CARROLL, *THE ANNOTATED ALICE*

4

THE REAL COMMENTARIES OF THE INCA; OR WHAT WE REALLY THINK ABOUT WHAT YOU THINK AND WHAT WE DO WITH IT

GUAMAN POMA and Garcilaso de la Vega are in a way opposites. Little is known about Guaman Poma's life, even less about who read the manuscript of the *NCBG* in Peru or after it made it to Europe. Garcilaso de la Vega, in contrast, was a very public figure and his writings, published either in Portugal or Spain, were widely known on both sides of the Atlantic.[1] However, when it comes to more substantial matters, they both have much in common. Both wrote about the state of culture and society in the Andes at the turn of the century. And both shared, as I aim to show, the same understanding that the problems of the Spanish colony in Peru were about race and coloniality. They thought also that these problems would be solved only by internal transformation. It was about changing peoples' eyes, how they saw the world and made sense of it. Perhaps their real differences can be found in the way they thought the process of change would occur and in whom they directed their discourse. While Guaman Poma sought to teach all people through a decolonial theology, Garcilaso focused mainly—although not exclusively—on offering Indians ways to exist beyond colonial scripts through postindian stories of survivance.

The *CRI*, Garcilaso's most famous work, was published in Lisbon in 1609. As in the case of the *NCBG*, most scholarly interpretations of the *CRI* use a two-cultures lens. Many scholars point out how it masterly weaves together Christian, humanist, and philosophical traditions to offer a complex portrayal of Inca history and culture. Rebuking demeaning Spanish representations of the Incas that celebrated the advent of the Spanish colony, the argument goes, the *CRI* highlights the existence of a common ground linking both civilizations, Incan and Western, and their joint contribution to history: the former brought the light of reason to the Andes while the latter brought the light of revelation. This common ground sustains the idea of complementarity between both parties, which expresses the renaissance ideal of *concordia* (concord, harmony) and perhaps the Andean ones of *tinku* (ritual battle of the opposite halves of a group) and reciprocity. Garcilaso was, in short, a translator or cultural mediator (Castro-Klarén 2016; Durand 1976; Duviols 1964; Fernández 2016; López-Baralt 2011; MacCormack 1991, 332–82; Zamora 1988).

When it comes to explaining the reasons driving Garcilaso's project, this line of thinking often points toward his urge to solve the discomfort of being neither an Indian nor a Spaniard but an in-between, conflicted mestizo, torn between one civilization and the other.[2] Some see Garcilaso as being able to achieve the reconciliation; others see it as an impossible goal. When it comes to the question of readership—who could follow such argument and its sophisticated weaving of different Western ideas and/or who would need to have the Incas explained—the answer is (explicitly or implicitly) an educated European reader. An Indian would not have needed to have the Incas explained. That is, Garcilaso mediated by translating from Indians to Spaniards. When it comes to the means Garcilaso used to achieve his goal, scholars largely focus on those provided by the well-established genre of *comentarios*. While the exact strand of the genre (philological, historical, religious, etc.) he adopted is a matter of some disagreement, his investment in the genre's ultimate goal is not: the restoration of the truth (Castro-Klarén 2016, 204; Durand 1963; Escobar 1971; Fernández-Palacios 2004, 23–55; Zamora 1988, 12–61). In this case, the truth is about Inca culture and history and its relationship with European civilization, which Spaniards misunderstood and/or misrepresented.

Another scholarly view of the *CRI* suggests that it is not a European-minded text but a syncretic one (Mazzotti 1996, 2016). It is a polyphonic chorus in which European and Inca cultural voices uneasily coexist; while the former are largely explicit and have been thoroughly studied, the latter are largely implicit and need anthropological and ethnohistorical lenses to be recognized. By "articulating" Western and Andean elements, the text expresses an "emerging mestizo subjectivity" (Mazzotti 1996, 101) and its cultural syncretism oscillates from moments of harmony to moments of contradiction and conflict. In this light, the question of intentionality (or goals) cannot be answered or is irrelevant (Mazzotti 1996, 21–22, 37, 50, 170). In a last instance, the text's syncretic nature manifests the agency of cultures in a colonial milieu. When it comes to the question of readership, it is on the American side of the Atlantic: *Criollos*, blacks, mestizos, and especially Indians in Peru, who could recognize in its cultural complexity the solution it offers to the problem of adaptation to a regime that demanded total assimilation (Mazzotti 1996, 334–38).

While these interpretations illuminate different angles of the text, they do not address its main claim and structure: I argue that it is mostly not about an object—be it European, Andean, or both—but about *what people think about the object and about what others do with those ideas*. As a multilayered text, the *CRI* had to be read not at the literal level of its content, be it explicit or implicit (or at least not at that level only), but at the meta-level of a comentario, i.e., what Spaniards and Indians thought about the content. The objects of the book were not cultural articulation and mediation but coloniality and race. It theorized what it was to be Indian in the Spaniards' eyes and what Indians could do with that idea. Its primary readership was Indian although it has a white audience in mind, too—"white" understood as people who think of themselves as white, as "a state of mind." In the first case, it sought to help Indians be Indian beyond the options Spaniards gave them. That is, to be postindians and as such "an active presence" (Vizenor 1998, 15). In the case of white readers, it offered the option to put aside colonial masks and see the world anew—a metanoia.

My alternative interpretation of Garcilaso's text brings to light its pervasive and manifold doubleness. By this I do not mean that it blends two cultural traditions but that the text is full of double meanings. One can see this imme-diately in the very title of the book, which can convey something other than what it is often taken to mean. Scholars tend to focus on the word "comentario," which they link to a genre well established at the time Garcilaso wrote the book. The rest of the title receives much less attention, perhaps because the words are taken to be self-evident. Garcilaso was writing about the Incas and he was an Inca; therefore, it was "de los Incas" ("of the Incas"). As for "reales," he was from royal blood and was talking about Inca kings, which aligned the *CRI* in the tradition of royal books (Thurner 2011, 57–81). All these ideas made the English translation *Royal Commentaries of the Incas* sensible.

I suggest that while this rendering of the title is good and true, it is wrong and false at the same time. In Spanish, "reales" can allude to what is "royal" but also to what is "real."[3] And "real" can qualify objects as much as intentions. In the first case, it refers to what is *verdadero* (true) as opposed to what is one way or another untrue. Thus, for instance, when Xerez titled his 1534 account *Verdadera relación de la conquista del Perú* (*True Account of the Conquest of Peru*), his goal was to discredit that of another conqueror, Cristóbal de Mena, which he implicitly cast as untrue. In the second case, "real" refers to the intention of a person—it distinguishes his actual goal from the apparent one. This is, for example, the use of the word made by the Marqués de Palacio, when he titled his 1811 book *Manifiesto . . . de su verdadera intención en el solemne acto del juramento que prestó en la . . . las cortes generales . . . de 1810* (Manifest . . . about his true intention during the solemn act of swearing at the General Courts . . . of 1810).

With these observations in mind, the title acquires a new meaning. It can be rephrased as *Reales comentarios de los incas* (Real commentaries of the Incas), or what the Incas *really* thought or meant to say about what others had to say about something. In fact, there was no need to choose—that is the beauty of doubleness. One could read the text either as the royal commentaries of a noble Inca about Inca kings or as what Indians who knew what Spaniards thought about Indians really thought about what the former thought about themselves and the latter. Meanings depended on the readers' eyes—what they could see, what they took words to mean, and why.

If the text was a relentless double comment on others' interpretations, for whose eyes did Garcilaso cast it and what was expected of such reader? Unlike Guaman Poma, Garcilaso did not aim to trouble expectations with a pedagogical end—his addressee was not a Christian reader but an inquisitive one. This was no exception to doubleness. In closing his explanation of the complexities involved in writing his text, Garcilaso told: "On my end, I have done what I could, not having done what I wished for. I beg *the discreet reader* to receive my intent, which is to please and content him, although the strength, or the ability of an Indian . . . cannot make it there" ([*1609*] 1995, bk. I, chap. 19, 51,; emphasis mine).[4] What characterized a *lector discreto* (discreet reader) and how was he supposed to read? Addressing the reader as *lector prudente* (prudent reader) was a well-established practice (Fernández-Palacios 2004, 47–53). According to the early seventeenth-century *Tesoro*, someone prudente is someone who "weighs all things with much accord" ("pesa todas las cosas con mucho acorde") (Covarrubias Horozco [*1611*] 2006, 1380). *Acorde* (accord) in turn came from *cuerda* (cord). As in an instrument, cords work together in consonance. In other words, the lector prudente was supposed to read texts as harmonic ensembles where all parts worked in unison. A lector discreto read differently. Discreto came from *discernir* (to discern), which meant to separate, to distinguish, and to judge each thing on its own terms: "discreet, the man . . . who knows how to ponder things and how to give each its own place" ("discreto, el hombre . . . que sabe ponderar las cosas y dar a cada una su lugar") (Covarrubias Horozco [*1611*] 2006, 717).

What were the things discreet readers of the *CRI* were asked to distinguish and assess on their own terms? There could be many since the entire text was a protracted exercise in doubleness. But, the overall guiding principle connecting that multiplicity was the difference between what Spaniards imagined about themselves and about Indians and what Indians did with those imaginings. This guiding principle can be further qualified. First, Spaniards thought they were talking about what was real; meanwhile, Indians knew Spaniards were not. Moreover, Indians knew that Spaniards were clueless about being ignorant. Second, the plural views had to work in unison—after all, all the actors inhabited the same world. But at the same time, they did not have to work in an ensemble—the different actors lived in different worlds, the ones they each could see. It all depended on what each took the word *mundo* (world) to mean. This in turn told readers that white actors and Indian actors were dissimilar not because of a cultural or epistemological difference—the issue was not the object—but because of a colonial one.

Which were the means Garcilaso used to convey double meanings? In an oft-quoted passage of the "Proemio," he explained his writing strategy as follows: "In the discourse of the history . . . we won't say anything big that hasn't been authorized by the same Spanish historians who touched upon it in part or in all. That my intention is not to contradict them but to serve them as their comment and gloss and translator of many Indian words that, as foreigners in that language, they interpreted outside what was proper to it" ([*1609*] 1995, Proemio, 4).[5] This quote revealed two points important to my argument: it explained the doubleness of Garcilaso's writing and it veiled the conflict that such writing inherently provoked. First, while scholars often relate the word *comento* to the genre comentario, Garcilaso stated that his text would work as a "comento y glosa." The authoritative 1611 *Tesoro de la lengua castellana o española*, the first Spanish dictionary, had no entry for "comento." But there was one for "glosa"—and it had two meanings. The first one was "notes or comments that declare the texts or any other writing, since they are like tongues or interpreters" ("anotaciones y comentos que declaran los textos o otra cualquier escritura, por cuanto son como lenguas o intérpretes") (Covarrubias Horozco [*1611*] 2006, 979). Given that *declarar* (to declare) meant "to make manifest what was by itself hidden, obscure or not understood" ("manifestar lo que estaba de suyo oculto obscuro o no entendido") (Covarrubias Horozco [*1611*] 2006, 669), these definitions could be read along the common interpretation of the text—although it would depend on *what* was taken to be "hidden, obscure, or not understood" and why. Considering the newness of coloniality and the fledging nature of Western race-thinking and feeling, perhaps some meanings were hidden because the words to articulate these concepts did not yet exist. The second meaning of glosa pointed elsewhere: "in lay terms, to gloss words is to give them meanings other than the one they seem to have, and sometimes other than the one intended by the one who spoke them" ("glosar las palabras, vulgarmente es darles otro sentido del que suena y a veces del que pretendió el que las dijo") (Covarrubias Horozco [*1611*] 2006, 979). That is, to gloss others' words could be an exercise not in restoring truth but in twisting words to have them say something other than what they literally meant or were meant to mean. Read this way, the quote situated the text at the level of a meta-discourse that ought to be read not at the literal level of facts but at that of how those facts have been rendered meaningful to then play with them. His would be a reflection on others' reflections, a glosa or comentario.

Second, the quote was important because it veiled Garcilaso's thinking about Spaniards' thinking. Attentive to colonial hierarchies and what they stated about the intellectual capacity of Indians and whites, Garcilaso claimed that his goal was never to contradict, only to *comment* on what the legitimate speakers had said, thus narrowing the act of commenting to its most trivial meaning. In fact, he further reduced the task to make it fit an acceptable intellectual practice: he would improve translations of Indigenous terms that Spaniards misunderstood and corrupted—a legitimate action, considering his race: "to stop this corruption, may it be licit for me, since I am an Indian, that I write this story as an Indian" ("atajar esta corrupción me sea lícito, pues soy indio, que esta historia yo escriba como indio") ([*1609*] 1995, Proemio, 5).[6]

Down the road, I will return to and flesh out the passages I just quoted. For now, it is important to note that all of the aforementioned characteristics made the *CRI* a text way ahead of its time. As a consequence, much of what I use to understand it comes not from sixteenth- or seventeenth-century tool kits (those of political theorists, philologists, theologians, or humanists) but from thinkers who would come centuries later: theorists of race, thinkers of coloniality, experts in double meanings, and masters of writing and living under censorship. They help me recognize and make sense of the different ways in which double meanings can be packed for the discreet reader to discern and for the censor to miss.

Garcilaso's writing strategies can be best explained through visual images. As suggested by my rereading of the title, the first image is that of layers. These layered meanings are perceptible (or not) to different readers depending on the ways in which each conceives abstraction and flatness. The advantage of thinking in terms of layers is that it echoes the Spaniards' own schema: one can have inteligencia material and be able to read only at the most elementary level of signification or can read additional layers and be able to see meanings built into the same words. Closely related to this idea of layers are methods of signification like irony, sarcasm, and parody which are commonly marked by what Bakhtin (1986, 79, 85–90) called "expressive intonation," one of many tools of the practices of "signifyin(g)" (Gates 1988). Clearly, throughout the text beauty is in the eye of the beholder. While in a movie or a radio show double meanings are easily perceptible, in written texts, the interpretive work lies entirely on the reader's desk. A theater script would be the only exception—and at times I will suggest that CRI has to be read as if it were one.

A related aspect of the text that comes to mind is its dizzying speed and density. If Guaman Poma has readers run a marathon, Garcilaso has them play ping-pong. At a breakneck speed, he mixes, flips over, and blurs meanings that in the sixteenth and seventeenth centuries and even often today are commonly taken to pertain distinctively to Indians or Spaniards, shocking readers and troubling essential images of difference. The images that best encapsulate these situations are electroshocks and Möbius strip. With electroshocks, the dizzying switches fluctuate between shocking the reader and appeasing him, only to shock him again. This is similar to TV cartoons in which the successive shocks are represented by the screen going black/white and then white/black, the bad dude turning into a pile of dust, and then the story continuing as if nothing happened. In many of these cases, Garcilaso switches from identifying with Indians to identifying with Spaniards and at the same time from using traits that allegedly convey Indianness to traits that convey Spanishness. And again, like in a Möbius strip, one's effort to stick tightly to one side (the inside or the outside) often has the unexpected result of finding oneself on the other.

A third aspect of Garcilaso's writing strategy worth highlighting is its dual structure. The CRI is (at least) two texts at once in yet another way. It tells the story of the Incas before the Spanish arrival but also recounts many stories of Indians in colonial times. Its overall topography resembles that of the *Super*

Mario Brothers video game: there is a surface world and several underworlds. The first one has a linear structure, marked by books and chapters with their respective titles (what Genette [1997] calls "paratext"), which direct the reading of the text to the sublimated Incas. But, there are also recurrent doors into other worlds or underworlds. These underworld stories are present always under the guise of anecdotes and although they seem comical, they are in fact ironic instances of repeated teasing. Readers can follow one path or the other or both at once. In fact, both are related: underworld stories lead back to the surface world sooner or later and they make readers see the latter in a different, often contradictory way, adding even more ways of signifyin(g).

The final image that comes to mind when I consider Garcilaso's *CRI* is the veil. It works in two distinct but complementary ways. First, it conveys the act of obscuring, preventing from being seen. Clearly, the veiling of meanings allowed Garcilaso to write safely what otherwise would either be censured or get him thrown into jail—after all, the *CRI* was published in seventeenth-century Spain and only after passing several layers of censorship. However, this kind of veiling has another function: that of projecting onto the veil. By mastering (and mimicking) the Spaniards' favorite tropes, rhetorical styles, and authoritative sources, the *CRI* met Spanish expectations and from this perspective appeared to be a soothing example of what good natives could eventually get to write—an Indian writing about Indians. That was, I argue, the movie colonialist readers celebrated. At the same time, by paying attention to who produced the movie, how he took the shots, and the arrangement of the room, screen, and chairs when the movie was shown, one could see in the *CRI* a critical exposition of or lecture about whiteness and manifest manners. Because the exposition was cast in a register Spaniards could perceive only by questioning their own ideas about themselves and their colonial others (that is, by questioning their projections on the veil), it was accessible to whites only at a high price—they had to abandon their whiteness. On the other hand, a reader who inhabited a double consciousness and was gifted with a second sight could also celebrate the film, although for entirely different reasons.

In what follows, I will shift emphasis from the content of the upper world (the history of the Inca civilization) to the practices of writing and implicitly of existing beyond colonial scripts. While I will try to flesh out what each case means, I am aware that there is much more in the text than I have managed to discern. I ask the discreet reader to forgive my shortcomings, for this is all the strength and ability a pale-skinned man could deliver.

IN THE UPPER WORLD

Although the beginning of the *CRI* often receives scant attention, I find it important because it locates the alleged subject matter of the text, the Inca Empire, within Garcilaso's larger project of doubleness.[7] The two first (and short) chapters of the first book addressed how the discovery forced a rethinking of all received knowledge about the world. The first chapter, titled "Whether there are many worlds; it also treats of the five zones," discussed the idea of a world divided into five different climate zones of which only the second and fourth (the template) were inhabitable and the third (the torrid) could not be crossed over. The second chapter, titled "About the antipodes," addressed questions deriving from the fact that the world was proven to be round—such as if people in the antipodes hung upside down or if the sky extended over the entire world.

To begin a book about the Incas in this way could be seen as nothing but following standard sixteenth-century Spanish practice. After all, widely read works by famous chroniclers of the Indies, like Gómara's *Historia general de las Indias* (*General history of the Indies*) ([*1552*] 2004) or Acosta's *Historia natural y moral de las Indias* ([*1590*] 2002), did it. So did the well-known work of knowledge popularizers, like Francisco de Thamara's *El libro de las costumbres de todas las gentes de mvndo, y de las indias* (Book of the customs of all the people of the World, and the Indies) (1556), and reputed geographers, like Hierónimo de Chaves's *Chronographia o repertorio de tiempos* (Chronography or repertoire of the times) (1584). And in a way, starting with a geography of the world and its sky made sense during this era. As is known, the empirical evidence triggered by the discovery of the Americas forced Europeans to challenge well-established understandings of the world—and having proved the ancients' geographic knowledge wrong deserved some self-congratulatory pages.[8]

But, Garcilaso did more in these two chapters than just intentionally inscribe the book in this well-established tradition. As it is consistently the case throughout the book, he pointed to one thing to talk about another—more specifically, he pointed to an object to talk about the ways in which different people saw the object and how they made sense of it. In the case of his introductory chapters, he talked about the world not because he was concerned with geographical or theological matters, as Spaniards were, but because he was concerned with Spanish understandings of the world. And by "world," I do not mean the earth but the conceptual apparatus that Western colonialism put into effect and the reality (the new normal) native peoples had to inhabit thereafter. As is always the case with the *CRI*, Garcilaso was talking about the object and how people thought about it at once; in this instance, both were el mundo. Questioning Western understanding meant then not questioning Western geographic or theological ideas but instead questioning the seeds of coloniality informing them—what Spaniards implicitly thought about themselves and Indians, their respective places and roles, prowess and limitations.

The key to understanding Garcilaso's exposition was to be extremely attentive to the words he used, which constantly invited double readings. The literal one, which was reinforced by his mimicking of accepted tropes and authors, blinded those who thought of Indians as people who could not see beyond their inteligencia material. The second reading, which most often required readers to grasp little doses of irony, told those who knew that some thought about Indians in that way how handle to that way of thinking. This narrative style required discreet readers to constantly exercise their discreción: to separate meanings, discerning the different ways of signifyin(g) at work. At times, they worked simultaneously as layers in the associative axis; at others, they followed each other in quick, dizzying succession in the syntagmatic axis. At the end of the day, these recurrent double meanings evoked different rewritings of the same core idea: Indians were the same as Spaniards but different. And, similarity and difference were not about precontact qualities (cultural, epistemological, or symbolic)—they were colonial in nature.

MY WORLD IS NOT YOUR WORLD
(ALTHOUGH, IN FACT, IT IS)

That the "discovery" of the "New World" triggered a number of reactions in the European mind is a well-known fact. It is common to find in Spanish colonial texts expressions of wonder, amazement, strangeness, or excitement, including the sudden realization of being God's chosen people. For example, Gómara told the reader in the preface to the king of his widely read *Historia general* that while reading history was always interesting, his was particularly *deleitosa* (delightful) because of the *extrañeza* (weirdness) of the matter ([*1552*] 2004, 17). He then proceeded to exult the greatness of that matter: "The greatest thing after the creation of the world, leaving aside the incarnation and death of the one who created it, is the discovery of the Indies; and thus they call them New World" ("La mayor cosa después de la creación del mundo, sacando la encarnación y muerte del que lo crió, es el descubrimiento de Indias; y así las llaman Nuevo Mundo") (Gómara [*1552*] 2004, 17). And he continued, trying to clarify: "and they call it new not so much because it is newly found, but because it is very large and almost as large as the old one. It can also be called new because all its things are very different from ours."[9] Such differences included its animals, plants, and to some degree, its inhabitants, who "although men like us . . . they do not have letters, or currency or beasts of burden" ("empero hombres como nosotros . . . no tienen letras, ni moneda ni bestias de carga") (Gómara [*1552*] 2004, 18). This diversity, he stated in his third preface, was part of the *maravilla* (wonder) of God's creation with which man was faced ([*1552*] 2004, 21).

Perhaps because he felt he had gone too far stressing the newness of the New World, Gómara devoted the first chapter of the *Historia* to make clear that he knew that there was only one world and not many, like some ancient thinkers had suggested.[10] After methodically rebutting authoritative authors who had said so, he summed up the task with a contradiction: "although I believe that there is not more than only one world, I will name many times two here in this my work, to vary words referring to the same thing, and to be better understood calling the Indies New World, about which we write" ([*1552*] 2004, 23).[11] That is, he "firmly believe[d]" that there was only one world but would talk about two. Why? Perhaps for the sake of style, to avoid using the same words over and over. But, what about to be better understood? What exactly was better conveyed by calling it the New World? Was it that it had been just discovered, that it was almost as large as the Old one, or that while its inhabitants were similar, its animals and plants were different, as he mentioned in his dedication to the King? The question remained.

Acosta, who often copied Gómara, also began by explaining the goodness of his text which he also related to its object. Much had been written about the New World, its "new" and "strange" things, he stated in the preface to the reader of his *Historia natural y moral de las Indias*, but no one had explained them. In this attempt, he claimed, resided the novelty of his book which was "jointly history and philosophy, and because it is not only about the works of nature, but also those of the free will, which are the deeds and customs of men" ([*1590*] 2002, Proemio, 58).[12] The stated double purpose of this explaining was divine so that in observing God's marvelous natural creation, man would be led to praise him, and so that in knowing the Indians' customs, man would be led to help efforts to convert the *gente tan ciega* (people so blind) whom God had finally brought to the light of the gospel.[13]

Continuing his imitation of Gómara's work, Acosta proceeded to rebut (although in many more chapters) those who said there was more than one world—and like Gómara, he too nevertheless called the Americas "New World" ("Nuevo Mundo") or "New Orbis" ("Nuevo Orbe") in contradistinction with the "Old World." And while Acosta did not address explicitly the contradiction, he also acknowledged the uniqueness of the New World—what made it new. After a long attempt to explain the origin of its plants, animals, and human inhabitants, he concluded that they were definitely different, and accepted that his attempts to reconcile this fact with the oneness of creation and the common origin in Ararat did not work—to believe that they did, he concluded, would be "to call an egg chestnut" ("llamar al huevo castaña") ([*1590*] 2002, bk. IV, chap. 36, 283).[14]

Acosta thus ran into the same problem as Gómara. He tried a scientific detour instead of linguistic convenience to explain it but could not really answer why he called it two worlds when it was one and why he talked about one when there were two. This tension between the object (there was only one world) and what the subject thought and felt about the object (there was the Old World and the New World) also transpired in general texts. Cosmographers like Hierónimo de Chaues or knowledge popularizers like Francisco Thamara ran into similar problems. When the former's 1584 *Chronographia o repertorio de tiempos* addressed the division of the earth, it stated that there were four parts: Europe, Asia, Africa, and the West Indies. While discussing the latter, he called it "mundo nuevo . . . and justly so, because this land does not proceed from any of the three we already named: but alone, by itself it is, distinct and away from them. And it is called new land, because the ancient never had notice about it" (1584, 87v).[15] The title of Thamara's 1556 book said it all: *El libro de las costumbres de todas las gentes de mvndo, y de las indias* (The book of the customs of all the people of the World, and the Indies). The "world" and the "Indies." The structure of the text clarified the problem: it was organized along the biblical historical model with the three sons of Noah peopling the world. But, that tripartite model could not account for the Indies—they did not fit. So, it was "the world" (no qualifications) and the "Indies." When the book addressed the latter, it clarified the matter further: by God's grace the Spaniards had "discovered and found another new world never before known, at least not in the ancient writers' memory" ("descubierto y hallado otro nueuo mundo nunca antes conocido, a lo menos en la memoria de los escritores antiguos") (Thamara 1556, 250).

In short, all these influential texts manifested an unresolved tension in different ways: the existence of two worlds when in good consciousness there was only one. The authors danced around this issue, never being able to solve it. And in all cases, the Indians were part of the novelty to be described, of that new thing that was there and was new. They were, to borrow Vizenor's terms, "discoverables" (Vizenor and Lee 1999, 85). Garcilaso began the double task of addressing the tension and redressing the ideas behind it in chapter 1 by establishing the self-reflexiveness that characterized the entire *CRI*:

> Having to address the new world . . . it would seem fair, according to the common custom of the writers, to address here, at the beginning, if the world is only one or if there are many worlds. Or if it is flat or round and if the sky is too. If all the earth is inhabitable or the template zones only. If it is possible to go from one template zone to another. If there are antipodes and which are of which. And other similar things that ancient philosophers treated at length and modern ones do not stop talking and writing [about], following each the opinion that pleases him the most. ([*1609*] 1995, bk. I, chap. 1, 9)[16]

That is, unlike so many contemporary colonial authors, who copied each other without acknowledging it, Garcilaso told the readers from the get-go that he was pondering imitating what others did. The self-reflexiveness behind the imitation established a critical distance between the object (a text similar to others) and the author, opening up the space for agency and autonomy—qualities Indians were not thought to have. Authorial intentionality got pushed to the forefront. At the same time, double meanings set the stage where intentionality would operate. In this case, the word "parece" ("seem") situated the project within the realm of the readers' expectations only to challenge them—"it would seem fair" meant the opposite. He then declared some of the reasons why it was not reasonable: because authoritative authors said whatever they pleased—they had no actual ground to sustain what they said, which meant that they were not authoritative, even less worthy of being imitated (and yet they were taken to be so). Also, by passing judgment on both ancient and current authors, he undermined one of the latter's main claims when they wrote about these matters: that they had superseded the former. They were all the same, Garcilaso implied. That is why they were worthy of imitation with a difference.

As he most often did after letting out bursts of dizzying irony, Garcilaso immediately appeased Western readers but only to mock them and then appease

them again, as if it were a cartoon in which one character gets repeatedly elec-
trocuted and the image flips from the character to its skeleton and back, from
black to white, all in quick succession: "But, because this is neither my main
intent nor can the strength of an Indian boast that much—and also because the
experience, since what they call New World has been discovered, has disabused
us of most of these doubts—we will briefly go over them to get elsewhere, to
whose final terms I am afraid I will not make it" ([*1609*] 1995, bk. I, chap. 1, 9).[17]
Garcilaso began the sentence by telling two things at once, depending on the
reader's field of vision. To a discreet reader, he told he would not entertain such
nonsense, even if it seemed apropos, and highlighted the fact that the nonsense
was not seen as such—in fact, it was celebrated. To a colonialist reader, Garcilaso
confirmed his sense of order: Indians did not address such complex matters (or
were ironic, for that matter); otherwise they would be boasting, thinking too
much of themselves. Then, he mocked him, pointing out the obvious: there was
no reason to engage in long discussions because by reaching the Americas, all
ancient geographical and theological speculations about the world had been
proved false. Therefore, devoting as many chapters to it as "revered" Spanish
authors did (Gómara spent nine chapters on it, Acosta thirty-nine[18]) was at best
futile and at worst said more about the authors—their vanity, how much they
boast and think of themselves—than about the complexity of the subject matter.

In other words, Indians and Spaniards were equal (they both might run the
risk of thinking too much of themselves) but they were also different. The former
ran that risk because they were Indians in colonial contexts; the latter ran that
risk because they were Spaniards on colonial matters. What each could afford was
different. Garcilaso immediately controlled the irony, neutralizing it. He closed
the sentence by stating that he would address the matter only briefly because, as
an Indian (Indians were inferior also in strength), he might otherwise not make
it to where he wanted to go and address that which was acceptable for an Indian
to address—i.e., the customs and history of the Incas (if you were an Inca).

In the rest of the short chapter, Garcilaso mainly refuted the idea that the
world was divided into five different climate zones—of which only the second
and fourth were inhabitable and the third could not be crossed over—but he also
devoted some lines to another key colonial assumption: the existence of a New
World and an Old World. When doing so, he signaled naming as an important
matter. In the passage I just quoted, he said, "what *they call* New World was
discovered" ("se descubrió lo que *llaman* nuevo mundo") (Garcilaso [*1609*] 1995,
bk. I, chap. 1, 9), not "the New World was discovered" ("se descubrió el nuevo

mundo"). This directed attention to the fact that the issue was not the New World itself but the fact that "they" called it so. He pointed not to the object but to how people made sense of it. Right after this, he addressed the issue more fully: "But trusting in *divine mercy*, I say about the former that it can be affirmed that there is no more than one world. And although we call it 'Old World' and 'New World,' it is because that one has been discovered anew *for* us, and not because they are two, but only one" ([*1609*] 1995, bk. I, chap. 1, 9; emphasis mine).[19] Two peculiar word choices stood out in this quote: "divine mercy" ("misericordia divina") and "for" ("para"). In what concerns the first, why did Garcilaso need to invoke divine mercy?

There was nothing remotely heretic in saying that there was only one world. I suggest that here "divine mercy" largely played the same role as "being an Indian" had done before: it seemed to appease the reader, only to pull his leg. Saying that he trusted God's mercy could be understood in two ways. It might mean that Garcilaso hoped that God would take pity on his (Indian) condition and help him do that which exceeded his capacity—a colonialist reading. Or, it might mean that he trusted God to do something else: to protect him for saying about Spanish authors that which Indians should not, exposing that which was clearly visible except to Spaniards. He then quickly neutralized the ambivalence and trivialized the point. "We" in "we call it so" ("le llamamos") told that he saw what Spaniards saw—he was one of them.[20] "Call it so" told that it was simple convention. He completed the cajoling of the reading by closing the paragraph with an apparent contradiction: "And to those who even today imagine that there are many worlds, there is no point in answering them, but to let them hold on to their heretic imaginations until they are undeceived in hell" ([*1609*] 1995, bk. I, chap. 1, 9).[21]

What about the second peculiar word choice, "for" in "for us" ("para nosotros")? To say that the New World was "newly discovered *by* us" would have made sense à la Gómara: it would have referred to the fact that it was not really new—it was that Spaniards called it new because it was new to them. But, Garcilaso did not say discovered "*by* us" ("*por* nosotros") but "*for* us" ("*para* nosotros"). This word choice triggered two immediate questions: if not the Spaniards, *who* did it and *what* for? The answers came just a few paragraphs down.

When closing the short chapter, Garcilaso spent some lines rebutting the ancient idea that some parts of the world were uninhabitable. This was common practice (Gómara and Acosta did it) and so was the argument he chose to rebut that idea—that it contradicted God's command to men ("Be fruitful and multiply. And fill the earth and subdue it" ["Fructificad y multiplicand, y henchid la tierra y sojuzgadla"] [Genesis 1:28]). What was not common was the way in which he closed the argument (and the chapter). He stated: "I hope that in his omnipotence that at its time he will discover these secrets (as he discovered the new world) *for* greater confusion and affront of the insolent that with their natural philosophies and human understandings want to assess God's potency and wisdom: that he cannot do his works but as they imagine them, there being such disparity from one knowledge to the other as there is from the finite to the infinite" ([*1609*] 1995, bk. I, chap. 1, 11, emphasis mine).[22] Garcilaso's conclusion answered the lingering questions triggered by "for" in the paragraph just examined (and then repeated here): what for and who did it. When he said "and although we call it 'Old World' and 'New World,' it is because that one has been discovered anew *for* us," he blurred agencies. The wording invited the reader to think that Garcilaso was talking about Spaniards all along—it was because they had discovered the Indies that they called it New World. The idea was not necessarily new: Gómara suggested that Spaniards thought of the Indies as new because they had recently discovered them. But, Garcilaso's consistency and the quote about God suggested a different reading: the Spaniards called it New World because it was new to them but they had not discovered it—rather, it had been discovered *for* them. In other words, the agent was not the Spaniards (Columbus, Cortés, etc.) but God.[23] Did that change anything?

A Spanish reader would likely have resented having the glory taken away in such casual manner but what was left would still have fit his providential frame: God had them discover because they were his instruments, his agents, in the universal scheme of things. The real problem in the Garcilaso passage lay in the "for." According to many reputed chroniclers—pro- and anti-Indian, conquerors' accounts and royal documents alike—God had Spaniards discover the Americas so they could fulfill their providential role: to bring his light to the Indians, opening their door to salvation. But Garcilaso pointed elsewhere, as always through double meanings. If one were to ask why he did it, it would be to confuse and shame the imprudent who thought he could only do things as they imagined—that is, the Spaniards—so that they realized how full of themselves they were, a point *los atrevidos* (the insolent) missed.

Clearly, the insolent were those who thought that they could know and explain God as if they were his peers while in good theology, there was as much distance from human intelligence to God's as there was from the finite to the infinite. As always, Garcilaso numbed through double meanings. The jab could be seen as directed at those who thought that not all the world was habitable—but those did not attempt to explain God, simply missed his point. Therefore, the reader was left (at dizzying speed) with a second option: the jab was directed at those who had the arrogance to explain God when they accounted for why the Americas had been discovered—the Spanish chroniclers. The direct target was likely Acosta, whose book combined natural philosophy and human understanding (*Natural and Moral History*) and who stated authoritatively "because it is not about what God could do, but about what is in accordance with reason and the order and style of human things" ("porque no se trata qué es lo que pudo hacer Dios, sino qué es conforme a razón y al orden y estilo de las cosas humanas") ([*1590*] 2002, bk. I, chap. 16, 97). God shamed "them" for their sin of arrogance: they thought their miserable philosophy—echoes of Marx—and limited human capacity could match God's as if he could only do things "as they imagined them." (I will return to Garcilaso's use of the world "imagination.")

The chapter seemed to settle the question of whether it was right to talk about one or two worlds with a definitive answer: there was only one. However, some lingering issues remained. First, it was not clear whether the doubt concerned the object or what people said about it. At times, it seemed to be one of simple convention ("we call it so"); at others it seemed to be one of deep misunderstanding as if to say New World and Old World meant that there was more than one world, questioning the oneness of creation. Second, although he stated that ancient and current authors concluded whatever they pleased about these issues, he seemed to adhere to that nonsense custom. Third, to make matters worse, in the (very short) second chapter, Garcilaso would say exactly the opposite: the New World was justly called so because it was, in many regards, entirely different from the Old World. It was not that it was new to Europeans—it was that there was more than one world.

The unpretentious title of the second chapter of the *CRI*, "About the antipodes," suggested that Garcilaso would do there another customary thing: answer those ancient thinkers who had deemed the existence of the antipodes impossible. As usual, Gómara and Acosta had done it, although in several chapters. Garcilaso also did it, albeit in one paragraph—more was not really needed, Amerindians were not hanging upside down. He then moved on to point out the unresolved conflict between the observable world and Spanish explanations of it—tension the Mercator map expressed by placing Germany in the center of the world when it was not and by making Europe larger than other continents

when it was not. In a down-to-earth, amicable language, as missionaries recommended, Garcilaso summarily stated:

> How those people so many and with such diverse languages and customs as
> those found in the New World have passed, neither is know for certain. Because
> if one says by sea, in ships, problems arise concerning animals that are found over
> there, that is to say how and why they were shipped, some of them being more
> dangerous than profitable. Then to say they could have gone by land, even greater
> problems arise: such as saying that, if they took over there the domestic animals
> they had here, why didn't they take those that remained here, some of which since
> then have been taken over there? And if it was because they could not take so
> many with them, how is it that there are none left here of the kind that they took
> over there? And the same can be said about seeds, legumes, and fruits, which are
> so different from those here that with good reason they called it "New World,"
> because it is thus in every way: in meek and fierce animals, as in meals, as in men—
> who are generally barefaced, with no beard. ([*1609*] 1995, bk. I, chap. 2, 11–12)[24]

These lines, which consider, rebut, and go beyond Acosta's speculations all at
once, were extremely problematic. First, they highlighted that Western explanations anchored in the Bible did not reconcile with nature. They thus shattered
the idea of a unique creation with one order and the readability of the book of
nature. Second, they pointed out the Spaniards' incapacity to solve the problem,
calling into question the Western claim of privileged vision, which was tied to
the world's alleged self-evidence. European superiority was, among other things,
a matter of their seeing and thinking prowess. The "new" in the New World
ceased to be a matter of style or convention.

As usual, Garcilaso quickly masked the radical nature of his critique, taking
another opportunity to insert a good dose of mockery and irony while at it:
"And because in such uncertain matters there is no use in trying to figure them
out, I will let them rest, because I am less sufficient than any other to inquire
about them. I will only address the origin of the Inca kings and their succession"
([*1609*] 1995, bk. I, chap. 2, 11–12).[25] Attentive to colonial hierarchies, he pointed
out the nonsense only to then declare that the matter escaped his competence—
experts would know better. However, the quote triggered two questions. First,
what was the referent of "such uncertain matters"? At first, it would seem that it
was the origin of the Amerindians. But, what came right before it was the explanation of why "they called it New World." So, the uncertainty could refer to

either how Amerindians came to the Americas or whether it was fair to say that it was a new, different world. The former would fit a geographical-theological question, like the question the soldier posed the rowers in the story Alvarez recounted (see chapter 1). The latter would fit the rowers' answer: it was about coloniality. Who was the other person more sufficient to handle these matters? Of course, it was none other than Acosta who, as we saw, could not reconcile the Americas' uniqueness with biblical history. The reader's field of vision and inter-textual knowledge secured or undermined the colonizer's ascendancy. And, the ironic reading was more complex than it first appeared: readers could only see it as such if they accepted that Garcilaso (the Indian) was smarter than Acosta (the Christian expert). And this, it went without saying, could not be true. In other words, it was a catch-22 played by Indians on Spaniards—a reverse of the usual situation (see Lamana 2008, 6–7, 23, 223–24).

In short, Garcilaso told in these two chapters that there was one world but there were two. This seeming contradiction was only so if one looked at the object instead of at how people made sense of it. If one considered the latter, it became clear that both statements rejected fundamental Spanish assumptions about the Americas and its inhabitants that underlaid coloniality's unconscious—the same assumptions that would underlie Hegel's theory of history a century later. By pointing out the conventional character of naming, Garcilaso rejected the idea that history had arrived in a ship, moving from East to West, from its privileged point of origin to new places. There was no particular-but-taken-to-be-universal point of reference from which the Americas was naturally a New World. It would have been oxymoronic to have Amerindians call it so. Universal history happened everywhere as Guaman Poma had stated, too. There was therefore not a New World and an Old World—just one world and one history.[26] At the same time, by pointing out that the New World was in fact new because it was different (its animals, plants, and humans were not the same), Garcilaso rejected the move that made Spaniards the lone incarnation of the universal eye, the one that could rec-ognize the true order of things regardless of where and when while others failed to do so. Even if Spaniards were unable to notice it, their hegemonic pulsations contradicted their alleged capacity to see the real as it really was. Furthermore, they were blind to their own blindness and as a result inhabited a different world, that of people who thought they were white. To repeat, there were two worlds but there was only one. And the issue was not about who lived where, but about what one took the word "world" to mean. It all depended on who one was and what one could see and imagine about the world.

FABLE AND ALLEGORY (IT IS NOT A GREEK THING)

In light of the text's pervasive doubleness, what can be said about what is often taken to be the object of the *CRI*, Inca culture and history? If, as I have argued, the key issue when reading the text is to understand what the *CRI* did and how it commented on others' ideas about the world, then the question had to be not just the particular image of the object (in this case, what the Incas had been and had done) but how the Incas—Garcilaso included—thought the act of representing what they had been and done vis-à-vis what Spaniards had been able to think about it.

This change of register interjected a layer of reflexivity, making narrative voices and structure (the switching from the explicit to the implicit) as well as irony and teasing the key elements to trace. In such a reading, Garcilaso defied the Spanish intention of mastering the visual field, of seeing Indians as creatures who could easily be pinned down and talked about, their own ideas brushed aside as superstition or nonsense. As usual, he did it with a good amount of humor, at once deploying and masking double meanings.

As is known, Garcilaso divided precolonial Andean history into two clearly different *edades* (ages): pre- and post-Inca rule. He gave to these ages the opposite values Guaman Poma did: pre- was quite preposterous while post- was almost perfect. The pivotal event connecting them was the origin of the Incas. After describing the Indians' barbaric state prior to Inca rule (in chapters 9–14 of the first book), he presented the origin of the Incas. The oft-quoted passage explained: "[seeing the Indians' miserable condition] our father the sun . . . felt pity and mercy for them and sent from the sky to the earth a son and a daughter of his so they would teach them about knowledge of our father the sun so that they would adore him and have him for their god" ([*1609*] 1995, bk. I, chap. 15, 41).[27] The mission of these two divine agents was to have Indians adore the sun and "that they live like men in reason and urbanity . . . like rational men and not beasts" ("que viviesen como hombres en razón y urbanidad . . . como hombres racionales y no bestias") (Garcilaso [*1609*] 1995, bk. I, chap. 15, 41).

Scholars point out that this divine act made the Incas part of providential history. The *praeparatio evangelica* (preparation for the gospel) frame comes next: the sun did it all "so that when that same God, sun of justice, considered for good to send the light of his divine rays to those idolaters, he would find them not so savage but more docile to receive the Catholic faith and teachings and doctrine of our holy mother Roman Church" (Garcilaso [*1609*] 1995, bk. I, chap. 15, 39).[28] Garcilaso stated, borrowing a line from Acosta (bk. 7, chap. 28), it had been proven that conversion happened readily in the case of Indians who had been governed by the Incas unlike in the case of those who had not. The origin story, the argument goes, was part of Garcilaso's larger casting of the Incas which had two goals. First, by presenting them as bearers of the light of reason, he built on the well-established view that a person's capacity to embrace Christianity went hand in hand with the development of his rational capacity. Natural reason would lead man to observe the natural law and then progressively to observe God. Second, by including divine intervention, he made the Incas part of an explicitly providential global history unlike in Las Casas's texts. In God's plan, the Incas were the apostles of reason while the Europeans were the apostles of faith (Duviols 1963; Zamora 1988, 85–128, 140–59).[29]

This interpretation fits the origin story in many regards but it is not without problems. First, there is an unaddressed contradiction: divine intervention does not align with an argument about the natural progression of man toward God. In theological terms, it is the opposite—it points not toward what is natural in man but toward what God gives him, the supernatural supplement without which man can do little. Second, the story is outlandish. In post-Trent Spain, nothing was more tightly policed than alleging direct contact with God.[30] To state that God had sent some agents (even worse, his children) straight from heaven down to earth to help do his work was either laughable or punishable. Third, and last but not least, there is a matter-of-fact problem: Garcilaso would disqualify the entire origin story down the road, saying it was made up. Why present it only to debase and refute it? (I will return to it.)

These problems suggest the need to look at the origin story in a different manner. One element that opens the door to new meanings is the structure of the narrative—who says what about whom and why. In the case in question (the divine origin of the Incas), the speaker was not Garcilaso but his uncle whom he quoted at length.[31] I suggest that the uncle and the issue of divine intervention were means to talk not about Incas but about Spaniards. Or better said, to talk about Spaniards talking about Incas and Indians. Garcilaso rarely did one thing without doing the other since his interest lay in the interplay of imaginings and expectations that characterized colonial interactions and cajoled what it was to be Indian. The key to accessing this reading was to follow Garcilaso's carefully interspersed references to the question of how to understand what Incas (and Indians at large) told about their history. In this case in particular, one had to look at what Garcilaso said Indians did with other peoples' beliefs about origin stories.

He devoted three chapters (15–17) of the first book to quote his uncle's narrative of the origin of the Incas and one chapter (18) to relate two other versions from non-Inca Indians. He consistently called them all *fábulas* (fables). Spaniards tended to misread them, taking them for vague, corrupted memories of universal events, he pointed out: "Some curious Spaniards want to say, hearing these stories, that those Indians had news of Noah's history . . . and that they said Paucartampu to mean the arc's window. . . . They want other things from one fable or another to resemble those of the Holy History, that it seems to them the two look alike" ([*1609*] 1995, bk. I, chap. 18, 48).[32] Down the road, when he explained that the Incas composed fables in poetry and prose, he stated that "Spaniards do not want [the stories] to be fables, but true histories, because they have some resemblance of truth. They mock many others because it seems to them that they are poorly conceived lies, because they do not understand their allegory" ([*1590*], 2002, bk. I, cap. 25, 119).[33] This observation seemed to fit well-known colonialist imaginings about Indian recollections of their past, part and parcel of the Indians' incapacity to think beyond and/or above what was presently in front of their eyes. Acosta summarized, "it all is full of lies and far from reason" ("todo va lleno de mentira y ajeno de razón") ([*1609*] 1995, bk. I, chap. 25, 119); they cannot even remember their origin, explained Alvarez ([1588] 1998, 147).

To these opinions, Garcilaso commented: "I plainly say the historical fables that in my childhood I heard my people say. Each shall take them as he wants and give them the allegory that suits him best" ("Yo digo llanamente las fábulas historiales que en mi niñeces oí a los míos. Tómelas cada uno como quisiere y deles la alegoría que más le cuadrare") ([*1609*] 1995, bk. I, chap. 18, 48). As always, the sentence accepted two readings. On the one hand, he claimed to present readers what he had heard without implying that he took it for a historical discourse about the real. On the other hand, he told readers that although fictitious discourses did not report real facts, they were not necessarily false. They might refer to things that were true but in a way that looked false because the meanings did not run at the literal level but at the allegorical. In that, they were, like the rest of the narrative, a *comentario*.[34] This had a ripple effect. If an Indian story was told by a Spaniard and explained (away) as a poorly remembered historical event, the story existed at the same level as the Indian: they were both objects for others of which to make sense. If, in contrast, a story was authored and told by an Indian, there was a distance, a space, between who the Indian was and what he thought and said to others about who he was through the telling of the story. In that space, meanings could unfold like an accordion's pleats—or perhaps like a jack in the box. Intention and agency—and therefore self-reflexivity—gained center stage. Reality was no longer simple nor were Indians and truth/falsity ceased to be the issue.[35]

In other words, by casting his uncle's words (and those of other Indians down the road) as something that had an allegorical significance, Garcilaso implicitly presented the Indians' capacity to detach themselves from the literal. Indians were not held capable of doing that for at least two reasons. First, deemed creatures of an *inteligencia material*, they were thought to lack mental capacity because their existence took place "does not lift one bit from the dust of the earth" ("no se levanta un punto del polvo de la tierra") (Alvarez [1588] 1998, 144). Conversely, Spaniards (people who thought of themselves as white) considered themselves the masters of abstraction, of *pensamiento elevado* (elevated thinking), figuration included. Second, eurocentrism and coloniality played an important role in solidifying these constructions. Allegory was a well-known and accepted idea, but only when it came to thinking about Old World stories, not about Amerindian ones. Coloniality made it look like some things had a proper place and were a province of a specific people—as it would happen four centuries later to the Mexican scholar Miguel León Portilla who was criticized for titling a book *Filosofía Nahuatl* (Nahuatl philosophy) (Mignolo 1999). It went without saying: allegory, like philosophy, was a Greek thing.

The structure of Garcilaso's historical narration intended to turn the tables when coloniality and eurocentrism were coming into being. His goal, like that of the Indians speaking with Santo Tomás and Alvarez, was to have his interlocutors partake of the shift. As he narrated the history of the Inca conquests and the development of the state system, Garcilaso returned to and fleshed out the relevance of his ideas of fable and allegory. When closing the narrative of the life of the first Inca, Manco Capac, Garcilaso explained the story of the origin of the Incas in his own secular terms:

> What I, according to what I saw and the nature of those peoples, can conjecture about the origin of this prince Manco Inca . . . is that he must have been an Indian of good understanding, prudence, and council who reached well the very simplicity of those nations and saw the need they had of doctrine and teaching for their natural live. And astutely and sagaciously, to be held in high esteem, he

faked that fable, saying the he and his wife were children of the sun: that they came from the sky/heaven and that their father sent them to indoctrinate and do good to those peoples. ([*1609*] 1995, bk. I, chap. 25, 61)[36]

At its simplest level, the paragraph told that the Inca developed stories as tools for good government—their fables were neither mistakes nor blurry memories. At another level, it presented a riddle: from where did its Christian elements come? Because, as a lector discreto might have noticed, even if Manco Inca invented the story, he was not supposed to know the elements. In turn, this suggests that either he had prefigured these elements, which made the dismissal of the story nonsensical, or the Incas in colonial times (or Garcilaso) had made up Manco Capac's making up to teach Spaniards through allegory—a fable inside a fable. And perhaps, what either of the former had wanted to teach the latter is that what was important was not the origin story itself, but the fact that it matched the Incas' deeds: "And as the benefits and honors he bestowed to his vassals confirmed the fable of his genealogy, they believed firmly the Indians that he was son of the sun who came from heaven/sky and they adored him as such. . . . Because there is nothing that that people pay attention to like to see if what their masters do conforms with what they tell them, and finding that they conform their life and doctrine no arguments are needed to convince them to do what they want to do of them" (Garcilaso [*1609*] 1995, bk. I, chap. 25, 161–62).[37]

Given that pointing out that the Spaniards talked the talk but did not walk the walk was ubiquitous in colonial texts, Garcilaso incited readers to compare Incas and Spaniards. In this case, the comparison was between someone who existed inside a story where he was superior to Indians, even a partaker of the divine, but acted nothing like it, and someone who was not, but acted as if it were the case (the Incas had not been sent by God to do good as they claimed but they acted as if they had). Equally if not more important, it was also an invitation to compare each people's agency and awareness vis-à-vis the stories that they are told. Spaniards inhabited them, unaware of their meanings; Indians knew that they were fables and related to them accordingly. Like in Guaman Poma's *NCBG*, Indians paid attention to doing, not to knowing: they noticed Spanish nonsense and rejected the invitation to be part of it. Garcilaso had used the same tactic when he followed the Spaniards' model to discuss the world(s) and then dropped it.

As Garcilaso narrated the Inca conquests, he gave actual examples of Inca fables and their allegories. Perhaps the most complete related to the Inca conquest of the Colla. As they did with each group they faced during their campaigns, the Incas sent messengers to the Colla asking them to peacefully accept their benevolent rule, which had been mandated by the sun. The Colla rejected the proposition and instead repeatedly attacked and berated the Incas. The latter, as always in those cases, abstained from using their superior power to overcome their enemy and only defended themselves, waiting for the Colla to realize their folly. One day, however, many Colla died during their attack on the Incas. Since they knew that the Incas only defended themselves, the rumor spread that the stones, arrows, and other weapons the Colla had used to attack the Incas had turned against them—another seeming case of divine intervention in favor of the Incas (Garcilaso [*1609*] 1995, bk. III, chap. 2).

Garcilaso then proceeded to tease out the different levels of agency and self-reflexivity at work in the fable. He explained, first what the Inca captains explained about it, "explaining the fable" ([*1609*] 1995, bk. III, chap. 3, 148). Tired of hearing the Colla's repeated insults and of having to repel their attacks, the Inca captains decided to teach them a lesson. They told their men to be fully armed and to inflict severe damage on the Colla when they attacked. The Inca warriors did as ordered. As a result, most Colla men died "[and] since until then the Inca's men had not fought to kill them but to hold them out they said that they had not fought that day. But that the sun, not being able to stand the little esteem in which the Collas held his son, had ordered that their own arms be turned on them to punish them, since the Incas had not wanted to do it" (Garcilaso [*1609*] 1995, bk. III, chap. 2, 149).[38] The Colla, simple people, believed the story, which Spaniards would have considered an example of Indian nonsense or the devil at work as they did with other fables. Garcilaso explained then the allegory of the false but nevertheless true fable: "The amautas (who were the philosophers), allegorizing the fable, said that because the Colla did not want to drop their arms and obey the Inca when it was requested of them, their arms had turned against them because they were the cause of their death" ([*1609*] 1995, bk. III, chap. 2, 149).[39]

In short, Garcilaso's history of the Incas differed from the one the Spaniards gave not just because of its content but more importantly because of how Incas and Spaniards made sense of it. The former saw, thought, and allegorized; the latter did not see, thought only what they could according to their limited imagination about themselves and Indians, and literalized or dismissed the fables. Both parties were similar but different, at once one and more than one—just like the world(s). Equally important, only Indians were aware of it.

5

UNDERWORLD STORIES AND UNTHINKABLE INDIANS

UCH OF the material of the *CRI* refers to the achievements of the Incas, their conquests, laws, and ideas. In fact, the explicit structure of the text—what Genette (1997) calls "paratext"—supports this reading: its books follow the lives of successive Inca kings as the expansion of the empire progressed and its chapters analyze specific aspects of the development of Inca rule. Those are the narratives I have critically examined in the previous chapter. At the same time, consistently interspersed throughout the text there is a different kind of material: stories about colonial times in which the protagonists are not Incas and the different ethnic groups being conquered but Indians and Spaniards. These stories have received limited scholarly attention. If analyzed at all, they are often seen as disconnected from each other. I suggest in this chapter that they form a coherent whole. They are, adopting the visual topography of the *Super Mario Brothers*, underworlds. Presented always under the guise of colorful anecdotes, these stories connect surface elements through alternative ways. Like the famous plumber, readers could see one dimension of the topography or two; they could follow the surface path only or both at once.

Each underworld colonial story is in some regards different from the others. Each addresses a specific colonial problem, unfolds in a particular spatial setting, and takes place at a precise moment of the colonial temporal sequence, from first contact to the actual writing of the book. At the same time, the stories have commonalities. The most salient is that they pretend to talk about Spaniards and Indians but in reality talk about the ideas Spaniards had about themselves and about Indians and what Indians did with these ideas. Literal meanings versus double meanings and irony pave each interpretive path. There is also the fact that Garcilaso did not simply tell tales but through the structure of their narrative intervened on the thorny colonial issues the stories addressed.

What was the purpose of these stories? It seems to me that it was double. On the one hand, they offered native actors in colonial times "postindian" (Vizenor 1999) tools for making life livable in the straightforward conditions of racial discrimination they faced. The limits the Spaniards' imagination set to both parties in colonial interactions were consistently fleshed out and undone. On the other hand, by repeatedly exposing the products of the Spanish imagination and their failure, the stories offered white readers (following Baldwin [2010], "people who thought themselves as white") the necessary critical distance for them to be able to see themselves and the Indians in a new light. That is, they encouraged change. Garcilaso's ultimate goal was not integration—to reform or open up colonial institutions to incorporate good Indians—but transformation: to radically change the field of colonial social relations. At a minimum, he intended to have Indians inhabit it as an "active presence" (Vizenor 2000); at maximum, he sought to have all parties abandon the faulty fundaments of the colonial world and start afresh.

SETTING THE STAGE: FIRST CONTACT AND IMAGINATION

After devoting the first three chapters of the first book to his sharp discussion about the existence of one or two worlds, Garcilaso addressed in the following three chapters the origin of the name of Peru. The explanation was part and parcel of the copying and parodying of Spanish pseudo-explanations about the names of the New and Old Worlds examined in the previous chapter. After all, the name "Perú" had not been used by those living in Peru, pretty much like "New World" had not been used by those living in the New World. In Spanish accounts, the places and its inhabitants were equally "discoverables" (Vizenor and Lee 1999, 85).

According to many scholars, Garcilaso's explanation of the name Peru followed a philological frame.[1] He began by stating that the term "Perú" did not exist in any Indigenous language prior to the Spanish arrival; he then proceeded to quote in detail diverse Spanish authors who acknowledged the fact that Spaniards used this name, not Indians; finally, he explained that when Spaniards named new places, they often corrupted words that existed in native languages without really understanding their meaning. In the case in question, if any native term should have been used to call what was by then known as Peru, it should have been the one the Incas used to call their empire, "Tawantinsuyu," which meant "the four parts of the world."

My argument is that this philological explaining happened in the surface world. In a short story inserted along the way, Garcilaso addressed something else: how the name came into being given that it did not exist—which no Spanish author explained. The story involved an Indian fishing, a river, and the importance of the imagination, all in a Spanish-Indian first contact scene. The elements were carefully chosen: most were present in passages of Acosta's and Gómara's accounts that made passing reflections about the name Peru. Gómara referenced it twice while narrating the Spanish conquest of the Inca Empire. The first time, he stated that "Perú" had been the name of a river ([*1552*] 2004, chap. 108, 198); the second time, he said that it referred to lands south of Túmbez city ([*1552*] 2004, chap. 110, 2002–03). As usual, Acosta developed Gómara's writing but changed little of its essence. In the midst of a long philological argument to prove wrong those who argued that Peru was the biblical Ofir, he stated that "Perú" did not designate a territory prior to the conquest—it was just the name of a river ([*1590*] 2002, bk. I, chap. 13, 91). Neither author addressed the question of how the name of a river had turned into that of a land or included Indian voices in their accounts.

Garcilaso redressed these problems in a short story in chapter four, appropriately titled "The deduction of the name of Peru" ("La deducción del nombre del Perú"). During the discovery and exploration that would eventually lead to the conquest of the Inca Empire, Garcilaso told, the crew of a Spanish ship sailing south along the coast of today's Ecuador saw an Indian fishing close to the mouth of a river. Eager to obtain information, a party of four Spaniards, all great swimmers, got off the ship to capture him. They plotted a particular trick. They approached the Indian stealthily, and before they laid their hands on him, they had the ship pass in front of him to divert his attention. The Indian "seeing in the sea such a strange thing, never seen before on that shore—as it was to sail a vessel at full sails—he was amazed and stayed bewildered and dazed,

imagining what could be that thing that in the sea he was seeing in front of him"
(Garcilaso [*1609*] 1995, bk. I, chap. 4, 15; emphasis mine).[2]

Taking advantage of the Indian's bewilderment, the Spanish party captured
him and brought him on board. After some attempts to calm him down, "they
asked him by signals and by words what land was that one, and how it was called"
("le preguntaron por señas y por palabras qué tierra era aquella y cómo se llam-
aba"). The Indian "understood that he was being questioned but not what he was
being asked. And to what he understood was the question, he answered quickly,
before they did him any harm. And he named his own name, saying 'Berú,' and
added another and said 'Pelú.' He meant to say, 'If you ask me what my name is,
I call myself Berú. If you ask where I was, I say that I was in the river'" (Garcilaso
[*1609*] 1995, bk. I, chap. 4, 16).[3] After explaining that "pelú" meant river in the
language spoken in that place, Garcilaso concluded: "the Christians understood
according to their desire, *imagining* that the Indian had understood them and
answered intentionally, as if he and they had spoken in Castilian" ("los cristianos
entendieron conforme a su deseo *imaginando* que el indio les había entendido
y respondido a propósito, como si él y ellos hubieran hablado en castellano")
(Garcilaso [*1609*] 1995, bk. I, chap. 4, 16; emphasis mine).[4]

One can begin the task of making critical sense of the story by examining its precise uses of the word "imagination"—an idea that in fact appears
in most of Garcilaso's underworld stories. The concept requires some fore-
grounding. There were mainly two ways of understanding it in sixteenth- and
seventeenth-century Spain. One of them related to demonic delusion. According to Aristotle-derived theological theories, the intellect functioned not on the
bases of direct sense perception but on "mental images" or "imaged concepts."
These images condensed or distilled the information the senses gathered and
carried it to the mind. The imagination played a crucial role in this process: it
mediated between raw sense perception (what was really there) and imaged
concepts (what the mind took as being there). As such, it was the devil's primary
target, a door through which he could mess with a person's mind, making him
believe that things that were not real actually existed—hence, demonic illusions
(MacCormack 1991, 15–35). This first meaning of "imagination" coexisted with
other more mundane meanings that resemble those it has today. Thus, the most
important seventeenth-century Spanish dictionary (Sebastián de Covarrubias'
1611 *Tesoro de la lengua castellana o española*) followed the Aristotle-derived definition by a lay one which defined "to imagine" as equal to "to think" or "to

occur" to someone and defined "imaginable" as that which can fit within the boundaries of what one can possibly conceive.[5]

While scholars study in detail the impact of the philosophical-theological apparatus in the Spaniards' understanding of Andean religion and Garcilaso's sophisticated response to it,[6] my interest lies elsewhere: in Garcilaso's (repeated and precise) use of both understandings of the word "imagination" to explain things unrelated to religion. Most often, he referred to imagination not to address the presence of the devil in the Andes or the Spaniards' ideas about the devil in the Andes but to explain how the Spaniards' minds worked—that is, a theory about the delusions of whiteness. The Spaniards' imagination limited their minds and as a result there was no true cognition or learning—exactly what, according to Spaniards, happened to Indians when they heard something new or when they observed nature.[7] The problem lay then not in abstraction per se, as Spaniards argued about Indians, but in something prior to it: in the mechanics underlying one's capacity of abstraction. In other words, there were different reasons why a mole could be blind and different kinds of impediments to seeing.

Returning to the case in point, of the Indian fishing in the river and the Spaniards who captured him, it was important to note that the story's two references to "imagination" signal (again) something that is the same but different and vice versa. Both the Indian and the Spaniards imagined. The Indian fishing by the river imagined when he tried to make sense of something of which he had not heard, something never seen before, which could hardly fit within the limits of his imagination; in other words, his *imaginando* (imagining) related to Covarrubias's second definition, the lay one. The Spaniards' imagining on the other hand worked along theologians' definition of it: they heard what did not exist, sounds got filtered into an imaged concept that did not match reality, and because of it, drove them to believe that what was not real was so. They were victims of their delusions—no devil involved—and because of it believed that the Indian confirmed their expectations. The same, one could argue, was happening time and time again some seventy years later when the *CRI* was published as Spaniards believed the devil to be running amok across the Andes, even if he did not exist according to anyone but them.

This story, set not by chance as first contact, sketches several important underworld ideas. First, Spaniards did not interact with Indians—they interacted with their imaginings about Indians. It was their expectations about Indians and the stories Spaniards told themselves about themselves and their others that controlled colonial interactions. Second, Spaniards were all along convinced that it was actually Indians who could not tell reality from delusion or error, imprisoned as they were by their limited knowledge and imagination, and therefore failed to have meaningful interactions with Indians. Third, a critical issue in such a setting was how Indians responded. In this particular case, a contact case, the Indian quickly devised a solution to get the weird guys off his back "before they did him any harm"—he chose to please the Spaniards. Even if the Spaniards missed that it was a choice and that it involved performance (and therefore agency), for discreet readers, the Indian ceased to be an absent presence as he was always in Spanish accounts. Fourth, Garcilaso was active in the story. While the chapter is titled "Deduction of the name of Peru," the deducing was done neither by the Spanish explorers, who could not deduce anything because they did not understand, nor by Acosta or Gómara, who offered no explanation, but by Garcilaso—and it worked not by following empirical evidence, as one would expect according to good deductive logic, but by following knowledge of the Spaniards' imagination. Fifth, Spaniards and Indians were the same but they were not. Both could imagine and both faced limitations—it was human. But while the Spaniards' imagination was constrained by coloniality, as was always the case, the Indians' imagination was constrained by the limits of the real—here, alluding to both the observable and that which others could imagine existed in reality. As in Guaman Poma's case, it was important to distinguish conceptual and factual limits when it came to assess what people did or did not, thought or did not think.

INTEGRATION? SAMENESS, DIFFERENCE, AND UNTHINKABLE INDIANS

The question of sameness and difference is at the heart of any colonial project. Colonialism is carried out in the name of turning the native into a Westerner, but in practice, it needs difference to prevail—otherwise, its raison d'être would cease to exist. Paraphrasing Bhabha a bit (1994, 86), colonialism's success is its strategic failure. This tension opens up the question of integration: if there are different peoples, how exactly are they going to live together? Being the same or being different? In either case, on which exact terms? In colonial Peru, during the second half of the sixteenth century, being similar but different or different but similar was actually a matter of fraught theological debate and a political and ecclesiastic power struggle that directly affected native peoples.

The power struggle had a clear result: it ended up shifting the official stance away from the positions and practices of the first evangelization toward those of the second. Different milestones consolidated the shift: the reorganization of the colonial system carried out in the 1570s by the Viceroy Francisco de Toledo, who annihilated the last Inca holdout and executed its king, Tupac Amaru, committed a history of the Incas that cast them as tyrants and idolaters and backed it all up with notarized historical inquiries; the 1583 Third Ecclesiastical Council of Lima, which made official the defeat of the first evangelization and was followed by its discrediting in important publications; the advance of the Jesuits over the Dominicans that led to the latter's loss of the rich Lupaca territory to the former; and finally, the general offensive against and persecution of Indigenous religious practices carried out through inquisition-like campaigns that started in the 1580s and extended well into the 1600s (Estensoro-Fuchs 2003, 139–370; MacCormack 1991, 249–80, 383–433; Meiklejohn 1988; Merluzzi 2014).

The theological debate in contrast was never settled. It could not have been because it involved legitimate diverging views of thorny theological problems that Christian thinking had wrestled with since the apostles (Alberro 1993; MacCormack 1989). As seen in more detail in chapter 1, these diverging views offered the others of Spanish colonialism two options: they could be the devil's puppets/partners, estranged peoples whose customs had little in common with Christians, or they could be somewhere behind Spaniards on the long path toward God, distant relatives who did Christian-like things in primitive and inchoate ways. Either way, Indians were considered simple and unreflexive people, which made them easy targets of the Spaniards' scopic regime.

When it comes to the parts native actors chose to play in colonial settings, it would be reasonable to think that they favored the less damaging of the two lousy options available. And in a way, that would seem to be the case in the *CRI* (and the *NCBG*): Garcilaso's Incas are the embodiment of natural reason. Their order and practices aligned with natural law, casting a ray of sunlight over the peoples of the *primera edad* (first age) in the Andes. However, that is not all that there is in the text. In some of his underworld stories Garcilaso consistently presented unexpected Indians. These were Indians whose Indianness was defined in ways that did not fit the two options Spaniards offered. Garcilaso made these Indians impossible to pin down—they observed and created, dodging both first and second evangelization ideas of Indians. As a result, the question of similarity and difference, which vexed clergymen and royal administrators alike during these years, acquired entirely new meanings, referring to something else altogether. And integration became a question with no set answer, except that it could not be discussed in the available terms.

NOT THE SAME (HOW TO SWEAR)

Although Garcilaso mentioned a large number of Spanish authors, in the *CRI* there was no reference to Santo Tomás. This may seem odd because it would have fit his portrayal of the Incas like a glove: the Dominican was a very important agent of the first evangelization in the Andes, an expert on Andean languages, and a philologist. I suggest that the absence expresses the fact that, while the options the first evangelization offered were better than those of the second, and in fact he used them extensively in the upper world, Garcilaso (like Guaman Poma) knew that the detrimental defense came at a price and he was not willing to pay it.

This dissatisfaction may explain why Garcilaso chose to address and challenge Santo Tomás's ideas in an underworld story and not mention him by name. He did it through extensive mimicry, in the third chapter of the second book, which focused on Inca religious beliefs. In its first two chapters, Garcilaso established Inca monotheism. He discussed the fact that the Incas had *rastreado* (tracked) the existence of a supreme God (whom they called Pachacamac) although they had no clear idea of who he was or how to adore him. This fit the first evangelization's idea that Indians could only attain a conocimiento confuso of God's existence. While the third chapter began by also following the first evangelization's path, it ended by presenting something totally different: an unexpected Indian, one whose Indianness was defined in ways that escaped all available offers.

The chapter has two parts. The first told that, prior to the Spanish conquest, the Incas had a marble cross in Cuzco that they venerated, although they did not know why—another case of vague knowledge. Garcilaso lamented that Spaniards did not use it to convert Indians—had they done it, they "would have gotten Indians interested in our religion with their own things, comparing them with ours, like it was this cross" ("aficionaran a los indios a nuestra religión con sus propias cosas, comparándolas con las nuestras, como fue esta cruz") (1995 [*1609*], bk. II, chap. 3, 73–74). In fact, he pointed out, Spaniards could have taken advantage of many Inca practices that matched the natural law and the commandments of the law of grace including mercy works—all first evangelization material. This critique was a clear jab to Acosta and Alvarez and a nod to Santo Tomás.

The second part of the chapter presented a story about a cross that blurred these neat lines. Garcilaso explained that the timing for this story was apropos given that he was just talking about the cross, but this justification veiled more than it enlightened. The story was only tangentially about a cross—it was rather about swearing and in fact went to the core of Santo Tomás's argument about Indians' mental prowess analyzed in chapter 1 and undid it. To review, Santo Tomás claimed, prior to the conquest Indians used juramentos execratorios because they had not known God. While after the conquest they did, they were still far from really understanding what it meant to be Christian and thought that imitating Christians was how to be one. Thus, when the Dominican asked a curaca what he knew of being Christian, he answered that he already swore like Christians did, stole a bit, and was learning to play cards. He thought this, Santo Tomás explained, because Indians were unable to distinguish the abstract truth from the concrete examples in front of them. This argument rendered Indian critical thinking invisible and presented the Spaniard as the only intelligent party in the duet, the one endowed with abstract critical thinking.

Mimicking Santo Tomás, Garcilaso set the stage in chronological terms, distinguishing pre- and post-contact times. Before the Spanish arrival, he told, Indians did not know what it was to swear. When it came to legal matters, they always said the truth because they knew well how the Inca punished liars. When it came to deities, they uttered the names of the sun or Pachacamac only to adore them, with much veneration. He thus made two arguments at once: first, Indians knew God; second, it was not because they did not know God that they did not swear invoking a witness. Santo Tomás got both things wrong and made the wrong argument—it was not that Indians did not lie because they were afraid that what they had sworn for would happen (e.g., the earth would eat them) but they did not do so because they were law abiding and kept religion to its rightful purpose.

Continuing his miming act, Garcilaso then went on to consider how things had changed after the Spanish arrival (which he did, also like Santo Tomás, through an ethnographic example). He told of a murder case in the province of Quechuas which had been assigned to a specially commissioned Spanish judge. When the judge called an Indian witness (a curaca or cacique, like in Santo Tomás's example), he presented the latter with a cross and asked him to swear to God and the cross to tell the truth. The ensuing dialogue was short but very revealing: "The Indian said: 'I have not yet been baptized to swear like Christians swear.' The judge answered saying that he should swear to his gods, the sun and the moon and the Incas. The curaca [cacique] answered: 'We do not utter those words but to adore them. And thus it is not licit for me to swear to them'" (Garcilaso [*1609*] 1995, bk. II, chap. 3, 75).[8]

The first line was a polite rejection to a request to do nonsense (very much like Garcilaso's when talking about the five zones). It is as if the cacique had said, 'Um, I am not a Christian, but I do know that swearing to God before the cross is something Christians do; therefore, there is no use in having me do it'—which should have been clear to the judge since baptized Indians could be identified because only they had Christian names. There was thus no Indian mistaking the act of swearing with being Christian, as Santo Tomás had had it. Rather, the absolute opposite occurred: the Indian saw the situation clearly, the Spaniard did not—unless of course the judge mistook swearing like a Christian with being one. After the Indian pointed out the obvious nonsense, the judge offered a substitution: 'Fine, given that you are not Christian, then swear for whatever you hold in great esteem: the moon, the sun, the Incas, anything.' The implicit idea was that the structure was valid; all that was needed was to replace the object. God or the Virgin do for Spaniards; the moon, the sun, or the Incas should do for Indians. The third line was a rejection of the offer by the curaca and as such the beginning of an unthinkable Indian: Indians did not treat their deities the way Spaniards treated God. Unlike the latter, the former uttered their names only to adore them and only in religious contexts; they did not to invoke them as witnesses when swearing and it did not even cross their mind to blaspheme. In short, there was no easy replacement because there was no easy equivalence. It was not that Indians did not understand what it was to swear the way Christians did, which was Santo Tomás's argument—it was that they did. Moreover, they knew that for Spaniards and Indians "swearing" (like "world" and "imagination") was the same but it was different, something Santo Tomás was not able to see.

The dialogue continued, fleshing out the point: "The judge said: 'What guarantee will we have that what you have said is true if you do not give us some security?' 'My promise will suffice,' said the Indian, 'and the fact that I understand that I am speaking directly before your king, since you come here to do justice in his name. That is how we did it with our Incas. But, to satisfy what you ask for, I will swear to the earth saying that it should open up and swallow me alive as I am if I were to lie'" (Garcilaso [*1609*] 1995, bk. II, chap. 3, 75).[9] In other words, the curaca's first explanation had fallen on deaf ears—the judge was still looking for a replacement: swear for something, anything we can hold as *prenda* (security), otherwise you may lie. The curaca then simultaneously explained to the judge the Indians' way of understanding truth and the reasons why they neither gave securities nor lied. He also stated, given that the judge (and Spaniards at large) did not get it, he would swear for the earth to open and eat him. This was revealing on two accounts. First, it told that *Indians did nonsense*, as Spaniards often argued, *but only on demand.* They did it to please Spaniards, who were not interested in the truth, but in having their expectations about Indians met. 'It is the satisfaction of your desire that is at stake, nothing more (and nothing less),' pointed out the cacique. 'You like to see us play Indian? Fine. We oblige.' Second, the mention of "shall the earth eat me" ("trágame la tierra") put into effect an astonishing and deep twist in the several layers of meaning governing the entire interaction and its context. It turned mimicry into parody.

A discreet reader may have noticed that there was no prior mention to a juramento execratorio in Garcilaso's example. Indians did not use it before the Spanish arrival, and the judge did not ask the curaca for it. The juramento execratorio (in particular "shall the earth eat me") was present only in Santo Tomás's example—that was, the Dominican stated, how Indians used to swear. This uncalled-for reference turned the implicit imitation into parody and changed the meanings both of the local exchange and the bookish one.

To examine the complexity of this situation, Geertz's (1973, 6–7) distinction between a twitch and a wink is useful. In a room in which two people each close one eyelid, the act can be the result of one's muscular reflex (a twitch) or of another's intentional act (a wink). Things can get more complex: there can be a third person in the room who deliberately copies the second and whose act of closing an eyelid is neither twitching nor winking but parodying. On the reception side, things are not simple either: the differences can be missed or can be interpreted as existing when they do not.

In the case in point, there were two interpretive contexts: the one in the dialogue and the intertextual one. The curaca was not twitching—he was either winking or parodying. Vis-à-vis the judge, he was saying something odd. It was not an option for him to swear with a juramento execratorio but the judge saw no intention in it. However, had someone in the room read the *Grammatica*, it would have been clear to him that the curaca was responding to Santo Tomás: "We do not swear with a juramento execratorio, you fool. We never did, still do not. We only do it to satisfy your imagination about Indians so you will leave us alone. Besides, when you swear to God, you are invoking his punishment if you lie; that is the same as what you want me to do with 'shall the earth eat me.'" And, there was more. Because this was a text, the curaca was Garcilaso's marionette: by saying "shall the earth eat me," the curaca was winking not to Santo Tomás but to the other curaca, the one in Santo Tomás's story, who was in fact winking—although Santo Tomás thought he was twitching. This transformed Garcilaso's curaca's wink into a parody (and Garcilaso himself into a satirist).

The story ended with the curaca answering the judge's questions and, seeing that the latter's questions did not allow him to explain the truth, interrupting the judge and telling him that, unless he told the entire story, he would be lying. That is, in spite of the fact that the judge told the curaca to stick to his questions, the curaca chose to tell the whole truth because he understood it at once in the same but in a different manner. Back in Cuzco, Garcilaso concluded, Spaniards admired the conversation between the curaca and the judge.

The story conveyed multilayered critical thinking. First, the Indian knew what it was to be Christian while the Spaniard seemed to have forgotten it and therefore the former had to remind the latter. Second, although the Indian rejected the substitution offer, he still satisfied the Spaniard's desires, which sprung from his limited vision. In doing so, the Indian expressed a high level of reflexivity—a far cry from the idea that Indians copied what they saw without really understanding it, as Santo Tomás stated. Third, the example was full of titillating similarities and differences, which turned into each other like the inside and outside of a Möbius strip. Swearing was different but it was the same; the truth was the same and it was different; relations with the divine were the same but different. Spaniards and Indians thought about it all in the same way but did not. While Indians knew it and acted accordingly, to Spaniards things were one way only and it was Indians who did not get it. Fourth, the example had little to do with Indian childishness or their lagging behind in the evolutionary scale, which valued Indians' way of being as a kind of age of innocence, another key element of Santo Tomás's schema. Instead, there was coevalness and an active presence driven by a clear sense of the past and the future. Fifth, Indians understood the complexity of the situation in a way Spaniards did not. The former could separate the abstract (what Spaniards thought about Indians and equivalence) from the concrete example in front of them (an Indian swearing in a trial) while the latter clearly could not. Or, Indians could tell a twitch from a wink while Spaniards could not (at least when it came to Indians). Agency was thus reassigned drastically. Sixth and last, all this opened up a space for social action, community solidarity, and making life livable, a space that was safe and sound and fostered survivance. There was room to let out a number of good laughs at the Spaniards expense, because when Indians winked at each other, Spaniards thought that they were twitching.

NOT SO DIFFERENT (A DECOLONIAL DUNG-PUSHING BEETLE)

After politely rejecting the paternalistic offer of the first evangelization and pointing a way out of its corset, Garcilaso proceeded to do the same with the second evangelization. He did it by inserting twitching and winking in a story narrated by the second evangelization's most prominent figure in the Andes, the Jesuit José de Acosta. Garcilaso engaged the latter's work in different ways. On the one hand, Garcilaso quoted Acosta's *Historia* (1590) when it supported his argument (praising Inca social order) and silenced it when it did not (condemning Inca idolatrous practices); on the other, Garcilaso drew a clear line separating Amerindian history into pre- and post-Inca rule which Acosta did not do (Brading 1986; Zamora 1988, 85–128).[10] But Garcilaso's *CRI* were neither the first nor the only text to highlight Inca order, silence Inca idolatry, and draw a pre/past divide. Cieza de León's 1553 *La crónica del Perú* also marked the divide and Hieronimo Roman, chronicler of the Augustinian order, did it as well in his chapters about pre-Hispanic Andean history in his *Republicas del mundo*. He also praised Inca order and laws, which were just and necessary, good enough to rule any Christian republic, and criticized Spanish conquerors along Las Casas's lines (Adorno 1993; Duviols 1963; Brading 1986). Printed in 1575 and again in 1595, it was a widely read and influential book. How were Garcilaso's ideas different then? Was he simply adding his work to those who disagreed with Acosta? Not quite. As it was the case of his dialogue with Santo Tomás, his debate with Acosta aimed not simply to correct the record but also to "stage conceptual jail breaks" (Smith 2009, 90). This became clear in another underworld story in which Garcilaso told something altogether different about Spanish debates over similarity and difference, the first and the second evangelization included, shifting sixteenth-century terms of the conversation.

In chapters 1–9 of the second book, Garcilaso discussed Inca religious beliefs and practices. He made two key points: the Spanish misunderstood most of them and the Incas were monotheist. Stating that the Incas had reached knowledge of the existence of a supreme god through natural light was part of Garcilaso's implicit argument about the compatibility of Andean and Western civilizations: the Incas had been on the way to Christianity. At the same time, Garcilaso repeatedly disqualified the Spanish view of Inca religion as one more case of the devil's hand at work. To do so, Garcilaso played the philological card, correcting Spanish misunderstandings of key Inca terms, like Pachacamac or huaca, and flatly rejected that Inca terms fathomed Christian mysteries.[11] Playing the Indian card, he stated that if these religious mysteries were beyond man's natural capacity, then Incas and Indians in particular were characterized by a material intelligence, being close to concrete, simple things—a statement that worked as ironic veiling.[12]

To further support his claim about Spanish misunderstanding of Inca religion, in chapter 6, Garcilaso quoted at length the Jesuit Blas Valera, who stated that reports of religious similarities made by Spaniards were the result of their poor understanding of native languages. When Spaniards asked Indians about religion, Valera explained, sometimes they understood exactly the opposite of what Indians told them; other times, they understood something but not exactly what was being said to them; and very few times, they got it right. As a result, "In this great confusion the priest or layman that asked them [the questions] picked according to his taste and chose what seemed to him the most similar and closest to what he wanted to know and to what he imagined that the Indian could have answered. And thus, interpreting them according to their imagination and whim, they wrote as true things Indians did not dream of" (Garcilaso [*1609*] 1995, bk. II, chap. 6, 83).[13] If there were actual similitudes, Valera concluded, it was because the devil had a hand in it—Acosta's argument.

Toward the end of the fifth chapter of this book devoted to Inca religion, Garcilaso interjected a seemingly out-of-place story. It was about non-Inca religious beliefs and from la primera edad. The anecdote thus seemed to violate the explicitly stated premise that pre- and post-Inca times and beliefs had to be clearly distinguished. This seeming contradiction was in fact another door into the *CRI* underworld, a story that at once deviated from and informed what happened in the surface world.

The story was about a dung-pushing beetle named Tangatanga. The chapter began by closing his argument about the many significations of Quechua words that related to the sacred, significations Spaniards missed because they spoke Quechua poorly and failed to recognize the different pronunciations that conveyed the different meanings. To support his linguistic claim, Garcilaso narrated a short personal anecdote that also foregrounded his argument about Spanish incomprehension that he would develop in the next chapter via Blas

Valera. He told that in the Dominican convent of San Pablo in Córdoba, he met several times with a friar, a well-regarded master and teacher of Quechua in Peru. Once, when they were talking about Quechua, the clergyman pointed out that the word *pacha* meant many different things—presumably a comment about Quechua's poverty of vocabulary and resulting imprecision. Garcilaso then asked him if he knew the different pronunciations of pacha so that it could actually convey those different meanings. The clergyman admitted to not know, to which Garcilaso replied sharply, "Having been a master of this language, you do not know this?" ("Habiendo sido maestro en la lengua, ¿ignora esto?"). He then proceeded to teach the "maestro" ([*1609*] 1995, bk. II, chap. 5, 80).[14]

Garcilaso's remark, sharp as it was, was even more so given the extremely deferential tone of the rest of the dialogue. I suggest that Garcilaso inserted these unsettling lines not by chance—they did the work of setting up a two-sided screen. On one side, he would project a movie that met the expectations of colonialist viewers about the restitution of racial hierarchies. On the other or through the other, Indians would see a much more complex and encouraging take of the same film.

Right after the dialogue, without transition, Garcilaso began a story about an idol called "Tangatanga, which one author says was adored in Chuquisaca, and the Indians said that it was one in three and three in one" ("Tangatanga, que un autor dice que adoraban en Chuquisaca, y los indios decían que en uno eran tres y en tres uno") ([*1609*] 1995, bk. II, chap. 5, 80). The "one author" who had said so was none other than Acosta, who in book 5 of the *Historia* discussed Amerindian religious beliefs and practices which, like Blas Valera, he systematically attributed to the devil. Chapter 28 in particular fleshed out the devil's role in the Incas' and other Indians' adoration of mocking resemblances of the trinity. Like Garcilaso, Acosta interjected firsthand knowledge about non-Inca beliefs in his discussion. For example, he briefly told that once in Chuquisaca "a very honest priest" ("un sacerdote muy honrado") told him that the Indians adored a Trinitarian idol, Tangatanga, "who they said that it was one in three and three in one" ("que decían que en uno era tres y en tres uno") ([*1590*] 2002, bk. V, chap. 28, 360). To the amazed priest, who had even carried out an *información* (notarial inquiry) about it, Acosta simply told "that the devil would steal all he could from the truth. . . . He did it with that infernal and stubborn pride with which he always wishes to be like God" ("que el demonio todo cuanto podía hurtar de la verdad. . . . Lo hacía con aquella infernal y porfiada soberbia con que siempre apetece ser como Dios") ([*1590*] 2002, bk. V, chap. 28, 360). In other words, in line with his simultaneous disavowal and disqualification of the theology and practice of similarity and continuity, Acosta cast the priest's ideas as naïve and the Indians as puppets.[15]

Garcilaso commented that the closest he could get to making sense of the name of the idol (which he was sure the Spaniards got wrong) was "Acatanca: which means 'beetle,' [a] name with much propriety composed of this name, 'aca,' which means dung and this verb tanca, which is 'to push.' Acatanca means 'the one who pushes dung.' [And he then added:] That in Chuqui-saca—in that first age and ancient gentility, before the empire of the Inca kings—they adored it as a god, would not shock me. Because . . . then they adored other equally despicable things. But not after the Incas, who banned them all" ([1609] 1995, bk. II, chap. 28, 80–81).[16] So far, the changes Garcilaso made to Acosta's story worked at two levels. At the most literal, he amended Acosta's data: Indians of the first age were barbaric, it was true, but the Incas had banned the adoration of low creatures, like beetles, and had directed Indians toward the sun/Pachacamac. Acosta failed to make that distinction and this misunderstanding led him to think that the devil had Indians mock the Trinity. At a second level, he discredited both Acosta's and the priest's knowledge. These two expert inquirers of native religion entirely missed the meaning of the idol's name, which led them to unwittingly engage in an eru-dite argument about the origin and causation of the alleged similarity between the dung-pushing beetle and the Trinity. Had they known, they would have noted that it was something from the first age.

One could say that this solves the apparent anomaly: an example about pre-Inca religion was present in a chapter about Inca religion because it followed the philological argument that applied to both pre- and post-Inca times. But, there was a third layer of meaning in Garcilaso's rendering of the story a discreet reader might notice. After cracking a laugh about Acosta's and the priest's scant language knowledge, such a reader would have wondered why and how in the first place the Indians of Chuquisaca told the priest that Tangatanga related to the Trinity. After all, Garcilaso made it clear that this was a vain belief of the first age, which the Incas had banned—and even if the memory had somehow survived, there was nothing about the Trinity in it. Where did it all come from then? Anticipating the question, Garcilaso shifted gears and switched focus from the object (religious beliefs) to what different peoples thought about it. He added: "That the Indians say that in one they were three and in three one, is a new invention of theirs, which they have done [made] after they have heard the Trinity and unity of the true God our Lord, to flatter the Spaniards by telling them that they too had some things resembling those of our holy religion" ([*1609*] 1995, bk. II, chap. 28, 80–81).[17] That is, Garcilaso took Blas Valera's idea and flipped it upside down—or took it one step beyond (and above). It was not that Spaniards understood (wrongly) what Indians said according to their imagination—it was that Indians told (sold) them what they knew Spaniards wanted to hear (buy).

But, if so, why would tracing parallels be a way of flattering Spaniards? It would seem rather a form of self-flattery since by establishing parallels, the Chuquisaca Indians jumped on the (alleged) universal train and close to the driver—a much better option than being the devil's puppets on a ride to nowhere. The question ceased to make sense if one looked not at the content or object, seeking correspondence, but at the act or conceptual practice, seeking power relations. Garcilaso went on: "All which is invented by the Indians [Trinity and other similarities], which the hope that, if just by likeness, some courtesy will be done to them. This I affirm as Indian, that I know the natural condition of the Indians. And I say that they did not have idols with the name of Trinity" ([*1609*] 1995, bk. II, chap. 28, 80–81).[18]

In other words, by marking similarities, Indians flattered Spaniards because they confirmed the latter's self-proclaimed mastery. In this case, the first evangelization's priest's desire that Indians conformed to and confirmed was the theology of continuity. While seeming to be about Indians (colonialist ideas of them), the story opened a door into the interior worlds of Latin America's colonial subjects that allowed seeing colonialism as they saw it. It was not a story about Indians, as it had been in Acosta, or about Spaniards seeing Indians, as it would have been in Blas Valera. It was about Indians seeing Spaniards who thought that they saw Indians. As a result, it no longer mattered whether the similarities were real or not or how Spaniards explained them. What mattered was that Spaniards liked to see themselves expertly seeing through Indian practices and fables, making sense of them, and being in a position of scopic mastery vis-à-vis their subjects/objects—and the latter knew it and obliged. What was at stake was the exercise of power, pure and simple. Or, as Humpty Dumpty famously put it, "The question is . . . which is to be master—that's all."[19]

While Spaniards believed they were the masters, they were blind to the fact that they were being helped to believe that such was the case. The Chuquisaca Indians crafted and sold sameness hoping that it would trigger the Spaniard's sympathy and they would be seen, if only momentarily, as human beings not objects—'we are like you.' This could be interpreted as a variation of the desire of the colonized to become the colonizer, as Frantz Fanon ([1952] 2008) analyzes in *Black Skin, White Masks*. However, Garcilaso's explanation made clear that it was not *just* a product but one so blatantly funny that, to a discreet reader, it could only indicate humor and reflexivity. After all, why choose such an outrageously hilarious name (Tangatanga, Acatanca, dung beetle) to claim knowledge of nothing less than one of Christianity's most complex mysteries, the Trinity? This at once pointed to difference—'we are not like you.' Spaniards were deluded into scopic mastery. They sat in their comfy seats, thinking that they were looking at little brown people, but they were not really watching little brown people—they were watching a movie about little brown people. The subjects of the film in turn watched their own spectacle: they were looking at the dangerous blind men watching the movie Indians had produced. In this scenario, whites were seen "undressed and from the back and side" (Du Bois [1920] 2015). The setting was still there as Spaniards imagined it but it was not: 'you are looking at us and think you see us but you do not—you see our performance.' As if having a "third eye" (Rony 1986), the Indians saw the veil and through it and replaced colonial simulations with postindian ones, reclaiming an agency they had been denied, and becoming an active presence.

To close, I stress three points. First, the difference between Garcilaso and the Spaniards (Blas Valera and Acosta) followed the *CRI*'s overall pattern: Garcilaso's text was about Indian reflexivity, self-awareness, and intentionality as well as Spanish blindness when it came to imagining Indian things. The Spaniards looked at Indians, who they thought they could diagnose, taxonomize, and explain away. They did not imagine a returned gaze, even less one that "sees the self through the eyes of the other"—a W. E. B. Du Bois déjà vu ([1903] 1990, 5). The Indians' third eye challenged the scopic desire at the core of Spanish colonialism. Once the observer turned into observed, the racist effect of the colonizer's gaze ceased. Second, there was irony as always. From the dung-pushing beetle to the act of telling lies to flatter, it was all about humor, about pulling the Spaniards' legs and jokingly telling how things really were without the (Spanish) audience noticing. There was no traumatic experience in being looked at, just annoyance and amazement at not being seen. Third, this story defined "being Indian" or Indianness as a moving target. It was not an essence, cultural, epistemological, or whatever else one may call it—it was the consciousness of and conscious practice toward political intervention informed by a particular way of experiencing and understanding the world, which was one and many at the same time. Sameness and alterity acquired entirely new meanings, decolonial ones—and so too did "to write like an Indian."

THE HEART OF WHITENESS
(MELONS AND RADISHES)

The order in which I am presenting the underworld stories of the *CRI* follows the same order in which the text progressed. This order reflected, I suggest, how Garcilaso organized his conceptual ethnography of whiteness. The ethnography began appropriately with a contact story. This initial fable set the stage in terms of white imaginings about Indians and painted the basic strokes of what Indians could do with those imaginings. The second set of fables illuminated angles of the theme of "integration." They presented the two main proposals Spaniards could make Indians—which resulted from the limited ways in which they could think about difference and similarity—and offered unexpected solutions. The final set of underworld stories of the *CRI* addressed the heart of the racial order of things: whiteness as a libidinal quest for superiority. They theorized the Spaniards' desire for Indians that confirmed their certainty of ascendancy and as always offered Indians creative ways of dealing with it.

The final book of the *CRI* (the ninth) had a peculiar structure. Its first fifteen chapters narrated the deeds of Huayna Capac, the last Inca emperor; its final eight, the conflict between Huayna Capac's sons, Huascar and Atahualpa (which was still ongoing when the Spanish conquest began). The sixteen chapters in between discussed the new things Europeans brought to Peru. At the beginning of chapter 16, Garcilaso explained this shift from history to ethnography by resorting to chronology: the narrative was getting close to the time of the Spanish arrival. To some extent, there was nothing notable about it. Ethnographic-like chapters in the midst of historical narratives were common in Spanish chronicles and so were comments about the new things Spaniards had brought to the Indies. There was, however, something peculiar about the way in which Garcilaso talked about the new things: "It will please present and future [readers] to know about all the things that there were not in Peru before the Spaniards won that land . . . so that it is seen and considered with how many fewer things—and seemingly so necessary to human life—those peoples made it through and lived very happily without" ([*1609*] 1995, bk. IX, chap. 16, 598).[20]

As it happened at the beginning of the *CRI*, with the experts talking about there being one or two worlds, *al parecer* (seemingly) was Garcilaso's way to state that what (white) people said made no sense and of announcing his intention to part company with them. As always, he did it at high speed and with irony. The quote began by praising Spaniards for the novelties they introduced and took to be ineluctable evidence of progress, and ended by telling them that, oh well, they were not so. The teasing contradiction drove the attention away from the novel things toward what Spaniards thought about them and implicitly about what they thought about themselves and Indians—and what Indians did with those thoughts.

The first implicit idea that Garcilaso discarded is that Indians had to be grateful for having been conquered since as a result their lives had improved. Either apologetically or unapologetically, in a celebrative or remorseful tone, Spaniards stated that they had brought to Indians important things they lacked. The main one was knowledge of the true religion, but the items mentioned included a range of things from iron to cows, wheat to writing, and melons and radishes to *humanidad* (humanity).[21] The second related idea was that Spaniards were superior to Indians. The novelties were material evidence of the former's greater mental prowess. And, the fact that they knew God and were in fact his agents often made that superiority partake of the divine.

Throughout the text, Garcilaso addressed these ideas in passing, skillfully weaving deference and difference; in two underworld stories of chapter 29 of the ninth book, he tackled them head on.[22] The stories were about melons and radishes and, Garcilaso declared, talking about them posed dilemmas that haunted him during the very writing of the book. As always, the narration was full of different voices—to the extent that they resembled theater scripts more than prose—and of irony, which made meanings dependent on what readers could interpret and what they took words to mean.

MELONS (HOW FULL OF IT YOU ARE)

The Spanish conquistador Antonio Solar, "a noble man," Garcilaso told, had an estate some leagues away from his residence in the city of Lima. One day, his Spanish *capataz* (foreman) decided to send him ten melons and a letter carried by two Indians. When they were ready to leave, the foreman warned the carriers: "Don't eat any of these melons, because if you eat any this letter will say so" ("No comáis ninguno de estos melones, porque si lo coméis lo ha de decir esta carta")

(Garcilaso [*1609*] 1995, bk. IX, chap. 29, 624). On their way, driven by *golosina* (relish), one of them told the other: "'Shouldn't we know what this fruit from our master's country tastes like?' The other replied: 'No, because if we eat any, this letter will say so, that is what the foreman said.' 'Well,' answered the first, 'let's dump the letter behind that wall. And as it won't see us eat, it won't be able to say anything'" (Garcilaso [*1609*] 1995, bk. IX, chap. 20, 624).[23]

The messengers ate the melon. Then, worried that their unequal loads might awaken the Spaniards' suspicion, they consumed another. When they arrived, their Spanish lord, Antonio Solar, read the letter and asked them about the missing melons. They denied ever having more than eight, to which Solar replied: "'Why are you lying? This letter says that you were given ten, and that you ate two!' The Indians were lost, seeing their master accusing them in full view of what they had done in secret. Thus, confused and convinced, they did not know how to contradict the truth. Then they left saying that with much reason the Spaniards were called gods, with the name Huiracocha, since they arrived at an understanding of such grand secrets" (Garcilaso [*1609*] 1995, bk. IX, chap. 29, 624).[24]

Garcilaso casted this *cuento gracioso* (amusing tale) as an example of Indian simplicity and, alluding to a similar story narrated by Gómara, concluded that this trait characterized Indians across the Americas—they attributed divinity to any actions committed by the Spaniards unknown to them "and because of that they called them gods" ("y por ende los llamaban dioses") ([*1609*] 1995, bk. IX, chap. 29, 625). Specialized scholars often share the casting. Some interpret this well-known story as an example of Indians' fetishization of literacy: since they could not understand the nature of writing, Indians turned letters into animated beings (Rosenblatt 1977, 30; Arrom 1991, 154–55; Ortega 1992b; Harrison 1994, 79), a case of Indian "simplicity" (López-Baralt 2011, 165). Others read it as evidence of the alliance between colonialism and literacy and the effect it has over oral societies (Chang-Rodríguez 1977; Degregori 1991, 13; Mignolo 1995, 172; Fuchs 2001, 80; Cornejo-Polar 2003, 96).

However, for these readings of the story to work, two important incongruences must be ignored. First, while the story allegedly celebrated Spanish superiority and pitied Indian inferiority, the Indians got away with what they wanted: they ate the melons and did not get punished. Second, the story seemed to follow a by now well-known pattern, but the end went astray. Spaniards, due to their elevated thinking, could understand that a letter was part of the human order of things; Indians, due to their material intelligence, could not and saw the supernatural where it was not. And yet, the story ended not with the Spaniards correcting the Indians' foolishness and error, as it should have, but with its celebration. How was all this possible?

To answer this question, a discreet reader would have to access the story's veiled message, which would become visible (and even necessary) if he adjusted the reading to the meta-level of a comentario. It would then become clear that the story of the melons signified Gómara's story about the potencies infusing writing and the divinity that Spaniards thought that Indians thought Spaniards embodied, rather than merely reiterating it. Garcilaso's rewriting of the contested trope of the "talking book" (Gates 1988) twice subverted the meaning of the original story: it reversed the colonial hierarchy it seemed to celebrate and it emptied it of any supernatural connotations.[25] At the end of the day, what was left was an example of colonial practice and subaltern writing.

As mentioned, in the closing lines of the story Garcilaso referenced a similar tale recounted by Gómara. The tale appears in chapter 34 of Gómara's 1552 *Historia general de las Indias*. Also titled *Hispania Victrix*, this widely read and immensely popular book at the time celebrated the glorious achievements of the Spanish colonial enterprise, defending the conquistadors' deeds before the so-called Indians' party critiques. The book's 224 chapters are chronologically ordered. The thirty-fourth is a very brief one, devoted to summarizing miracles that paved the way to Indian conversion during the Spanish conquest of Cuba—a way to make clear the hand of God behind Spanish actions.[26] Such miracles included the following: demons that stopped appearing to Indians once the holy host was consecrated; a cross that healed many and that warlike Indians could not demolish despite concerted efforts; an Indian lord who became dumb and bald after intentionally sinning in a church; three Indians who were struck by lightning during a storm after having taunted Mary while the one who commended himself to her survived; and finally a brief story about the magic of alphabetic writing: "Literacy and the letters that Spaniards sent to each other also helped much [in conversion] because Indians thought that they had spirit of prophecy—since without seeing or talking with one another, they understood each other—or that paper spoke, and they [the Indians] were bewildered and abashed because of it" (Gómara [1552] 2004, chap. 34, 72).[27] To have spirit of prophecy means to possess knowledge not accessible to ordinary people, knowledge inspired by direct contact with the divine. Since reading allowed Spaniards to talk about what they could not know in a manner that was cognoscible to Indians, they appeared to the latter to be divinely inspired—like prophets. Gómara then gave an actual ethnographic example of it, to which Garcilaso referred:

One Spaniard sent another one a dozen pieces of cold cuts. . . . The Indian who
was taking them fell asleep . . . on the way, and it took him a long time to arrive,
and thus he was hungry or tempted to try the cold cuts, and so . . . he ate three
pieces. The letter he brought back in response thanked him for the nine pieces. . . .
The master scolded the Indian. He denied it . . . but since he understood that the
letter spoke it, he confessed the truth. He remained abashed and wary, and spread
among his people that letters spoke, so that they would be watchful. ([*1552*] 2004,
chap. 34, 72)[28]

While the similarities between Garcilaso's and Gómara's stories are clear, I want
to stress the differences. The key distinction is that in Gómara's tale the divine
was unmediated; it was the Indian messenger who, unable to understand the
nature of writing, thought that letters were animated beings. There are some
objects that speak; no explanation is needed to understand that it is a manifestation of the supernatural. And even if it was the weakest of all the miracles that
Gómara mentioned—in the sense that, unlike in all other examples, what the
Indian attributed to divine manifestation was only a human skill—in the last
instance, the Indian understood what Gómara intended to convey: that there
were agencies other than human ones. That is why each and all these events
paved the way to conversion. In other words, what mattered to Gómara was a
pedagogy of the nonhuman order, not of the sociological order. This concern
also explained the other distinctive characteristic of Gómara's short story that
I want to point out: it could only work at a literal level as there were no voices
explaining what things were. They simply *were*.

In contrast, Garcilaso's story worked at a meta-literal level and what mattered
to him was a pedagogy of human relations, in particular colonial ones. Everything in his story was mediated by what its characters (well fleshed out, unlike
Gómara's) explained about what they did and thought and about how they
expected others to proceed. This introduced a layer of reflexivity: the story was
not simply about the facts but equally about what the actors in it thought and
had to say about those facts. The plot unraveled at the meta-level of a comentario: the interpretation of others' interpretations of what happened. Because
of this—and despite all appearances to the contrary—the magic of literacy was
in fact desacralized, rendered trivial by the explicit and repeated references to
it. The difference is like that between having people talk at length about God
(and elaborate how mighty he is) and having them witness a miracle. The end

result was an inversion of Gómara's priorities: here, everything took place in the sociological realm of human action.

In this terrain, the question was what people of unequal power standing did in colonial contexts with what others thought—a theory of postindian practice. From the start, the foreman used the allegedly ubiquitous belief in the supernatural character of writing to try to control the Indians' behavior, thereby affecting colonial hierarchy. This aim was directly expressed in the prohibition against Indians eating melons, a foreign fruit they grew but had no opportunity to taste, and indirectly in the Spaniards' desire for control. The expectation behind the foreman's explanation was that letters could work as portable Panopticons. As is the case in Jeremy Bentham's prison model—in which guards invisibly observe inmates from a central tower—once the disciplining gaze is internalized, the energy spent in controlling is economized (Foucault 1975, 159–99, 228–64). The foreman (Spaniard) would not need to be present to police the messengers (Indians); the latter's imaginings about the former (powered by letters) would do the job. Yet from the messengers' point of view, when the foreman declared the power of letters to them, he was in fact telling them what Spaniards expected Indians to believe about letters and implicitly about the Spaniards themselves. The key to the story was as much what happened to the melons (its conventional reading) as how this parallel set of expectations unfolded.

To take advantage of a good opportunity to eat melons, the messengers put to good use the Spaniards' belief in Indians' gullibility and simplicity. They concocted a great story, in fact a fable, that met Western expectations about Indians to exculpate themselves and get away with it. The main interpretive cue to this alternative reading lay in the temporal relations between narrative and story—what Genette (1980, 31) in his study of narrative discourse calls "tense." In Garcilaso's story, unlike Gómara's, the timeframe of the narrated events did not coincide with that of the narrative—there was an anachrony at work in the text. The way in which Garcilaso related this story of Indian simplicity— particularly the order in which he presented the events and the voices through which they became known to the reader—veiled the fact that the hilarious tale of the Indians hiding the letter (so that it could not see them eat the melons) became known to the Spaniards *only* from the messengers' mouth and *after* the action was over. The Indians themselves related this act to their master once they returned to his house in order to defend themselves after eating the melons, in spite of the warning.

This writing strategy becomes a colonial postindian practice once one makes sense of the fact that, despite the story's twists and turns and its amusing elements, there is a discrepancy between its alleged celebration of Spanish superiority and the fact that the Indians were not punished for their acts. That is, they got away with what they wanted. I argue that they were successful because they understood that what was at stake for the Spaniards was not the melons but rather their expectations about their divine superiority and the Indians' gullible inferiority. The colonial fable is best explained in the form of a dialogue. Alonso Solar, the master, after receiving the melons, asked the Indians: 'Why did you eat the melons when you were told that the letter was going to tell us? Did you think that what we say about letters is not true?' If the nobleman Solar lied and told the messengers that the letter saw them eating the melons, it was because this act of consumption threatened the Spaniards' desire for an ascendancy partaking of divinity that the magic of literacy allegedly made manifest. The Indians essentially responded with an amusing and amazing explanation: 'No master, we did not intend to challenge you nor to disrespect the letter. We put it behind a wall to make sure that it would not see us but it did not work. Oh, how silly we are!'

After paying homage to the Spaniards' fascination with literacy and confirming their ideas about Indian inferiority, the messengers left, telling the Spaniards that they were justly called gods. And as with everything else in the story, the meaning of its denouement was not what it seemed at first. Rather than an example of Indian naïveté and Spanish superiority, it constituted an example of subaltern irony and Spanish blindness. When Garcilaso had the messengers say that "with much reason the Spaniards were called gods, with the name Huiracocha," he played with the fact that, while Spaniards argued that Indians called them Huiracochas because they saw them as being divine, which in turn made the reference seem coherent, he had explained earlier that Huiracocha was not a native deity but something Indians had made up with the specific aim of flattering Spaniards ([1609] 1995, bk. V, chap. 21, 302).[29] The literal interpretation of the utterance ceased to be at odds with my reading once one takes into consideration what Bakhtin (1986, 79, 85–90) calls "expressive intonation." In this case, it was playful and ironic. When, after getting away with eating two melons, the Indian carriers said, "With so much reason the Spaniards were called gods . . . since they arrived at an understanding of such high secrets," they were not praising their divine status but making fun of them, celebrating the fact that because Spaniards thought so highly of themselves, they could not see things otherwise.[30]

RADISHES (HOW COMICAL YOU CAN BE)

To dig further into the meanings of the story of the melons and understand its implications for an incipient theory of whiteness, its context has to be considered. It appeared in a chapter devoted to "the monstrosity, greatness, and abundance" (Garcilaso [*1609*] 1995, bk. IX, chap. 29, 623) of some European garden produce in Peru. As always, the trope and the objects fit the genre: chronicles often had a section about the Americas' extraordinary features, its marvels and monsters, including what happened with transplants (Ortega 1992). The mimicry worked as part of a veiling: while disguised under familiar tropes, the placement of the melon story suggested that writing and the talking book belonged neither to the goodies that testified to the accomplishments of Spanish colonialism nor to evidences of Spanish superiority, divinity included, but to things people could happily live without. They were, in short, not signs of mental capacity, as Europeans thought. Or, they might well have been—it all depended on how mental capacity was conceived.

The fable of the melons is the second of two featured stories in chapter 29. The first one, which told of a *rábano gigante* (giant radish), had two clearly distinct parts. It began with a 1556 anecdote. On his way south from Lima, Garcilaso explained, the newly appointed governor of Chile, don García de Mendoza, was told about "a radish of such strange greatness that under the shadow of its leaves five horses were tied" ("un rábano de tan extraña grandeza que a la sombra de sus hojas estaban atados cinco caballos") ([*1609*] 1995, bk. IX, chap. 29, 622). Wanting to see the radish by himself "so that he had something to tell," don García paused his trip. The governor was not disappointed. The radish was in fact so big that a man's arms could not reach around it and yet it proved tasty and tender once it was dug up. Then, with no transition, Garcilaso switched to the story's second part: a May 1595 dialogue, contemporary to the actual writing of the chapter, in which he presented the trouble he then faced. The setting was very solemn: "the holy Cathedral Church" of Cordoba. There, "talking with a nobleman [*caballero*] called don Martín de Contreras" about the writing of his work, Garcilaso confided to the latter "that he feared writing down the greatness of the new things of grains and legumes that grew in my land because they were incredible for those who had not left theirs" ("que temía poner el grandor de las cosas nuevas de mieses y legumbres que se daban en mi tierra porque eran increíbles para los que no habían salido de las suyas") ([*1609*] 1995, bk. IX, chap. 29, 623). The knight's response matched the gravity of the setting and the seriousness of Garcilaso's concern:

Do not leave unwritten, on that account, what happens. Let them believe what they will, it is enough to tell them the truth. I am eyewitness of the greatness of the radish of the Azapa valley, because I am one of those who made the journey with don García de Mendoza. And I testify, as noble knight, that I saw the five horses tied up . . . and later ate some of the radish with others. And you can add that in the same trip I saw in the Ica valley a melon that weighed four arrobas and three pounds, and to that effect it was taken as faith and testimony before a public notary, so that such monstrous things will be credited. ([*1609*] 1995, bk. IX, chap. 29, 623)[31]

Garcilaso presented reporting on the greatness of garden produce to a Spanish reader as if it were a problem that scared him. By doing so, he pushed to the extreme and caricaturized the Spaniards' demand for a narrative of authorization—a variation of Bhabha's "*tell us why you, the native, are there*" (1994, 99). That demand explained the setting: it was solemn to indicate seriousness and confessional to convey interior (true) conflict and feebleness. The nobleman's response revealed the efficacy of the colonizer's need for a returned gaze that satisfied and secured the self—Bhabha's "*tell us why we are here*" (1994, 100). Vis-à-vis the native's impeccable performance, the humanist civilizer felt obliged to take on the burden (the *White Man's Burden* [sensu Rudyard Kipling]) of having to alleviate an Indian's fears. In other words, Garcilaso appeared to embody Sepúlveda's ideal natives: those who justified the colonialist burden and were grateful for it. That is why they were there and so were the Spaniards. The same reason but different.

Garcilaso's narration of the radish episode encapsulated some aspects of his critical thinking: it offered a theory of Western colonial expectations, as just seen, and at once explained how to make those expectations livable. As a theory of postindian practice, it allowed a reader gifted with a second sight to enjoy the force of the Spaniards' projections on the veil. Such a reader could see in don Martín de Contreras, a *caballero hijodalgo* (knight), resolutely testifying to the greatness of a radish, the ridicule of Spanish pretentiousness and pomp. The pairing of nobility and radishes was even more effective and funnier in light of the Spanish idiomatic expression "me importa un rábano," which literally translates to "it matters a radish to me"—meaning something in between "I do not give a damn" and "I couldn't care less." That is, if vegetables were things of little prestige, the growth of a root crop, a subclass of little prestige within veggies, they were even more so idiomatically. The readers could also perceive the possibility of inverting meanings: "let them believe what they will, it is enough to tell them the truth" paraphrased biblical passages that became a key tenet of conversion. While the truth had to be revealed to them—that was the Spaniards' mission—Indians could not be forced to believe. In this case, the truth was not the right way, but the size of a radish and the roles were inverted since here it was the Spaniards who refused to believe.

The two fables were, in short, about the opposite of what Garcilaso seemed to state. Rather than about Indian simplicity and Spanish greatness, they were about how Indians could pull the Spaniards' legs and prevent them from noticing the mocking that inverted the colonial power structure. Antonio Solar, the man who lied about the nature of writing, was "a nobleman," one of Peru's renowned and respected first conquistadors. Don Martín de Contreras, the caballero hijodalgo, invoked the quality of his blood to testify to as grave a matter as the size of a radish and also subjected literacy in its most formal mode, that of legal writing, to an absurd end: giving a notarized testimony—not unlike the one Garcilaso demanded from Acosta—about the size of a melon. One can only imagine the notary setting up (in the middle of nowhere) his table, chair, ink, and plume and getting on with the important task at hand. The absurdity, as a commentary about the power of writing, was even more meaningful if the discreet reader considered that Garcilaso's writing was full of significance.

Both stories tied back to elements present throughout the book. First, the "parece" that sets the scene for the melon and radish stories—in the CRI introduction to the things "seemingly so necessary to human life"—resonated with the "parece" of the opening chapter about one or two words. In both cases, Garcilaso pushed intentionality to the forefront: it may seem reasonable to do nonsense but he would not. Second, there was the repeated problem of stating what Spaniards could not take but was true. His call for the Spaniard to assuage his fear of telling the truth about the size of a radish resonated with his invoking divine mercy to tell the truth about there being one or two worlds. Third, there were the many questions about the divine. Gómara's story about the letter resonated with Manco Capac's about the origin of the Incas. Both were lies about the divine that still achieved what they meant to do; that is, they were fiction but also true—unlike the story about the melons, which had very little to do with the divine and a lot to do with what some people thought about themselves and the divine. Alonso Solar's lie achieved nothing (except perhaps self-delusion), it was not true, and it was not a fable either. The icing on this cake came not surprisingly through irony. Garcilaso's sixteen chapters on novelties were preceded by a prophecy about what Huaina Capac, the last precolonial Inca emperor, allegedly said before dying. In it, the Inca emperor foretold the fall of the Inca Empire to a new people, who would be superior to the Incas (Garcilaso [*1609*] 1995, bk. IX, chap. 15, 596). The prophecy echoed one that Caribbean native priests allegedly made and that Gómara reported, one wonders if by chance, also in the chapter prior to telling the story about writing. In the *Historia*, both elements aligned and testified to the supernatural in the conversion of Indians. But in the *CRI*, they did not align and therefore testified to Spaniards' delusion about their divine standing—and its ridiculing.

To close the underworlds, it is important to note the fact that the messengers delivering the melons were not punished and that the *CRI* was published in Europe and well received suggested a striking parallel: Garcilaso was the messenger. Both worked in the same way: they satisfied the Spaniards' expectations about Indians, blinding them, and did what no Indian could in theory do. They challenged the master and made him swear about radishes. The key to the messengers' success was the same for Garcilaso's writing. They both had the capacity to operate at two levels at once, seeing through a veil and seeing what was projected on it—a second sight. If the story of the radish was made of images seen through a camera, we might say that Garcilaso used the presence of the nobleman to suggest the possibility of adjusting the focus of the lens, making the radish blurry and the observer himself sharp. The same happened in the previous case, which was not really about the letter and the melons—it was about the foreman and the nobleman, what they believed Indians thought about them, and what the latter did with the formers' expectations. In short, both cases were particular instantiations of his general theory of whiteness as a state of mind and his repertoire of postindian practices. Of course, readers could adjust the focus and read these stories and the *CRI* at large on a literal level and see only a story about a giant root vegetable or a story about Indian simplicity—soothing images, nothing else.

EVERYWHERE: UNTHINKABLE OFFERS

The material presented above suggests the need to reexamine Garcilaso's goal and readership. Scholars often identify Garcilaso's in-betweenness as one of the driving forces of the text. In her extensive study of the *CRI*, Margarita Zamora points out that, unlike European texts, which either marginalized or condemned Indigenous cultures, Garcilaso "sought to reconcile the oppositions and contradictions that he perceived in those discourses in order to achieve the Renaissance ideal of concordia, or the conciliation of opposites" (1988, 3). Garcilaso achieved this ideal by suggesting that the Incas and the Spaniards were complementary: the former brought the light of reason to the Andes, the latter the light of revelation. Castro-Klarén argues that Garcilaso proposed a "theory of universal harmonization" (2016, 2018) that highlighted the presence of the same principles of human life in European and Inca civilizations, thus questioning the existence of hierarchical differences between them. Other scholars have more negative views of the same set of images. Cornejo-Polar (1993) and Ortega (2003) see the *CRI* as a discourse of the "impossible harmony" and Mazzotti (1996, 97–98, 171, 326, 352–53) considers it as a text in which harmony and contradiction are never too far from each other. When it comes to Garcilaso's narrative strategy, Zamora (1988) argues that he based it on the nascent discipline of philology, adopting the idea of exegesis, of restoration of true meaning, which was achieved through a good command of the original language in which that meaning was encoded. Thus, he wrote "like an Indian." Others see in Garcilaso's claim of writing like an Indian either a statement of cultural specificity (the way in which Spaniards write is alien to him [Mazzotti, 1996, 45]) or a statement of authority (unlike Spaniards, he spoke Quechua and knew the Incas firsthand—that is why he could be a mediator, someone who translated Inca civilization to Westerners [Durand 1976; Duviols 1964; López-Baralt 2011; MacCormack 1991, 332–82; Zamora 1988]).

But if one reads the text as a multilayered example of a consciousness of coloniality and emerging race-thinking, a different meaning of the very same set of ideas emerges. In this light, the *CRI* was also aimed at reconciling opposites, Amerindian and European, but the difference between them was not cultural. And, the text was not about the Inca past or not only about it—it was equally about the present. Concordia was not achieved by finding an overarching solution to which all parties contributed equally and knowingly. It was achieved by a particular reenactment of the colonial condition that allowed Indians and Spaniards to achieve their differing goals in spite of power asymmetries. Indians had to reassure Spaniards that they conformed to their ideas about Indians and what they thought of Spaniards. In exchange, Spaniards could be blinded and Indians could eat melons. Opposites were neither reconciled to achieve synthesis nor amalgamated through cultural syncretism—they were colonially accommodated and remained in inherent tension. To write like an Indian meant at once to veil, expose, and laugh, intentionally mimicking colonialist imaginings and outdoing the terms they set.

This alternative interpretation of the goal forces one to look anew at Garcilaso's intended audience. A view that posits that the text articulated different cultural traditions suggests that his readers were on the American side of the Atlantic—Creoles, mestizos, and especially Indians (Mazzotti 1996, 334–37). A philological task of mediation, on the other hand, required an expert reader trained on the intricacies of humanist thought. Clearly, illiterate Europeans were excluded and so were Peru's mestizos and Indians, who "would not have needed Garcilaso to interpret indigenous history for them" (Zamora 1988, 9). While philology-geared or culture-geared readings of the text may make either of these conclusions reasonable, a reading from coloniality and race tells a different story: a text directed toward expectations and practices in a colonial context had at least two sets of readers and two sets of goals.

On the one hand, learned European readers may have appreciated the sophistication of Garcilaso's image of Inca history and culture, the material of the upper world. But, native actors could make good use of that image, too. They could see in it a particular discursive articulation of the competing cultural traditions, as Mazzotti (1996) suggests, or they could see in it a tool for political dispute. After all, the Incas of the *CRI* had much in common with those being publicly displayed in portraits and ceremonies in Cuzco at the turn of the century. These public representations indigenized Christianity rather than Christianized the Andean past—shift Spaniards noticed and found unsettling (Dean 1999).[32]

On the other hand, understanding what Garcilaso did in the underworld stories did not necessarily require a vast knowledge of colonial narratives. For sure, that knowledge would have illuminated the intertextual games in which he engaged but the stories and their meanings stood by themselves. One only has to recall the dialogues in Santo Tomás's, Alvarez's, and Acosta's texts to realize that the dialogues in Garcilaso's stories were common colonial currency. The kind of ironic teasing the stories built on and the critiques they conveyed made sense (or not) independently of any intertextual gymnastics.

Indian readers could see in these underworld examples a fledgling theory of whiteness as a state of mind and tools for postindian survivance. I say "Indian" because Garcilaso, like Guaman Poma, used this term and I think for similar reasons. Indians were all the same neither because the Spaniards called them so nor because of an alleged cultural commonality but because they saw reality in the same way. It was a colonial commonality or one about coloniality that made some native actors "Indians." As it happened with the *NCBG*, the *CRI* was "ethnographic" in a conceptual manner. Its examples addressed precise colonial problems in sharp and creative ways, consistently highlighting that Indigenous actors could be something other than what was expected of them. More to the point, they were clearly urged *not* to be what Spaniards offered them because there would be little to gain from that gamble—an echo of what Du Bois, Fanon, Malcom X, and Baldwin, each in his own way, would state centuries later.

What about the Spanish readers of the underworld stories? In them, Spaniards were recurrently cast as incapable of seeing outside the limits set by their cognitive model of reality and the tales they told about themselves and their others. There was no crack in their whiteness. One could argue then that like Acosta's Indians seen in chapter 1, Garcilaso gave up on white people. Or at least, as Baldwin (1979) put it, as long they continued to think that they were white, they were "irrelevant." There was no use in talking to them, hoping for a worldview change. In this light, Garcilaso wrote as he did, inviting a literal reading of the *CRI* and veiling other meanings, to dodge censorship and reach Indian readers alone. Because of the ways in which his underworld stories questioned the basis of the Spanish ideas about the order of things in the colonies, he had to write this way. But one could also argue that in the relentless double meanings of the text, there also was an invitation to Spanish readers. They were offered good reasons to change the way in which they imagined the world. As in the case of the *NCBG*, the offer could not be taken lightly: Spaniards would have to laugh about themselves and let their colonial sense of reality crush to then start again in a world in which things look radically different—a metanoia.

Most often, Garcilaso made this offer in a veiled manner: as he faced Western readers with examples that contradicted their ideas, stories, and expectations about themselves and their others, it was the readers who had to slow down, connect the dots, and laugh. Laughter would mean the beginning of the end of the delusion of whiteness. But at times, Garcilaso made the offer straightforwardly. For instance, as he told that in precolonial times Indians took Manco Capac and their decedents for sons of the sun because of their good deeds and as such venerated them, he switched to present tense:

I say that they adore them today as they did then. . . . And if they reprehend them, telling them why they do it—since they know that they were men like them and not gods—they say that they have already been disabused of their idolatry, but that they adore them for the many and grand benefits that they received from them. That they treated their vassals like Incas sons of the sun—and not less. That if they were now shown other men like them, they would also adore them as divine. ([*1609*] 1995, bk. II, chap. 1, 68)[33]

The reference to Spaniards, to what they thought of themselves and expected Indians to think of them, was clear and so was the irony, as always. But, this case was also different. Garcilaso stated that Indians did not make the *mistake* of adoring past kings as divine, tricked and blinded by the devil, as Spaniards argued.[34] They *willingly* and *knowingly* adored them. Adoring Inca kings in colonial times begged the question and as such it was an open invitation to a frank dialogue—beyond colonial scripts, with no masks. Garcilaso's Indians knew what Spaniards thought about it and about them and yet did it. It follows that they awaited the Spaniards' reaction, even invited it, to then make a point, saying what they otherwise could not. In other words, Garcilaso, who was always the Indian of his examples, turned the alleged mistake into an intentional act—not all that different from what the "ignorant" and "material" Indians did with Santo Tomás and Alvarez. The offer may still be out there.

CONCLUSION

Fixed Stars, "Indians," and Colonialism as Living a Lie

THE MAIN argument of this book has been that, to Garcilaso de la Vega and Guaman Poma de Ayala, the problems of the colonial world in the Andes had more to do with the emerging race-thinking and coloniality than with the tension arising from the differences between two cultures. That is the reason why their ideas and those crafted centuries later by figures like W. E. B. Du Bois, James Baldwin, and Gerald Vizenor had much in common. The two native intellectuals wanted to change the world and to do so, they concluded that what needed to be changed was the way people saw it, one pair of eyes at a time. They not only wrote about whiteness and described coloniality centuries before any of those ideas even existed but they also began to resignify what being Indian meant way before the idea of Indianness came into existence.[1] They laughed and did it in different ways and proposed diverging, postindian futures, which made them definitely un-Indian. They were (some of) the first Indians—and in particular some of the first Indigenous activist intellectuals, writing at the very beginning of the centuries-long Western global expansion. What were the main characteristics of that colonial beginning in the Andes?

The Spaniards' images of being Indian and being white played a central role in Spanish proto-racism and the justification of the colonial enterprise at large. Despite the many differences and strong polemics among Spaniards, including their more positive or negative views of Indians, the latter were unanimously considered inferior. As such, they were one of the Spaniards' "fixed star[s]" (Baldwin 1993, 9) that helped anchor white images of the world. Spaniards believed they operated on the basis of a reality that was readable and they were its best interpreters. While no one had full access to the order of the logos, being Christian guaranteed immense superiority. Christian order was the one that resembled the perfect order the most, and Christian rationality was the one that resembled absolute reason the most. In that conceptual map of the world, non-Christians had a specific role: they had to be the living proof of that superiority. The fifteenth century started well. The reconquista and the discovery fed that certainty of superiority. It was seen as proof that Spaniards were God's chosen people and agents. The fact that the sixteenth century got messier in Europe (Spaniards did not get the upper hand against Turks and Protestants) made the conquest of the Aztec and Inca Empires even more meaningful.

The second element that characterized the birth of race-thinking and coloniality in the colonial Andes was the unavailability of manifestly inferior Indians and the surplus of manifestly faulty Spaniards. In colonial Peru, Spaniards often acknowledged that they talked the talk but did not walk the walk. It was public and notorious that few acted like Christians should—there was no denial about it. Perhaps precisely because in the Andes at the turn of the sixteenth century few behaved as if they were white, Spanish proto-racist characterizations of Indians and Spaniards focused not on content (what people did or their achievements) but on the process of thinking itself—unlike Spaniards, Indians could think very little, if at all. They were flat creatures with an inteligencia material. Unlike Spaniards, they looked but could not see. They lacked the conceptual map that would help them differentiate the accidental reality in front of them from the real, absolute reality.

And to make matters worse, Indians were not aware of the fact that they did not know. It followed that there was not such a thing as Indian agency. Whatever Indians did was the mechanical reproduction of what they had ended up being, not the result of an option. Agency—if one could call it so—would have been that of culture (mental structures, epistemologies, or ontologies in today's academic terms, *costumbres* [customs] in sixteenth-century parlance). Cultural achievement did not matter either because it was a reflection of the ceiling of that past, not of the flexible mental prowess needed for the future. Indians were stuck in an early evolutionary stage—one of rudimentary cognitive capacity and limited awareness—and they had a long way ahead of them to catch up. Proof of it was that when they faced the truth/modernity, the results were ugly and comical, which gave birth to the colonial problema del indio.

Or so the story went. Because, as the very dialogues Spanish authors gave to prove Indian limitations laid bare, an important problem Spaniards in sixteenth-century Peru encountered was that Indians were not incapable of abstract thinking and certainly did not lack a conceptual map. And, the dialogic examples of critical thinking Spaniards considered good examples of Indian inferiority were not exceptions that proved the rule but instead intellectual expressions of a larger picture. On arenas as different as the economy, politics, or religion, there was domination but no dominance. In fact, this had been the case since the conquest. Spanish colonialism in the Andes, at least during the sixteenth century, had been more about repressing competition in the modern enterprise than about helping Indians become modern.[2] Spaniards denied and/ or failed to notice this.

In other words, Spanish proto-racial theory in Peru developed precisely when Indians were not heroically clinging to their traditions or in desperate need of a helping hand that would remedy their misery but actively competing with Spaniards. It was the tension between the Spanish certainty of superiority and the evidence provided by reality on the ground that powered and shaped Spanish proto-racism in the Andes. That tension, relevant to understand Guaman Poma's and Garcilaso's ways of theorizing inchoate whiteness and of imagining solutions, meant a particular kind of challenge: if one is certain of one's superiority but the other does not confirm or validate that feeling of superiority, what options are there? I can think of five.

The first one would be to blame the others for it. There was something inherently wrong with them that prevented them from seeing it like it was. Because they could not see it, they could not acknowledge Spanish superiority. This idea was clearly at work across the board from one end of the Spanish political spectrum to the other. The second option would be to question the methods. Indians did not acquiesce, because the teaching was done poorly. In the same way that children cannot really be blamed for not knowing and drawing crazy inferences, Indians were not the ones at fault if their *maestros* (masters) failed to uplift them. This was also clearly at work both in the first and the second evangelization, each with its own definition of what the right way of teaching had to be. The third option would be to deny it. Spaniards did not register or acknowledge the lack of confirmation either because they did not want to or because they could not. The word choice is always difficult because it determines consciousness. Denied, disavowed, ignored, or silenced implies awareness; unac-knowledged, unseen, or unnoticed does not. Either way, this third path to facing the problem was clearly at work, too.

The three options just outlined kept Spanish superiority in place. The following two would put it at risk. Although they were never at work (to my knowledge), they prove important when it comes to thinking of the Indigenous responses to white demands of confirmation. The fourth option would be to say that the frame was right but the one carrying out the correspondence was a poor executioner. There would still be absolute truth and being as close to it as possible would still be the goal. But, it would mean that the colonizer had lost the capacity to see and act in consequence. The downside, less dramatic in existential terms, is equally clear in political terms: there would be no European superiority because whatever thing Europeans thought or did was outdone by the natives. The fifth option would the most drastic: to question the frame. There would be no single truth, no absolute order of which the colonizers were (or not) its closest embodiment. There would be other ways of conceiving the world which were equal or superior to the West's. The downside is obvious: there would be no superiority and all the premises on which the Spanish sense of self were based would go out the window.

SIXTEENTH-CENTURY CRITICAL RACE THEORY AND POSTINDIAN IMAGINATIONS

How did the Indigenous intellectuals studied in this book conceptualize the emerging race-thinking and feeling? What avenues did they envision for changing those who saw themselves as white regardless of the color of their skin? What were the suggestions they had for native actors who had to live in a world that was organized by coloniality? Guaman Poma's *NCBG* and Garcilaso's *CRI* have several common elements. First and foremost, the key issue was not the object but how people thought about it. Colonialism on the ground was bad but the real problem was the twisted ways in which people who thought of themselves as white made sense of it and wanted others to do so, too. The cornerstone of Spanish proto-racism was the fact that Spaniards (thought that they) could really see Indians, who did not know that they did not know, and therefore could not see themselves for what they truly were. That is why Garcilaso and Guaman Poma targeted the seeing (and not being seen), the knowing and being aware of it (and the lack of knowledge and awareness). Second, since they both thought the problem was not in the object but in the eyes of those making sense of it, they concluded that rewriting culture alone would not do the job. They both cast Amerindian civilizations in a much better light than Spaniards did and did their best to explain the former to the latter—but they knew that corrective images could only go so far. They would still be seen as the expression of what Indian material intelligence, characteristic of their evolutionary stage, could achieve. They would not change the frame and Indians would continue to be an absent presence. Third, these two Indigenous intellectuals shared an understanding of the fact that the problem of facing Spanish proto-race-thinking and feeling and coloniality was made worse by the simple fact that Indian predicament was an ironic reversal of the one Spaniards thought they faced. Spaniards thought they were facing people who could not see the real, whose eyes had to be fixed, who could not be abstract thinkers, who could be comical but not funny. As a result, Indian thinkers—as the dialogical examples in Spanish texts, the *NCBG*, and the *CRI* all show—had to talk to people whose world would have been turned upside down had they been able to see/acknowledge the Indian point of view. Fourth, in both texts there was the idea that Spaniards and Indians lived in the same world and they were equal—yet they lived in different worlds and were different. This difference was racial and colonial, not cultural or related to the pre-Hispanic past. Fifth and last, they both rejected the offer of the detrimental solution made by those in the so-called partido de los indios. Guaman Poma asked for the full package, no discounts. Garcilaso pointed out that it was all the same—the same racist premises were present in the ideas of Indian sympathizers as well as in those of Indian haters.

Although Guaman Poma and Garcilaso wrote their texts to change the way people—both those who saw through whiteness and those who had to endure that lens—saw the world, each had his own way of conceiving the best way to achieve that change and how things would look like after the change had succeeded. Guaman Poma's way of tackling the colonial problem was essentially pedagogical. To change the way in which incipient whiteness made the world a contorted place, he confronted readers who thought of themselves as white with repeated instances of seeming contradiction—conceptual puzzles that could be solved only if the one seeing could realize that the premises guiding his sight were wrong and could let them go. In other words, he did not question the frame but people's relationship to it. To help those with a visual impediment realize that they had failed to make sense of the accidentally real, and as a result, had drawn crazy inferences, he resorted to two seemingly contradictory moves.

First, through a decolonial use of Granada's theology, he asked his cristiano lector to shift the focus from knowing—to know, everybody knew—to doing. This implied doing away with race-thinking as the guiding principle used to make sense of the colonial world. That drastic restructuring of the field of intelligibility had consequences in terms of how the past and the present had to be understood. His heterodox but absolutely orthodox explanations of the pre-Colombian past and world history, his rewriting of the conquest, and in particular the role of the hand of God, miracles, and grace, showed that the world was readable, just not in the ways most Spaniards and some natives in the colonies read it. The latter's material success in spite of their bad deeds was not a reward that confirmed their superiority; rather, it proved that they were going downhill at a very high speed. By the same token, the hardships of those who had to endure the results of that apparent success were not the consequence of their sins nor evidence of their inferiority but instead proof of them walking the narrow path and therefore evidence of their superiority. Second, he deviated from Granada's theology and showed in many ways that the problem was not the ceguera del mundo but the ceguera de la colonialidad. Spaniards did in the Americas what they did not do in Spain—they found reasonable in the Americas what they would never in Europe. They acted against reason not because they knew and chose not to act accordingly but because they did not know and thought that they did. These rewritings of the past and the present set discussions about the future straight: Indians did not have a problem, Spaniards did. They had a long way to go to fix their eyes and acts; until then, they had to stay away from native peoples and let them be because the latter had never been white and did not want to be.

While Guaman Poma chose the fourth option, doubling down on the frame and asking for absolute correspondence, Garcilaso took a different path, closer to the fifth option. He questioned the frame itself. In a way, it was the logical next step to Guaman Poma's analysis: what mattered was the Spanish desire for superiority, plain and simple. It was not the greed for material riches—they did not care that much about the melons—it was the libidinal surplus that being a colonizer gave them, the high they got out of seeing themselves being masters. Whiteness was for Garcilaso as much a state of mind as an emerging structure of feelings. The price of the ticket was that Spaniards did not see. They did not interact with Indians—they interacted with their imaginings about them. If Guaman Poma confronted Spaniards over and over with the discrepancy between how they said the world was and how it really was, Garcilaso confronted them over and over with the discrepancy between how they thought Indians were and what Indians did with those ideas (which proved the ideas wrong). This was also a way of having Spaniards face the fact that things were not as they saw/thought. The range of meanings words had served as disturbing evidence to support this idea.

The *CRI* confronted white readers (readers who were seeing the world through whiteness) with the fact that it was as easy to satisfy their libidinal drive as it was to frustrate it. In example after example, when Spaniards demanded confirmation of their delusions, Indians deferred and differed. Meanings could not be pinned down. By doing so, Garcilaso had Spanish readers face the fact that the veil was an unreliable piece of machinery. Their imaginings did not necessarily secure ascendancy but they could also undermine it. He wanted Spaniards to realize that the veil could make Spaniards appear superior and Indians fools but it could also make Spaniards look childlike in their refusal to acknowledge and comically laughable although definitely not funny. This had the potential effect of Spaniards recognizing that the world was not as they thought it was. It was neither about *what* they said it was (it was not about the real and accidentally real) nor about *how* they said it was (reason defeating nonsense). In that brave new world, Spaniards not only did not have the upper hand but also had a long way to go. There were no easy shortcuts, no points of arrival, just the practice of doing. It was a theory of practice that required a different conception of reality.

What about Guaman Poma's and Garcilaso's projects insofar as those who were seen through whiteness were concerned? Following Du Bois, one could say that the projections on the screen—the offers Spaniards made—prevented natives from achieving self-consciousness. The "nigger" and the Indian would be twentieth-century examples of such simulations. Guaman Poma and Garcilaso made other offers available and tried to expose the mechanism, hoping to disarm it. In terms of content, both presented much better images of being Indian than Spaniards did. As long as they were not white, Indigenous actors in the *NCBG* talked the talk and walked the walk. The same is true about Garcilaso's upper world: the Incas were the incarnation of natural reason. At the same time, both thinkers were aware of the fact that what needed to be disarmed was the mechanism of whiteness, not just its contents. As long as people saw the world through whiteness, corrective images and denunciations of abuse would only have marginal effects.

Guaman Poma showed native actors that the root problem of the colonial order of things was that it was upside down: although Spaniards were the ones who could not see it for what it was, they told Indians that it was them and forced them to adjust their lives and sense of self accordingly. Paraphrasing Gloria Anzaldúa, one can say that Guaman Poma stated that "the worst kind of betrayal lies in making us believe that . . . [we are] the betrayers" (1987, 22). That is, the worst accomplishment of Spanish proto-racism would have been to have natives believe that there was something wrong with them, to get them to accept the lie and take it as part of their self-consciousness. To prevent native actors from internalizing that twisted perception of the world, the *NCBG*'s conceptual ethnography fleshed out permutations of that nonsense, making their contra-venes scream. In the real world, Indians found validation, not condemnation. Through the *NCBG*'s unthinkable rewritings of the order of things, Indigenous readers saw that they were "on the side of justice" and those who saw the world through whiteness were lost sheep, people who did not know that they did not know. There was nothing racial about it—race was a lie, although whiteness was not. It was about the truth and behaving accordingly, and at that, everybody was equal, even if some deluded themselves about it.

Garcilaso also showed native actors that colonialism was a contrived beast— that while Spaniards said Indians were blind, Spaniards were really the ones who could not see. But he did not direct his conceptual ethnography to flesh out and correct nonsense like Guaman Poma did; instead, he sought to make available ways of existing and feeling other than those Spaniards offered and demanded. He showed that even in the best cases, Spanish simulations were dead ends that instilled inferiority and inadequacy and gave numerous examples of how to stage conceptual "jailbreaks" (Smith 2009, 90). In those escapes, Indians were an active presence. They produced both for Spaniards and for themselves and they questioned the way in which Spaniards implicitly told Indians to think about the world and be in it. It was not about the truth and correspondence—it was about playfulness and outsmarting. As a result, to be Indian was radically different from what it was often thought: it was a practice—close to Baldwin's idea of blackness being a condition but different at once. If life was scripted—or, as Vizenor would state it, if it is a simulation—then Garcilaso told Indians to create their own scripts and be Indian in postindian ways. His was a theory of practice but a transformative one because it involved an alternative theory of reality. According to it, Indians were funny and knew it; Spaniards, on the other hand, were comical and clueless.

To conclude, I want to stress that Garcilaso and Guaman Poma were by no means exceptional thinkers or examples of a project that was possible only at a certain point in time. The native actors that engaged in conceptual conversations with the Spaniards in Alvarez's, Santo Tomás's, and Acosta's texts had the same kind of ideas in mind. And, one can find them centuries later, too. During the 1750 revolt in the town of Huarochirí, southeast of Lima, commoners besieged the Spanish local authorities. Under constant attack, the latter tried to run for safety. Most failed and were caught and killed. One of the last ones to make a run for it was the former corregidor, don Francisco de Araujo y Río. As he tried to escape, he was discovered by a commoner, who stopped and told him: "You are my corregidor; I have always loved you, and you me. Come with me and I will defend you. But you know that the Indians hate you because you made them carry stones, and in order to appease their anger put this stone on your back and carry it" (Spalding 1994, 285). Although Araujo promised to donate a large amount of money to the local church, the commoner had him walk several blocks carrying a heavy rock on his back. When he reached the edge of town, still carrying the rock, he was stoned to death by natives awaiting him (Spalding 1994, 285). As Spalding points out, the stoning was a ritual debasement, a return of both the humiliations native peoples endured when forced to work for Spaniards and the hypocrisy of saying that Indians were forced to work for their own good. But, there is another aspect of the story that is relevant, too: its ironic exposure of the fact that to live under Spanish colonialism was "to live in a lie" (Havel 1987). When the commoner, in such an unsettled moment of violence, took the time to tell the Spaniard "you are my corregidor; I have always loved you, and you me," he made a point of saying that he was aware of the bullshit and wanted to reverse it. He did not simply denounce Spanish injustice to then deliver punishment. He first gave the Spaniard a taste of his colonial contrivance knowing that the situation was unique. In ordinary circumstances, Indians were never able to expose the lie. Now the tables were turned: the Spaniard was in no position to call the lie for what it was and he had to swallow the nonsense and adapt, like Indians always had to do. In short, the ironic reversal tackled the cornerstone of Spanish coloniality. Numerous Indians had done the same at the turn of the sixteenth century and others continued doing it much later, even in pongos' dreams. They have been waiting for people who think of themselves as white to realize it.

GLOSSARY

ALCALDE: Mayor; judge on the city council, or *cabildo*.

AYLLU: A localized Indigenous social group based on extended kin.

CABILDO: Municipal council. There were *cabildos de indios* in rural Indigenous areas and *cabildos de españoles* in urban areas.

CACIQUE: Caribbean word imported by the Spaniards, equivalent to *curaca*.

COMPAÑÍA: A conquest company; a private enterprise that had obtained the Crown's legal authorization to pursue the conquest of a given territory.

CORREGIDOR: A district administrator appointed by the Spanish Crown. *Corregidores de indios* had jurisdiction over rural Indigenous areas while *corregidores de españoles* were in charge of urban populations.

CORREGIMIENTO: Area over which a corregidor had jurisdiction.

CURA: Secular priest of the Roman Catholic Church.

CURACA: Native political lord.

DOCTRINERO: The Catholic priest in charge of a *doctrina,* or Indigenous parish.

ENCOMENDERO: Holder of an encomienda grant.

ENCOMIENDA: Encomienda grants were cessions from the Crown to conquerors of its right to collect tribute from its vassals; in exchange, the awardees had to be ready to defend the king and care for their Indians' spiritual well-being.

HANAN: The half of the highest rank of a dual sociopolitical entity.

HUACA: Sacred, powerful being/shrine, with many possible embodiments.

HURIN: The half of the lowest rank of a dual sociopolitical entity.

MITA: Rotational labor service.

MITIMAE: Members of an ethnic group residing away from the groups' main settlement.

MANDÓN: A person with some degree of authority over a group of Indigenous workers. Most often, mandones responded to local authorities or persons in a position of power.

TAMBO: Inn, lodging site for travelers.

YANACONA: A native retainer, someone without local ayllu affiliation.

NOTES

INTRODUCTION

1. Much has been written about it. For overviews of some important aspects of the debate, see Adorno 2008b; Brading 1993; Hanke 1949; Pagden 1987; Pietschmann 1989; Seed 1995.

2. "Que preguntando una vez en cierta provincia a un cacique si era christiano, me dixo: 'aún no lo soy, pero ya lo comienço a ser.' Y preguntándole yo qué sabía de [ser] christiano, me dixo: 'sé ya jurar a Dios, y jugar un poquito a los naipes, y comienço ya a hurtar.'"

3. "A lo que yo entendí, devía pensar aquel pecador que, como ser sastre no era más de lo que ellos comúnmente veen hazer a los sastres, que es coser, y lo mismo en los demás officios, assí creía que no era más ser cristiano de lo que ellos comúnmente a los christianos avían visto hazer."

4. It took time for Amerindian intellectuals, who were used to non-alphabetic writing systems, to learn to express themselves in written Spanish. The process was slower in the Andes than in Mesoamerica, perhaps due to the radically different materiality of the quipu (Boone and Mignolo 1994; Brokaw 2010; Mignolo 1995).

5. For references to scholarship on each author's work, please see the chapters in which I analyze them in detail.

6. Studies of Indigenous intellectuals in colonial Spanish America at large—including those who defended before Spanish courts the rights of the communities they represented or the claims of the lineages to which they belonged—also see them as people who straddled cultures and knowledges, who had one leg in each

world (Indigenous and European), and who had to constantly move from one to the other (Boone 2014; Ramos and Yannakakis 2014; Rappaport and Cummins 2012). Studies of the colonial process in the Andes, especially when they concern Indigenous peoples, also tend to frame questions with an ethnic or cultural lens— what social actors in the colonial context did or thought is rendered intelligible to a large extent by their precolonial cultural affiliation.

7. E.g., Burns 2010; Charles 2010; Mazzotti 2010; Ramos and Yannakakis 2014; Rappaport and Cummins 2012. For colonial uses of quipus in particular, see Brokaw 2010 and the essays on colonial material in Quilter and Urton 2002. For colonial mural art as quillcas and thus forms of local knowledge, see Cohen Suarez 2016.

8. While Quijano had a straightforward answer to the question of the origin of race, what exactly characterized it, and its function, these matters are hotly debated by specialized scholars. For overviews of current debates in what concerns the Hispanic world in particular, see Eliav-Feldon, Isaac, and Ziegler 2009; Hering Torres, Martínez, and Nirenberg 2012; Feros 2017; Heng 2018, especially chapter 3.

9. See the work of the influential sixteenth-century thinker, entrepreneur, and administrator Polo Ondegardo (Lamana 2012).

10. To remind readers of the artificial nature of the term and what is wrong about it and to stress its complicity with Western dominance, Vizenor proposes to italicize it and not to capitalize it (*indian*).

11. For a study of the complex history of the word "Spaniard" and its relation to race, see Feros 2017.

12. For a detailed discussion of whiteness in Baldwin's work, see Pavlić 2016, chapter 10. Baldwin did not consider the effect of those stories on white people to be absolute or the same in all cases. White people may at times believe them and delude themselves while in other cases they may know they are not true but refuse to acknowledge this. That is why whiteness can on occasion be "a moral choice" (Baldwin 2010, 157). "I'd like to say that when I say 'white' I'm not talking about the color of anybody's skin, I'm not talking about race. It is a curious country, a curious civilization, that thinks of it as race. I don't believe any of that. White people are imagined. White people are white only because they want to be white, and they want to be white only because they don't want to be black. They all turned white when they came across the ocean. White is a metaphor for power; that is all it means, absolutely all" (Baldwin 1979, 1). Although in a different way, Du Bois also linked white supremacy to colonialism (see [1920] 2015).

13. Assadourian 1994; Estenssoro 2005, 1–178; Goldwert 1955–56; 1957–58; Lamana 2008, 2012; Lohmann Villena 1966; MacCormack 1991, 1–248; Morong Reyes 2016; Spalding 1984, 106–35; Stern 1986, 27–50; 1992.

14. For different angles of Toledo's reforms see Estenssoro 2005, 178–308; Merluzzi 1996; MacCormack 1985, 1991, 249–80; Stern 1986, 71–113; Spalding 1984, 136–67. I say "practical end" because, since it went to the core of the justification of the structure of the colonial system, the *Polemics of Possession* (Adorno 2008) was a

perennial issue. Toledo annihilated the last Inca stronghold and produced extensive anti-Inca juridical and intellectual products. He also shifted the weight of the argument about the Spanish presence from causes to consequences—that is, the key question was no longer if Spaniards had the right to do what they did but what bad results their eventual departure would trigger. Finally, he strengthened the colonial state apparatus to the detriment of encomenderos and defined in legal documents the Indians' status as inferior beings who could not be entrusted with much and certainly not, above all things, with self-government.

15.   For different angles of the mining labor problem, see Assadourian 1993; Bakewell 1984; González Casanovas 2000, 1–126; Saignes 1995; Tandeter 1992. Several texts penned during those years have been published by Vargas Ugarte 1951 and Aldea Vaquero 1993. See also Agía 1604; Castaneda-Delgado 1983. For texts in favor of the perpetuity of the encomiendas in particular, see Coello de la Rosa 2014; Jurado 2013; Ortiz de Ceruantes 1619.

16.   For different views of religious dynamics after Toledo, see Acosta 1987a and 1987b; Barnadas 1993; Duviols 1977 and 1988; Estenssoro-Fuchs 2003, 178–516; Gose 2008, 161–238; Griffiths 1995; MacCormack 1985, 1991, 249–455; Mills 1997; Silverblatt 1987, 159–215; 2004; Urbano 1993, 1999.

CHAPTER 1

1.   The scholarship on the *NCBG* and the *CRI* will be examined in detail in parts 2 and 3.

2.   At least as far as humans were concerned. No human could see or know as much as God, of course.

3.   For studies of language and colonization in the Andes, see Cerrón Palomino 1995, 1998, 2013a, 2013b; Dedenbach-Salazar Sáenz 2013; Durston 2007; Mannheim 1991; Taylor 2000, 2003.

4.   In addition to these two texts, Santo Tomás also wrote and sent to Las Casas an important report about Indigenous religious practices. The two also worked together to support Andean peoples' resistance against the project of making perpetual all grants of *encomiendas* (native labor) and giving Spaniards jurisdiction over native peoples' affairs in the fashion of medieval lords (e.g., Assadourian 1994, 151–304; Lamana 2012).

5.   "pues según el philósopho, en muchos lugares no ay cosa en que más se conozca el ingenio del hombre que en la palabra y lenguaje que usa, que es el parto de los conceptos del entendimiento."

6.   "Now, that man is more of a political animal than bees or any other gregarious animals is evident. Nature . . . makes nothing in vain, and man is the only animal who has the gift of Speech" (Aristotle 1996, 7–9). While *The Politics*, in which Aristotle makes a clear connection between language, civilization, and barbarism, was widely available in the sixteenth century, only fragments of Aristotle's full theory of language survived (see Modrak 2001), which makes it much less likely a source

of Santo Tomás's reference. See also Gera 2003 for Greek ideas about language and civilization.

7. In addition to Latin, Greek and Hebrew were thought of as having retained more of the lost rationality and expressivity of the Adamic language (Breva Claramonte 2008a, 2008b; Eco 1997; Kelly 2002; Modrak 2001).

8. There are five términos: terms Indians use when they swear, terms they use when they greet each other, kinship terms, personal names, and terms used to describe the sounds animals make.

9. "Que preguntando una vez en cierta provincia a un cacique si era christiano, me dixo: 'aún no lo soy, pero ya lo comienço a ser.' Y preguntándole yo qué sabía de [sic]

**please note italics christiano, me dixo: 'sé ya jurar a Dios, y jugar un poquito a los naipes, y comienço ya a hurtar.'"

10. "A lo que yo entendí, devía pensar aquel pecador que, como ser sastre no era más de lo que ellos comúnmente veen hazer a los sastres, que es coser, y lo mismo en los demás officios, assí creía que no era más ser christiano de lo que ellos comúnmente a los christianos avían visto hazer."

11. That is why he is told that Indians "believe" something that is not true—and not just any Indian but a cacique, who Spaniards considered to know more and be better at thinking than ordinary Indians.

12. "No dexaré de notar aquí una cosa para gran confussión de los malos cristianos, y es que para maldezir o blasphemar a lo que ellos falsamente tenían por dios . . . [los indios] no tenían términos, y no solamente no los tenían, pero ni aún les pas-sava por imaginación tan gran irreverencia y maldad . . . sino que con grandíssima reverencia y temor tomavan en la boca los nombres de las cosas que ellos tenían por dioses."

13. The repartimiento of Aullagas was one of the three belonging to the corregimiento of Paria—the other two were Quillacas and Paria itself. Alvarez had also been cura de indios in the repartimientos of Sabaya, Potosí, and Lupacas (see Villarías Robles and Martín Rubio 1998; Martín Rubio 1998).

14. "así como es necesario entendimiento—y que el entendimiento forme el concepto satisfactorio, para haber de creer—asimismo tiene necesidad el hombre de tener vocablo o término que signifique lo que es la fe; de suerte que, entendida la signifi-cación del término, entienda lo que quiere decir en esencia o en sustancia—aunque sea en confuso—percibiendo satisfactorio concepto del todo de aquello que el término expone."

15. "máxime, con el ejemplo material de sus visibles uacas, porque viéndolas y engañán-dose unos a otros . . . y no creyendo ni teniendo ciencia ni inteligencia más de las cosas que ven, no pueden venir en conocimiento de la verdad por los vocablos y doctrina que se les enseña. Porque toda la significación dellos es de cosas espiri-tuales inteligibles, ques duro negocio persuadirles a que lo crean por ser su inteli-gencia toda material."

16. "Un soldado, caminando por el mar en una balsa que remaban dos indios, les pre-
    guntó diciendo: 'A puestas del sol decidme, ¿adónde va el sol?' Dijeron: 'va a donde
    está Dios, a quejarse por nosotros, porque nos tratáis mal.' Y preguntó el español:
    'pues, ¿dónde está Dios?' Dijeron: 'allá donde vosotros venís, ¿no decís que está
    Dios? Pues allá va, a decir que vengan los ingleses a mataros, porque nos dejéis y
    no nos tratéis mal.'"
17. Which may also suggest that the Spaniards are not good Christians while the
    English are—and that is why he will send his instruments to deliver justice.
18. For the idea of playing Indian at work in other contexts, see Deloria 1998; Raibmon
    2005; O'Toole 2012, 64–87.
19. This colonial denial of coevalness had little to do with Jerusalem or space in general,
    as in Fabian's formulation, and a lot to do with knowledge/vision, correspondence,
    and self-awareness. For the idea that the Western other was initially conceived in
    spatial terms and only in the eighteenth century in temporal terms, see Mignolo
    2011, 153.
20. "If they studied correctly and truthfully, they would then know that, in the same
    way that our senses minister our intellect and reason, thus those sensible things
    minister that intelligible being who governs it all, God" ("Si estudiaran recta y fiel-
    mente, luego conocieran que así como nuestros sentidos son ministros de nuestro
    entendimiento, y raçón, así aquellas cosas sensibles son ministros de aquel inteli-
    gible bien que lo govierna todo, que es Dios") (Torquemada [*1615*] 1986, vol. II, bk.
    VI, chap. 12, 27a).
21. Natural law, Sepúlveda argued in his *Tratado de las casusas justas de la guerra contra
    los indios*, is "una participación de la ley eterna en la criatura racional," a law God
    wants preserved and to that end he has provided man with reason. This recta razón
    embedded in man's heart tells not only Christians what is wrong and what is right
    but also "todos aquellos que no han corrompido la recta naturaleza con malas
    costumbres y tanto más cuanto cada uno es mejor y más inteligente" (Sepúlveda
    [1551] 1975, 67). In other words, since natural law reflects God's law, is perfect and
    the only one, and is a built-in feature of man, it follows that an absolute distinc-
    tion can be made between those who recognized and followed the natural order
    of things (Christians, with few exceptions in practice) and those who were unable
    to—Indians among them. Because the latter did not know and deviated from what
    nature itself dictated, as in the case of idolatry or sodomy (Sepúlveda [1551] 1975,
    123), the use of force against them was granted if they refused to obey those who
    knew more about the right order of things than they did and were superior to them
    in any regard (Sepúlveda [1551] 1975, 83–85).
22. Thus, for instance, Santo Tomás began his explanation of the second kind of térmi-
    nos for which he considered necessary an extended explanation, that of greetings
    among Indians, as follows: "Since Indians lived in their first and natural simplicity
    they did not have many ways of talking to, or greeting, each other . . . but they
    treated and welcomed each other with that ancient simplicity we read about in
    ancient books, either about sacred doctrine or secular ones" ("Como los indios

bivían en la primera y natural simplicidad no tenían muchas maneras de hablarse o saludarse . . . sino que se tratavan y rescebían con aquella antigua simplicidad que leemos en los libros antiguos, assí de doctrina sagrada como de los profanos") ([*1560*] 1995, fol. 68v, 141).

23. In Spain during these years, the word *ingenio* (ingenuity) had a very precise meaning related to science and wisdom (see Juan Huarte de San Juan's *Examen de ingenios para las ciencias*).

24. "a esto contradize su insuficiencia en casos de pintura y lo mal que se aplican a formar en ella rostros humanos que es cosa a que jamás dan punto, pues aunque los demás animales pintan con gran imperfeción, eso muy peor, y assi es cosa que no se sabe que ellos lo usassen."

25. , Precolonial Andean pictorial systems of representation were largely abstract while, as the example shows, Spaniards translated this difference into a lack of abstract intelligence. A similar problem was reported by the Third Ecclesiastical Council of Lima. In the case of religious images, for instance, the represented is detached from the representation: an action upon the representation will have no effect on the represented; order will remain intact. Christians know it—that is why they do not mistake one thing for the other, the third Concilio points out, while Indians, as Alvarez would say due to their inteligencia material, do (*"Tercero catecismo"* [*1585*] 1991, 690).

26. See De la Cadena 2000, 44–85.

27. "pues no se puede creer sean heridos de amorosa flecha con diferencia alguna de las bestias . . . [sino] conforme a sus ingenios, cuyos conceptos jamás se levantan del suelo, ni sus pensamientos de la tierra."

28. "[la] memoria de lo passado, gouierno de lo presente, y prouidencia en lo futuro, y por la razón entender las cosas, distin[g]ir, concluyr, persuadir y consultar."

29. All these ideas were already present in one of the writings of one of the most influential Spanish colonial thinkers, Polo Ondegardo. Polo was very influential in colonial times—Acosta acknowledged that all his writing on Incas follows Polo— and his influence has continued into the present (see Lamana 2012).

30. Much of the conceptual groundwork to justify Indian forced labor was laid by two important colonialist thinkers in the 1560s, Polo Ondegardo and Juan de Matienzo (see Lamana 2012; Matienzo 1967; Morong Reyes 2016).

31. This statement reflects a tradition highly reminiscent of some twentieth-century *indigenista* lawyers, academics, and politicians (see De la Cadena 86–130; *Informe Uchuraccay*). See also the Indians as legal minors (Oré [*1598*] 1992, 199).

32. I say "what was often considered" because some scholars have convincingly argued that much of what was labeled idolatry was rather the result of changes in the way of considering or assessing whether some practices were idolatrous or not, changes that were related to political struggles within the Peruvian church (see Urbano 1993, 1999).

33. Acosta 1987a, 1987b; Duviols 1977; Estenssoro-Fuchs 2003, 311–70; Gose 2008, 161–238; Griffiths 1995; MacCormack 1991; Mills 1997; Silverblatt 1987, 159–215; 2004.

34. While it was published in Lima in 1621, drafts of the text had been circulating extensively several years before.
35. See Mills 1997, 27–31, for a detailed description of Avila's auto de fe.
36. "ya que no se les pueden quitar delante de los ojos [las huacas], porque son fijas e inmóviles, se les procura . . . quitárselas del corazón, enseñándoles la verdad y desengañándoles de la mentira."
37. Arriaga primarily blamed Indians' persistent ignorance on lousy priests ([*1621*] 1999, chap. 7, 72) and, like Acosta, found good teachers crucial to "explain to, and teach, such ignorant people the mysteries of our holy faith" ("dar a entender y enseñar a gente tan ignorante los misterios de nuestra santa fe") ([*1621*] 1999, chap. 12, 115). The task would be slow mainly because it would take several generations to "deshacer y refutar los errores tan connaturalizados a su capacidad" (Arriaga [*1621*] 1999, chap. 12, 115).
38. Alvarez also proposed the papagayo image, although for him it was rather a matter of reluctance to learn and faking to do it than of plain incapacity.
39. "errores, trastocando o mudando algunas palabras o letras, con que hacen muy diverso sentido, como en el credo por decir *Hucllachacuininta*, que es la comunión o junta de santos, decir *Pucllachacuininta*, que es la burla o trisca de los santos." For a reading of this passage as being about linguistic misunderstanding, see Saignes 1999, 114.
40. Likely a play with the idea of "to be such (idiots, fools, etc.)" ("ser unos [idiotas, tontos, etc.]") and "ser uno," meaning to be alike, indistinguishable from each other.

CHAPTER 2

1. No scholar takes a single analytical path. However, he or she develops one to different extents. With no intention of presenting a comprehensive list, for the former path, see Adorno's many articles and books (e.g., 1989, 2000) and Quipe-Agnoli 2006; for the latter, see Cox 2002; López-Baralt 1988, 1992; Ossio 1977, 2008; Wacthel 1973. Also rooted around the question of cultural difference is the argument that much of what is often taken to be distinctively Andean in the *NCBG* can be found in European texts of the time or expresses technical constraints and conventions (Duviols 1983, 1987; Graulich and Núñez-Tolín 2000; Holland 2008; Plas 1996; Van De Guche 1992).
2. My argument is not affected by another notable source of disagreement, the one between scholars who say that Guaman Poma was not the actual author of the text and those who refute that position and attribute it instead to a number of Jesuit conspirators (see Adorno 2000, xi–lxi; 2008a, 231–95; Alberdi Vallejo 2010; Cantú 2001; Hyland 2003, 195–236; Lurencich Minelli 2005; Miccinelli and Animato 1999; Mumford 2000).
3. "el dicho libro . . . es muy útil y prouechoso y es bueno para emienda de uida para los cristianos y enfieles, y para confesarse los dichos yndios y emienda de sus uidas y herronía, ydúlatras, y para sauer confesarlos a los dichos yndios los dichos sacer-

dotes y para la emienda de los dicho comenderos de yndios y corregidores y padres y curas de las dichas dotrinas y de los dichos mineros y de los dichos caciques principales y demás yndios mandoncillos, yndios comunes y de otros españoles y personas."

4. Santo Tomás's 1560 *Grammatica* is an exception that confirms the rule—in it, "cristiano lector" refers to Spaniards alone.

5. The questions of bien vivir and bien morir, current at the time of Guaman Poma's writing, had a long history in European and Spanish thinking (Eire 2002; Martínez Gil 1996; Montayés 1557; Rey 1952; Rey Hazas 2003).

6. "entre estas dos partes que para bien vivir son necesarias, la segunda es tanto más necesaria y excelente que la primera . . . pues todos saben y conocen lo bueno, mas no todos arrostran a ello, por la dificultad que hay en ello"

7. "And being (as they are), the Indians, new and inexperienced people in the doctrine of the gospel, and it being common among them to not have high and elevated understandings . . . it is necessary . . . that the doctrine that is taught them is the basic of our faith. . . . Because presenting Indians with other materials of the sacred scripture is a thing excused for now . . . Since, such solid food, and that requires teeth, is for men grown up in the Christian religion and not for beginners" ("Y siendo (como son) los indios gente nueva y tierna en la doctrina del Evangelio, y lo común de ellos no de altos y levantados entendimientos . . . es necesario . . . que la doctrina que se les ensena sea la esencial de nuestra fe . . . Porque tratar a indios de otras materias de la Sagrada escritura es cosa por ahora excusada . . . Pues, semejante manjar sólido, y que ha menester dientes, es para hombres crecidos en la religión cristiana y no para principiantes") (*"Tercero catecismo" [1585]* 1990, 625–26).

8. As is known, Las Casas presented Spaniards as bad Christians and Indians as good proto-Christians. The entire *Brevísima* was an exercise of this reversal. In other words, Las Casas wrote from the Spanish/Indian split: he flipped the coin and made Spaniards the bad guys and Indians the good guys—but the coin and its theological-political implications remained. In a last instance, it reasserted the geopolitics of knowledge that sustained Spanish privilege, which he wanted to question. Guaman Poma followed this model at times but most often challenged it frontally: there were good and bad Spaniards as there were good and bad Indians or blacks. Or, put differently, there were good and bad Christians and it had nothing to do with their being Indian, Spanish, or black. That is why, in spite of the many similarities between Las Casas's account of Andean pre-Hispanic peoples and Guaman Poma's, which scholars have mentioned, I suggest that Las Casas represented in many ways a conceptual dead end to Guaman Poma.

9. The insufferable conditions expressed by these soldiers is closely related to the idea of "colonial normal" (see Lamana 2008).

10. "así como imprimió en los corazones de los hombres una inclinación natural para amar y reverenciar a sus padres, así también imprimió en ellos otra semejante inclinación para amar y reverenciar a Dios como a padre universal de todas las cosas y sustentador y gobernador de ellas."

11. "Por esta lumbre no podemos cognoscer más de que hay dios, a quien los hombres son obligados adorar y servir como verdadero señor y criador. Pero que sea uno que sean muchos por razón natural no se puede fácilmente alcanzar, como exceda la capacidad de nuestro entendimiento en infinita manera. . . . Por eso decimos que aquel cognoscimiento que por la lumbre natural alcanzamos es muy confuso."

12. Ignorancia invencible was a medieval Thomist concept that acquired new significance once peoples who had not received the good news were "discovered." The notions of *implícito* (implicit) and *explícito* (explicit), which applied to both knowledge and faith, were also central to the detrimental defense (see Méndez Fernández 1993, 274–346).

13. "aunque las tinieblas de la infidelidad tienen escurecido el entendimiento de aquellas naciones, pero en muchas cosas no deja la luz de la verdad y razón algún tanto de obrar en ellos, y así comúnmente sienten y confiesan un Supremo señor y hacedor de todo."

14. For the question of the supernatural and Thomist thinking, see Alfaro 1952; Méndez Fernández 1993.

15. For an early seventeenth-century summary of the conversation, see Gregorio García's 1607 *Origen de los indios del nuevo mundo e indias occidentales.*

16. "Mandó Dios salir desta tierra [Ararat], derramar y multiplicar por todo el mundo de los hijos de Noé; destos dichos hijos de Noé, uno de ellos trajo Dios a las Yndias; otros dizen que salió del mismo Adán. Multiplicaron los dichos[s] yndios, que todo lo saue Dios y como poderoso lo puede tener aparte esta gente de indios."

17. For the identification of a scholastic origin of the Indians' knowledge about God, see Adorno 1987, xxvii; 1989, 105; Farías 2008, 149, 179, 188.

18. "Mira, cristiano letores, mira esta gente, el terzero hombre, que fueron a más con su ley y hordenansas antiguas de conocimiento de Dios y criador. Aunque no le fueron enseñados, tenían los dies mandamientos y buena obra de misericordia y limosna y caridad entre ellos."

19. For the distinction between truths of different kinds or degrees of complexity—and therefore simpler or harder to figure and understand—see Méndez Fernández 1993, 123–33.

20. "They worshipped . . . God, and thus God did not send his punishment to this people" ("adoraua[n] . . . a dios, y ací no le[s] enbiaua Dios su castigo a esta gente") (Guaman Poma [ca. 1615] 1987, fol. 59[59], 56).

21. There are many references to the multiplication of Indians (e.g., Guaman Poma [ca. 1615] 1987, fol. 49[49], 46, fol. 55[55], 52, fol. 58[58], 54–55, fol. 61[61], 58) and the abundance of nature in general, all being proof of God's explicit approval (Guaman Poma [ca. 1615] 1987, fol. 73, 68).

22. The role of the supernatural was a common and controversial issue among Spanish authors interested in the Americas While providential Spanish accounts of history made the Spaniards instruments of God (Colón, Cortés, Xerez, etc.) and described their acts as divinely ordained, theologians that addressed in critical terms the Spaniards' discovery and conquest of the Americas worked hard to explain the

role of the divine in satisfactory terms. Their solutions were more elaborate and comprehensive: they included a theology of the supernatural that cast it as the final point in a long, *suave* (smooth), natural path through which all men went. In Vitoria's work, this affected both individual development and that of all peoples (Méndez Fernández 1993). In this way, these theologians managed to largely remove the supernatural from the discussion about Amerindians—remember Las Casas's emphasis on Pachacuti's resort to luz natural. Vitoria explicitly stated that no supernatural events had taken place during the conquest, which he used to prove that Indians could not be expected to convert when first contacted ([1539] 1989, 90–93).

23.   See, for instance, Cabello Valboa 2011, 131, 145, 215; García 2005.

24.   The same structure is present in Cristóbal de Molina el Almagrista's *Relación* ([ca. 1553] 1968) and Salinas y Cordova's *Memorial* ([*1630*] 1957).

25.   Although, Las Casas had the Incas as the ones to whom restitution was due (Adorno 2000, 13–35, 59–61).

26.   The historical record tells that by the time the Spanish company reached Túmbez, Atahualpa had sent a high-rank Inca, who was as much an envoy as a spy. Guaman Poma, conversely, made no explicit reference to guess work or any uncertainty surrounding the envoy or the meeting (see Lamana 2008, chap. 1).

27.   In the precontact chapters, Guaman Poma mentioned in passing that the Incas had been told about the Old World (Rome, Castile, even Turkey) by their huacas and hechiceros ([ca. 1615] 1987, fol. 111[111], 104, fol. 114[114], 108) and that Inca kings had prophesized the arrival of Europeans ([ca. 1615] 1987, fol. 262[264], 254, fol. 378[380], 384). Guaman Poma's solution is not unlike that made by Alva Ixtlilchotlil: Amerindians were always part of world history and were aware of it. The resource to prophecies (a much-debated issue by current scholars) is no evidence of a *mal agüero* or a proof of inferiority—it is one more way in which Amerindian authors question the geopolitics of knowledge that organizes Spanish texts and acts.

28.   "Y fue bentura y pirmición de Dios que, en tanta batalla y derramamiento de sangre y pérdida de la gente deste rreyno, saliese los cristianos. Fue Dios seruido y la Uirgen María adorado y todos los sanctos y santa ángeles llamado de que fuese la conquista en tanta rrebuelta de Uascar, Atagualpa, Yngas."

29.   A good example of this comes in Acosta's *Historia Natural y Moral* already-quoted passage: "as they were deserving of their sins [the Indians'], the almighty God left them under the power of their enemy, whom they chose as their god and shelter" ("mereciendo sus pecados [de los indios] que les deje al altísimo Dios en poder de su enemigo, a quien escogieron por dios y amparo suyo") ([*1590*] 2002, bk. V, chap. 10, 321).

30.   "Sepa que la causa porque Dios ha permitido que los indios seáis tan afligidos y acosados de otras naciones, es por ese vicio [sodomía] que vuestros antepasados tuvieron, y muchos de vosotros todavía tenéis. Y sabed que os digo de parte de Dios que si no os enmendáis, que toda vuestra nación perecerá. Y os acabará Dios y os raerá de la tierra."

31.   The observation needs some qualification. The Incas are not just evil according to Guaman Poma. Following a well-established frame laid down by Polo Ondegardo ([1571] 2014) and widely used by other influential Spanish thinkers (Lamana 2012), Guaman Poma splits Inca rule into good government and bad religion. It is true that they had close contact with the devil and as a result idolatry began in the Andes. But, on the other hand, they were the best exponents of good government and their moral order followed natural law closely. What no other author did however was to insert this split within a historical narrative that was also dual.

32.   "gente nueva en la fe" o gente "de cortos y tiernos entendimientos" (*"Tercero catecismo"* [*1585*] 1990, 625).

33.   See Guaman Poma [ca. 1615] 1987, fols. 235[237]–300[302], 228–98.

34.   For the emergence of the miraculous tradition, see Duviols 1962.

35.   From Colón to Cortés to Pizarro, Spanish narratives present their achievements against all odds as a mix of divine intervention and faith (of the hero); implicit is that there is a virtuous circle in which good acts are rewarded with grace, which fortifies the self and produces new, even greater deeds, etc. There is a one-on-one relationship. In contrast, in the *NCBG*, there are no heroes. Not only that, but Spanish conquistadors are presented in the least favorable light possible. Hence, it is clear to the reader that there can be no virtuous circle. Accordingly, Guaman Poma's acts of direct divine intervention, unlike those of Spanish accounts, cast heroes who are strictly divine: the Virgin, Santiago, saints, the Holy Spirit, etc. The conquerors' demise tells that they are not to be rewarded in the afterlife (a theological claim) in the same way that they should not be rewarded on earth (a political claim).

36.   "Of these two parts that are necessary to live well, the second is much more necessary and important than the first in that it is more the spirit than the body, the gospel than the law" ("Entre estas dos partes que para bien vivir son necesarias, la segunda es tanto más necesaria y excelente que la primera cuanto lo es más el espíritu que el cuerpo, y el evangelio que la ley") (Granada [*1565*] 1994–95, vol. II, 15–16).

37.   "con todo eso nos dize Dios que nos acordemos y llamemos, y en cada hombre y en cada casa enbía Dios al mundo su castigo para que lo llamemos y denos gracia para que nos lleue a su gloria adonde uiue la Santícima Trinidad."

38.   "El castigo que merecen éstos es el que Dios les da, que es el mayor que se puede dar, que es dejarlos andar en este juego toda la vida hasta que llegue la muerte, donde les acaezca lo que suele acaecer a los que nunca hicieron penitencia verdadera."

CHAPTER 3

1.   "aués de conzederar que todo el mundo es de Dios, y ancí Castilla es de los españoles y las Yndias es de los yndios y Guenea es de los negros. Que cada déstos son lexítimos propietarios. . . . La ley de Castilla . . . *que a razon de los yndios que se quenta y le dize por la ley*, y la de llamar [de] estrangeros, y en la lengua de los yndios, mitmac, Castilla manta samoc, que uinieron de Castilla."

2. Although not necessarily thinking exactly along Guaman Poma's line, see Cartledge and Cheetham 2011; Keller , Nausner, and Rivera 2004; Shorter 1999; Wafula, Mombo, and Wandera 2016.

3. "deuen pagar el pecho de su Magestad, pues que fue la ley de Castilla y son hijus de pecheros; aunque fuese conquistador deuen pagar y es justo que paguen."

4. One could argue, as some scholars do, that this claim reflects "Indigenous" categories of the world: the conflict between a "static" Inca system versus a "fluid" European system (Ossio 2008, 2016, 217–220). But, for one thing, it is as hard to argue that the Inca system was static (there were Incas of privilege and ethnic subjects could achieve high-status, honor-carrying positions) as it is to argue that the European system in the 1500s was fluid (blood was the cornerstone of the noble society).

5. "As I have said, the good knight in the world should be honored and be given precedence and space. Even if you hold an office or position by royal appointment, even if you are a doctor, a learned man, do not want to be more than you are by blood and lineage. No matter how poor he may be, one should honor and [give] distinction and authority to the knight and God's and his Majesty's servant" ("Como dicho tengo, al buen cauallero en el mundo se deue honrrar y desuiar y dalle lugar. Aunque tenga oficio o cargo de su Magestad, aunque sea dotor, lesenciado, no queráys ser demás de lo que soys de sangre y linage. Por más pobre que sea, se le deue onrra y primenencia y facultad al cauallero y seruidor de Dios y de su Magestad") (Guaman Poma [ca. 1615] 1987, fol. [951]937, 1032).

6. For an overview of the mining problem and the debate about forced Indian labor, see Assadourian 1993; Bakewell 1984; González Casanovas 2000, 1–126; Saignes 1995; Tandeter 1992. Several of the texts penned these years have been published by Vargas Ugarte (1951) and Aldea Vaquero (1993). See also Agía 1604; Castaneda-Delgado 1983; Coello de la Rosa 2014; Jurado 2013; Ortiz de Ceruantes 1619.

7. The 1601 royal decree mentions that Spaniards with no occupation should also work for the king but there is no conceptual shift involved and the idea, which never went beyond being a line in this document, is no longer present in the 1609 royal decree that amended the 1601 one.

8. That Castile law superseded all native customs was a founding fact of the colonial system. About the fact that pecheros ceased to pay taxes once in the Americas, see Pollack 2016.

9. "Saued que las hordenansas . . . son buenas para yndios, que no para españoles. Que las hordenansas y leys están en Castilla de los españoles. Somos libres. Y ací te digo que no [o]s canséys. Texe, hila deprisa. Con eso acauaréis y se contentará ellos."

10. "que más quería yr ellos cargados que cargalle a los pobres yndios, lo qual en la ley de cristiano y en Castilla no se cargauan a cristiano, cino a cauallo, animal. Que para ello le dio Dios a los animales, que en Castilla no se daua mitayo ni guía. Y ací temo a Dios."

11. "si bosotros en tu tierra fuese un yndio dacá y os cargase como a caballo y os arrease dándoos con palos como a bestia animal y os llamase caballo, perro, puerco, cabrón,

demonio, y fuera desto os quitase buestra muger y hijas y haciendas e buestras tierras y chacaras y estancias con poco temor de dios y de la justicia, conzedera destos males qué dixérades christianos. Me parese que le comiérades bibo y no estubiérades contento."

12. "yndios ausentes y cimarrones hechos yanaconas, oficiales siendo mitayos, yndios uajos y tributarios, se ponían cue[l]lo y bestía como español y se ponía espada, y otros se tresquilaua por no pagar tributo ni seruir en minas. Ues aquí el mundo al reués."

13. "A man has a camel hair suit made for him but the next day goes back to the tailor and says, 'The sleeve's too short.' The tailor replies, 'You can't recut a camel hair suit, but just hold your arm like this [over-extended] and no one will notice.' The man goes out with his arm like that, but the next day returns to say the right leg is too long. The tailor tells him to hold his leg like this–bent up–and no one will notice. Well, this goes on until the guy is walking around with his limbs every which way. A couple see him, and the woman exclaims, 'Look at the poor deformed man!' And her husband says, 'Yeah, but doesn't his camel hair suit fit great!'" (Nelson 1999, 178–79)

14. For Guaman Poma's faith in the power of writing, regardless of whether the king would read his text or be able to carry out reform, see Castro-Klarén 2011, 19–65.

15. Espíritu y atención, humildad, fe y confianza, obras y buena vida, pedir bienes espirituales, and paciencia y perseverancia.

16. "para probar nuestra fe, para ver si por tardarse aquello acometemos buscar el remedio por ilícitos y malos caminos, o para que más conozcamos nuestra necesidad, o para encender en nosotros mayor fervor de oración con esta dilación." The prayers and calls for God that Guaman Poma utters throughout the book are not just any prayers—they largely are taken from Granada's *Memorial* (e.g., [*1565*] 1994–95, vol. I, 25, vol. II, 53).

17. "protégenos de las justicias, corregidor, alguacil, jueces, pesquisidores, padre, encomenderos, escribano, mayordomo, teniente, españoles del tanbo, despojadores de hombres y ladrones."

18. Spaniards corrupt Indians by not giving them time to do good deeds ("everything is hindered by the said priests of the doctrines and the magistrates and comendero and Spaniards with their dealings and earnings . . . that occupy them in all the kingdom" ["todo le estorua los dichos saserdotes de las doctrinas y los corregidores y comendero y españoles con sus tratos y grangerías . . . que les ocupa en todo el rreyno"] [Guaman Poma 1987 [ca. 1615], 836]), by taking them through the wrong path ("had they been taught good things, the said women would have been saints, but they were taught bad things, and at midnight they were sent out through the streets and they saw all the bad things, and thus they turn out approved whores" ["si le enseñara cosa buena las dichas eseñoras fueran santas, pero enseñale cosa mala y a media noche enbía fuera por las calles y uen todo lo malo, y ancí salen putas aprouadas"] or "and thus leave the good and learn the bad and have a good time with it . . . And thus there are no saints among them, only idolatry" ["y ancí

dexan lo bueno y apriende lo malo y se huelga de ello . . . Y ancí no ay santo de ellos, cino ydúlatra"] [Guaman Poma [ca. 1615] 1987, fol. [838]824, 882]), and by forcing Indians to confess that they embrace idols when they know they do not, leaving them no other choice but to become idolaters (Guaman Poma [ca. 1615] 1987, fols. [1121]1111–[1122]1112, 1187–1212).

19.   "Esto espero sepas: que en los postreros días vendrán tiempos peligrosos. Que habrá hombres amadores de sí, auaros, cudiciosos, gloriosos, soberuios, maldicientes, desoberdecedores de sus padres, ingratos, impuros. Sin afecto, desleales, calumniadores, destemplados, sin mansedumbre, sin bondad . . . amadores de los deleytes mas que de Dios. Teniendo el apariencia de piedad, mas negando la eficacia de ella; y a estos evita. Porque destos son los que se entran por las casas y lleuan captiuas las mugercillas cargadas de pecados. . . . [Hombres] que siempre aprenden y nunca pueden acabar de llegar al conocimiento de la verdad."

20.   "Ansí que tu está firme en lo que tu has aprendido y te ha sido encargado, sabiendo de quien has aprendido. . . . Requiero . . . que prediques la palabra, que apresures a tiempo y fuera de tiempo; redarguye, reprehende duramente, exhorta con toda blandura y doctrina. . . . Tu . . . vela en todo, trabaja, haz obra de euangelista, cumple tu ministerio."

21.   As he walks toward Castrovirreyna poor and naked, the Virgin provides him with food, a sign of God's grace (Guaman Poma [ca. 1615] 1987, fol. [1115]1105, 1182)—and yet the miracle was lost on his son who, seeing him so poor and with no means to sustain himself, runs away from him while an Indian servant takes advantage of him and steals a chair and other things from him.

22.   The many parallels between Guaman Poma's ideas and late eighteenth-century Andean rebellions, especially the one led by Tomás Katari, testifies to the fact that, at least for some, they worked.

23.   "que uenía seruiendo a un hombre graue llamado Cristo-bal, por decir Cristo, metía deciendo 'bal,' aunque dixo Cristóbal de la Crus. Decía los hombres que quién era este dicho Cristóbal de la Crus, que ci era minero o rico. Respondía que auía cido gran minero, y es rrico ahora y poderoso señor su amo. Pregunta: '¿no ueremos a este hombre?' Responde el autor: 'Aý viene alcansándome. Aý le encontrará se lo busca vuestra merced.'" Cristo-bal shows Guaman Poma's humor once again, as if he were winking to the vision-impaired reader while explaining the situation and asking him, 'Get it?' (For humor in Guaman Poma, see Paupeney Hart 1996.)

24.   "¿Qué mayor ceguedad que, sabiendo tan cierto que habemos de morir, y que en aquella hora se ha de determinar lo que para siempre ha de ser de nuestra vida, vivamos tan descuidados, como si siempre hubiéramos de vivir. . . . ¿Qué mayor ceguedad, que por la golosina de un apetito perder el mayorazgo del cielo, tener tanta cuenta con la hacienda y tan poca con la conciencia . . . ? Destas ceguedades hallarás tantas en el mundo, que te parecerá estar los hombres como encantados y enhechizados, de tal manera que, *teniendo ojos, no ven, y teniendo oídos, no oyen, y teniendo la vista más aguda que de linces para ver las cosas de la tierra, tiénenla más que de topos para las cosas del cielo.*"

25. "Y no es menos de considerar . . . aquel cansancio de Cristo, [que] estaba . . . solo, cansado, asolado, despeado, fatigado del trabajo del camino y de las hambres y de la sed, como cualquiera de los otros hombres pobres y flacos. Quien fuera tan dichoso que acertara en esta coyuntura a pasar por aquel lugar y, considerados los caminos y cansancio deste señor, se llegara humilmente a él y le preguntara: Señor, *¿Qué vida es esta que vivís? . . . ¿Qué buscáis por tantos caminos y carreras? ¿Qué manera de vida es esta tan trabajosa que tenéis, caminando de lugar en lugar . . . sin que ni los cansancios de los caminos, ni las contradicciones del mundo os aparten deste propósito?* Nunca reposáis, nunca tomáis una hora de descanso; de día andáis por los lugares, de noche por los montes orando. Pues, *¿Qué tesoro es este que buscáis con tanto trabajo?*"

26. "Lo que a esto se podía responder es, que como buen pastor andaba en busca de su ganado descarriado. Dolíale mucho su descarriamiento y perdimiento; y por esto no había camino ni trabajo que no se pusiese por reducirlas a su majada."

27. There is also a fine contrast: Granada's imaginary person had been "blessed" to be able to ask unlike Guaman Poma's passersby who simply "run" into him.

CHAPTER 4

1. For a biography of Garcilaso, see Castanien 1969; Fernández 2016; Hernández 1991; Miró Quesada 1945, 1994; Porras Barrenechea 1955; Varner 1968.

2. Castro-Klarén identifies Garcilaso's "postcolonial situatedness" (2016, 203) at the roots of his project, not simply his cultural in-betweenness.

3. To my knowledge, only Rivarola (2001, 24) points that out; however, according to him the verdadero refers to the philological or truth-value of the content, not to intention, irony, or double meaning.

4. "De mi parte he hecho lo que he podido, no habiendo podido lo que he deseado. Al *discreto lector* suplico reciba mi ánimo, que es de darle gusto y contento, aunque las fuerzas, ni la habilidad de un indio . . . no puedan llegar allá."

5. "En el discurso de la historia . . . no diremos cosa grande que no sea autorizándola con los mismos historiadores españoles que la tocaron en parte o en todo. Que mi intención no es contradecirles sino servirles de comento y glosa, y de intérprete en muchos vocablos indios que, como extranjeros en aquella lengua, interpretaron fuera de la propiedad de ella."

6. In this light, "being Indian" ground his competence as a philology-informed translator, as scholars often argue; however, like with anything else in the text, "being an Indian" could mean more than one thing. Garcilaso often uses it to simultaneously deauthorize himself, confirming a Western reader's certainty of superiority and the Indians' inferior, feeble condition, only to turn around these positions. Thus, when discussing the question of the crossing over of climate zones, while he declares, "because this is not my main intent, not the strength of an Indian can presume that much . . . we will briefly go over them to arrive elsewhere, to where I am afraid of not making it" ("porque no es este mi principal intento ni las fuerzas de un indio pueden presumir tanto . . . pasaremos breve-

mente por ellas por ir a otra parte, a cuyos términos finales temo no llegar"), he
in fact contradicts, discredits, and deeply questions Spanish ideas about the world
and what they take words to mean.

7.   Exceptions are Mazzotti (1996, 53–54), who analyzes it in terms of human unicity
and cultural diversity, and Castro-Klarén (2016), who offers a postcolonial take on
the idea of the oneness of creation according to Garcilaso.

8.   For an analysis of the Western ideas underlying the "discovery" of the Americas,
see O'Gorman's classic *La invención de América ([1958] 2006)*.

9.   "Y no tanto le dicen nuevo por ser nuevamente hallado, cuanto por ser grandísimo
y casi tan grande como el viejo. También se puede llamar nuevo por ser todas sus
cosas diferentísimas de las del nuestro."

10. The chapter is titled "El mundo es uno, y no muchos, como algunos filósofos
pensaron."

11. "aunque creo que no hay más de un solo mundo, nombraré muchas veces dos aquí
en esta mi obra, por variar de vocablos en una misma cosa, y por entenderme mejor
llamando Nuevo Mundo a las Indias, de las cuales escribimos."

12. "juntamente historia y filosofía, y por ser no solo de las obras de naturaleza, sino
también de las del libre albedrío, que son los hechos y costumbres de hombres."

13. "The purpose of this work is that by the of news of nature that the Author so wise
of all nature has made, it gives praise and glory to God the almighty" ("El fin de
este trabajo es que por la noticia de la naturaleza que el Autor tan sabio de toda
naturaleza ha hecho, se le dé alabanza y gloria al altísimo Dios") (Acosta [*1590*]
2002, proemio, 58). Gómara also links observation and praise to God in the preface
to the first chapter.

14. Acosta addresses these issues in book 1, chapters 16–24, and book 4, chapter 36.
Spaniards had debated at length both the ways in which Indians had arrived to
America and from whom they descended, at times devoting entire books to the
topic—one of them written by Garcilaso's friend, Gregorio García's *Origen de los
indios del Nuevo mundo e indias occidentales* (1607). Regardless of their many differences, they had two elements in common: the first, one of two ways to get to
America was proposed by sea, as most argued, or by land; the second, the Indians'
arrival was seen as part of the larger peopling process of the earth which had as
point of origin the long, universal spreading apart of Noah's sons that followed
their landing in the Ararat mountains.

15. "y con razón, porque esta tierra no procede de alguna de las tres que ya nombramos:
sino sola por sí está distincta y apartada de ellas. Y llámase nueua tierra, por razón
que nunca los antiguos tuuieron noticia cierta della."

16. "Habiendo de tratar del nuevo mundo . . . parece que fuera justo, conforme a
la común costumbre de los escritores, tratar aquí, al principio, si el mundo es
uno solo o si hay muchos mundos. Si es llano o redondo y si también lo es el
cielo. Si es habitable toda la tierra o no más que las zonas templadas. Si hay
paso de una templada a otra. Si hay antípodas y cuáles son de cuáles. Y otras
cosas semejantes que los antiguos filósofos muy largamente trataron y los mod-

ernos no dejan de platicar y escribir, siguiendo cada cual la opinión que más le agrada."

17. "Mas, porque no es este mi principal intento ni las fuerzas de un indio pueden presumir tanto–y también porque la experiencia, después que se descubrió lo que llaman nuevo mundo, nos ha desengañado de la mayor parte de estas dudas– pasaremos brevemente por ellas por ir a otra parte, a cuyos términos finales temo no llegar."

18. Gómara devoted the first nine chapters of his *Historia general de las Indias* to the issues of the climate zones, whether the world is round, if the sky stretches all over it, etc. Acosta, who followed and developed Gómara's frame, devoted to these topics two of the seven books of his *Historia*, thirty-nine chapters in all.

19. "Pero confiado en la *misericordia*, digo que a lo primero se podrá afirmar que no hay más que un mundo. Y aunque le llamamos 'mundo viejo' y 'mundo nuevo' es por haberse descubierto aquel nuevamente *para* nosotros y no porque sean dos, sino todo uno."

20. Although he reintroduced ambivalence by saying "aquel" when it should have been be "este," geography soothes the grammatical riddle.

21. "Y a los que todavía imaginaren que hay muchos mundos no hay para qué respond-erles, sino que se estén en sus heréticas imaginaciones hasta que en el infierno se desengañen de ellas."

22. "Yo espero en su omnipotencia que a su tiempo descubriera estos secretos (como descubrió el nuevo mundo) *para* mayor confusión y afrenta de los atrevidos que con sus filosofías naturales y entendimientos humanos quieren tasar la potencia y sabiduría de Dios: que no pueda hacer sus obras más que como ellos las imaginan, habiendo tanta disparidad de una saber a otro cuanta hay de lo finito a lo infinito." (The modern edition I follow says "de lo infinito a lo infinito," which does not make much sense; the original 1609 edition says "de lo finito a lo infinito," which does.)

23. Garcilaso had already prepared the terrain for this ambivalence by stating "se des-cubrió lo que llaman nuevo mundo" (and not "se descubrió el Nuevo Mundo"). He directed the unstated agency to Spaniards who are the ones who name things (and clearly, Indians would not call their own land "New World"). By doing so, Garcilaso invited attributing agency to discovery in a similar manner.

24. "Por dónde hayan pasado aquellas gentes, tantas y de tan diversas lenguas y cos-tumbres como las que en el Nuevo Mundo se han hallado, tampoco se sabe de cierto. Porque si dicen por la mar, en navíos, nacen inconvenientes acerca de los animales que allá se hallan, sobre decir cómo o para qué los embarcaron siendo algunos de ellos antes dañosos que provechosos. Pues decir que pudieron ir por tierra, también nacen otros inconvenientes mayores: como es decir que, si llevaron los animales que allá tenían domésticos, ¿por qué no llevaron de los que acá que-daron, que se han llevado desde entonces acá? Y si fue por no poder llevar tantos, ¿cómo no quedaron acá de los que llevaron? Y lo mismo se puede decir de las mieses, legumbres y frutas, tan diferentes de las de acá, que con razón le llamaron 'Nuevo Mundo,' porque lo es en toda cosa: así en los animales mansos y bravos

como en las comidas, como en los hombres—que generalmente son lampiños, sin barbas."

25. "Y porque en cosas tan inciertas es perdido en trabajo que se gasta en quererlas saber las dejaré, porque tengo menos suficiencia que otro para inquirirlas. Solamente trataré del origen de los reyes Incas y de la sucesión de ellos."

26. For a different take on the question of there being one world that sees the statement as part of Garcilaso's critique of the inferiority of the Americas and their inhabitants, see Castro-Klarén 2016.

27. "[viendo la lastimosa condición de los indios] nuestro padre el sol . . . se apiadó y tuvo lástima de ellos y envió del cielo a la tierra un hijo y una hija de los suyos para que los doctrinasen en el conocimiento de nuestro padre el sol para que lo adorasen y tuviesen por su dios."

28. "para que cuando ese mismo Dios, sol de justicia, tuviese por bien de enviar la luz de sus divinos rayos a aquellos idólatras, los hallase no tan salvajes sino más dóciles para recibir la fe católica y la enseñanza y doctrina de nuestra santa madre Iglesia Romana."

29. For a reading of the creation myth as expressing also Inca tropes, symbols, and politics, see Mazzotti 1996, 135–39, 174–202; 2016. For it as expressing at once Andean and European ideas of love as reciprocity and caritas, see Castro-Klarén 2016.

30. See, for instance, the cases against *alumbrados* and other sixteenth-century religious practices the inquisition labeled heterodox and prosecuted (Beltrán de Heredia 1949; Huerga 1978; Telechea Idígoras 1977).

31. It is not that scholars have missed the figure of the uncle; the question is his function. Some see the reporting of the conversations with his uncle as a means to establish language competence; Garcilaso got the history straight from the source and in the original language (Zamora 1988, 44–46; Rivarola 2001, 41–43). Others take it to authenticate the culturally appropriate legitimacy of the history; an elder Inca is the right speaker to approach such matters (Mazzotti 1996, 104–18). Another view is that it expresses an affective connection, the love Garcilaso felt for this paternal figure, who stood for his mother's family (López Baralt 2011, 173–75, 253–55).

32. "algunos españoles curiosos quieren decir, oyendo estos cuentos, que aquellos indios tuvieron noticia de la historia de Noé. . . . Y que por la ventana de arca de Noé dijeron los indios la de Paucartampu. . . . Otros pasos de una fábula y de otra quieren semejar a los de la Santa Historia, que les parece que se semejan."

33. "las cuales quieren los españoles que no sean fábulas sino historias verdaderas, porque tienen alguna semejanza de verdad. De otras muchas hacen burla por parecerles que son mentiras mal compuestas, porque no entienden la alegoría de ellas."

34. Probably not by chance, *allegoría* and *fábula* are the concepts with the most entries in the *tabla de las cosas más notables* (index) of Garcilaso's 1590 *La tradvzion del indio de los tres Dialogos de Amor de Leon Hebreo*. For Garcilaso's use of *fábula* in the *Historia general del Perú*, see Zanelli 2016.

35. Of course, there are always readers who miss the point and historicize the fables, making them flat again.

36. "Lo que yo, conforme a lo que vi y naturaleza de aquellas gentes, puedo conjeturar del origen de este príncipe Manco Inca . . . es que debió de ser algún indio de buen entendimiento, prudencia y consejo que alcanzó bien la mucha simplicidad de aquellas naciones y vio la necesidad que tenían de doctrina y enseñanza para la vida natural. Y con astucia y sagacidad, para ser estimado, fingió aquella fábula, diciendo que él y su mujer eran hijos del sol: que venían del cielo y que su padre los enviaba para que doctrinasen e hiciesen bien a aquellas gentes."

37. "Y como los beneficios y honras que a sus vasallos hizo confirmase[n] la fábula de su genealogía, creyeron firmemente los indios que era hijo del sol venido del cielo y lo adoraron por tal. . . . Porque es así que aquella gente a ninguna cosa atiende tanto como a mirar si lo que hacen los maestros conforma con lo que les dicen y hallando conformidad en la vida y en la doctrina no han menester argumentos para convencerlos a lo que quisieren hacer de ellos."

38. "y como hasta entonces los del Inca no habían peleado para matarlos sino para resistirles dijeron que tampoco habían peleado aquel día. Sino que el sol, no pudiendo sufrir la poca estima que de su hijo hacían los Collas, había mandado que sus propias armas se volviesen contra ellos y los castigasen, pues los Incas no habían querido hacerlo."

39. "Los amautas (que eran los filósofos), alegorizando la fábula, decían que por no haber querido los collas soltar las armas y obedecer al Inca cuando se lo mandaron se les habían vuelto en contra, porque sus armas fueron causa de la muerte de ellos."

CHAPTER 5

1. See detailed studies of the philological argument in Zamora (1988, 67–69) and Thurner (2011, 1–26). See also Cerrón-Palomino (2013, 27–68) for a study of language corruption according to Garcilaso.

2. "viendo en la mar una cosa tan extraña nunca jamás vista en aquella costa–como era navegar un navío a todas velas–se admiró grandemente y quedó pasmado y abobado, *imaginando* qué pudiese ser aquello que en la mar veía delante de sí."

3. "entendía que le preguntaban mas no entendía lo que le preguntaban. Y a lo que entendió que era el preguntarle respondió aprisa, antes que le hiciesen algún mal. Y nombró su propio nombre, diciendo 'Berú,' y añadió otro y dijo 'Pelú.' Quiso decir: 'Si me preguntáis cómo me llamo, yo me digo Berú. Y si me preguntáis dónde estaba, digo que estaba en el río.'"

4. This reference to (the illusion of) a defacto universal translator anticipates *Star Trek* fiction and edges on the satiric as it seizes on the absurdity embedded in what passed as accepted truth.

5. "No pasarle por la imaginación una cosa, es no haber tenido pensamiento della ni primer movimiento. . . . Imaginar, pensar. Imaginable, lo que puede caber en la imaginación" (*Covarrubias Horozco* 1611, 1091).

6. MacCormack's 1991 book is about vision and imagination in the Andes. She devotes the prologue and the first chapter to the Western conceptual scaffold and

chapter 8 to Garcilaso's complex rejection of the Spaniards' argument about its influence on Andean religion.

7. The most relevant mention to the presence of the devil in the Andes comes in book II, chapter 2, when Garcilaso refuted the idea that the Andean god Pachacamac was in fact the devil (see Estenssoro 2003, 200–201, 252–53; Mazzotti 208–22; MacCormack 343–46; Zamora 77–78, 146–47). When it comes to the presence of Spanish ideas about the devil in the Andes, the most relevant example comes in book VII, chapter 28, where Garcilaso tells the story of a Spanish priest's thoughts about the amazing Inca fortress of Sacsayhuaman. In both cases, "imagination" refers to Spaniards imaginings, not to the devil or Indians.

8. "Dijo el indio: 'Aún no me han bautizado para jurar como juran los cristianos.' Replicó el juez diciendo que jurase por sus dioses el sol y la luna y sus Incas. Respondió el curaca: 'Nosotros no tomamos estos nombres sino para adorarlos. Y así no me es lícito jurar por ellos.'"

9. "Dijo el juez: '¿qué satisfacción tendremos de la verdad de tu dicho, si no nos das alguna prenda?' 'Bastará mi promesa,' dijo el indio, 'y entender yo que hablo personalmente delante de tu rey, pues vienes a hacer justicia en su nombre. Que así lo hacíamos con nuestros Incas. Mas, por acudir a la satisfacción que pides, juraré por la tierra diciendo que se abra y me trague vivo como estoy, si yo mintiere.'"

10. For an original analysis of other angles of the Garcilaso-Acosta dialogue, see Padrón 2010.

11. Extensive philological discussions of Quechua words play a key role in Garcilaso's explanations of Inca religious beliefs and practices. The most complete study of the philological argument is Zamora 1998. See also Miró Quesada 1974; Escobar 1971; Durand 1949. For a recent in-depth study of Garcilaso's actual linguistic and language knowledge, see Cerrón Palomino 2013. For a discussion of religion and imagination, see MacCormack 1991, 332–82.

12. There are numerous references to inteligencia material in the *CRI*. See, for instance, [*1609*] 1995, 29, 117, 121–22, 127.

13. "en esta confusión tan grande el sacerdote o seglar que las preguntaba tomaba a su gusto y elección lo que le parecía más semejante y más allegado a lo que deseaba saber y lo que imaginaba que podía haber respondido el indio. Y así, interpretándolas a su imaginación y antojo, escribieron por verdaderas cosas que los indios no soñaron."

14. Garcilaso may be referring to Santo Tomás or Gregorio García. Neither idea is without problems, however. See Cerrón Palomino (2013, 44–45) for a discussion of the different possibilities.

15. Acosta's works disavowed the theology of similarity and silenced its actual evangelical practice. By arguing that Amerindian religions were the direct result of devil's work, the *Historia* discredited the idea that similarities between Christian beliefs and other peoples' religious ideas and practices were the result of man's natural drive and progression toward God. In *De procuranda Indorum salute* (1588), the colonial religious practices and ideas of Amerindian peoples are cast as idolatrous and their

"persistence" as evidence of the fact that prior clergymen had been bad teachers, either too lazy, too greedy, or too lousy to do their job well, silencing the church's long-standing practice of using similarities as evangelical tools through a strategy of progressive substitution/activation that saw the same practices as works in progress.

16. "Acatanca: que quiere decir 'escarabajo', nombre con mucha propiedad compuesto de este nombre, aca, que es estiércol y de este verbo tanca, que es 'empujar.' Acatanca quiere decir 'el que empuja estiércol.' [And then added:] Que en Chuquisaca–en aquella Primera Edad y antigua gentilidad, antes del imperio de los reyes Incas–lo adorasen por dios, no me espantaría. Porque . . . entonces adoraban otras cosas tan viles. Más no después de los Incas, que las prohibieron todas."

17. "Que digan los indios que en uno eran tres y en tres uno es invención nueva de ellos, que la han hecho después que han oído la Trinidad y unidad del verdadero Dios nuestro Señor, para adular a los españoles con decirles que también ellos tenían algunas cosas semejantes a las de nuestra santa religión."

18. "Todo lo cual [Trinity and other similarities] es inventado por los indios, con pretensión de que siquiera por semejanza se les haga alguna cortesía. Esto lo afirmo yo como indio, que conozco la natural condición de los Indios. Y digo que no tuvieron ídolos con nombre de Trinidad."

19. "'When I use a word,' Humpty Dumpty said, in rather a scornful tone, 'it means just what I choose it to mean—neither more nor less.' 'The question is,' said Alice, 'whether you can make words mean so many different things.'
"'The question is,' said Humpty Dumpty, 'which is to be master—that's all.'" (Carroll 2015, 251)

20. "a los [lectores] presentes y venideros será agradable saber las cosas que no había en el Perú antes que los españoles lo ganaran . . . para que se vea y considere con cuántas cosas menos–y al parecer cuán necesarias a la vida humana–se pasaban aquellas gentes y vivían muy contentos sin ellas."

21. See, for instance, Sepúlveda (ca. 1551) 1975, bk. II, chap. 25, 76–77; Gómara (1552) 2004, chap. 224, 385.

22. Toward the end of book 1, for instance, when describing some Inca customs, he mentioned that some things the Spaniards brought really made a difference—just not the ones they imagined. For example, the Incas wore very short hair and since they had only stone cutting devices, "They sheared themselves with much work, as one can imagine. For that reason, seeing later on the ease and gentleness with which scissors cut, an Inca told one of our writing and reading co-disciples: 'If the Spaniards, your fathers, would have done not more than bringing us scissors, mirrors, and combs, we would have given them as much gold and silver as we had in our land'" ("[t]rasquilábanse con mucho trabajo, como cada uno puede imaginar. Por lo cual, viendo después la facilidad y suavidad del cortar de las tijeras, dijo un Inca a un condiscípulo nuestro del leer y escribir: 'Si los españoles, vuestros padres, no hubieran hecho más que traernos tijeras, espejos y peines les hubiéramos dado cuanto oro y plata teníamos en nuestra tierra.'") (Garcilaso [1609] 1995, bk. I, chap. 22, 54). He here ridiculed a related idea sustained by Spaniards critical of the con-

querors' behavior: that the Indians hid much of their treasures once they figured that the conquerors were guided not by grace but by greed and that if treated well, Indians would gladly give the king all hidden riches.

23. "'¿No sabríamos a qué sabe esta fruta de la tierra de nuestro amo?' El otro dijo: 'No. Porque si comemos alguno lo dirá esta carta, que así nos lo dijo el capataz.' Replicó el primero: 'Buen remedio: echemos la carta detrás de aquel paredón. Y como no nos vea comer no podrá decir nada.'"

24. "'¿Por qué mentís vosotros? ¡Que esta carta dice que os dieron diez y que os comisteis dos!' Los indios se hallaron perdidos de ver que tan al descubierto les hubiese dicho su amo lo que ellos habían hecho en secreto. Y así, confusos y convencidos, no supieron contradecir a la verdad. Salieron diciendo que con mucha razón llamaban dioses a los españoles, con nombre de Huiracocha, pues alcanzaban tan grandes secretos."

25. In the Andean context, the reference to alphabetic writing and Cajamarca is ineluctable (see Lamana 2008, 27–64; 2010; MacCormack 1989; Seed 1991).

26. This was incidentally Gómara's hidden polemics with the critical writings of Fray Francisco de Vitoria, who stated that since no miracles had occurred during the Spanish conquest of America, Indians could not be expected to convert when first told of the true religion ([1539] 1989, chap. 2, 90, 92).

27. "Hicieron también mucho al caso [a la conversión] las letras y cartas que unos españoles a otros se escribían; ca pensaban los indios que tenían espíritu de profecía, pues sin verse ni hablarse se entendían, o que hablaba el papel, y estuvieron en esto abobados y corridos."

28. "Un español envió a otro una docena de hutias fiambres. . . . El indio que las llevaba durmióse . . . por el camino, y tardó mucho en llegar a donde iba, y así tubo hambre o golosina de las hutias, y . . . comióse tres. La carta que trajo en respuesta decía como le tenía en merced las nueve hutias . . . el amo riñó al indio. Él negaba . . . mas como entendió que lo hablaba la carta, confesó la verdad. Quedó corrido y escarmentado, y publicó entre los suyos cómo las cartas hablaban, para que se guardasen de ellas."

29. Acosta stated that Indians called Spaniards "Viracochas" "because they had them for sons of the sky/heaven, and like divine" ("por tenerlos en opinión de hijos del cielo, y como divinos") ([1590] 2002, bk. V, chap. 3, 303). There is much debate among scholars about Viracocha including whether it was a true Andean deity or a tweaked version of an Andean deity made for Europeans. See, for instance, Demarest [1981] 2004; Duviols 1993, 1997a, 1997b; Itier 1993; Mazzotti 1996, 208–22; Zuidema 1997a, 1997b.

30. A literal reading would not be free of complications either. It was their *being deluded* by the Spaniards (who said about literacy what was not true) that drove Indians to think that the former were so superior—not the fact that they *actually were superior*. In this light, Spanish greatness was the ability to lie and deceive Indians, making them believe that they had a power they did not—which was in

fact the devil's modus operandi (see this parallel as a mode of Amerindian critical thinking in Lamana 2010).

31.   "'No dejéis por eso de escribir lo que pasa. Crean lo que quisieren, basta decirles verdad. Yo soy testigo de vista de la grandeza del rábano del valle de Azapa, porque soy uno de los que hicieron aquella jornada con don García de Mendoza. Y doy fe, como caballero hijodalgo, que vi los cinco caballos atados . . . y después comí del rábano con los demás. Y podéis añadir que en esa misma jornada vi en el valle de Ica un melón que pesó cuatro arrobas y tres libras y se tomó por fe y testimonio ante escribano para que se diese crédito."

32.   Literacy would not be an obstacle to this interpretation; there were literate natives around 1600 and the practice of reading was likely oral and communal, as it often was in Europe (e.g., Chartier 1987, 1992; Chartier and Paire 1993).

33.   "Digo que hoy los adoran como entonces . . . Y si les reprenden que por qué lo hacen—pues saben que fueron hombres como ellos y no diosesem dashicen que ya están desengañados de su idolatría, pero que los adoran por los muchos y grandes beneficios que de ellos recibieron. Que se hubieron con sus vasallos como Incas hijos del sol—y no menos. Que les muestren ahora otros hombres semejantes, que también los adorarán por divinos."

34.   See, for instance, Acosta (*1590*) 2002, bk. V, chap. 6, 311; (*1588*) 1987, vol. II, bk. V, chap. 9, 247–59.

CONCLUSION

1.   For critical reflections about being Indian in the twentieth-century Andes that echo in many ways the material in this book, see De la Cadena 2000.

2.   For some examples of competition in the colonial Andes, see Assadourian 1994, 151–304; Dean 1999; Estenssoro-Fuchs 2003; Lamana 2008, 2012; Larson 1995; Saignes 1995; Stern 1986, 1992, 1995; Tandeter et al. 1995.

REFERENCES

ABBREVIATIONS

CBC: Centro Bartolomé de Las Casas.
CSIC: Consejo Superior de Investigaciones Científicas.
FCE: Fondo de Cultura Económica.
IFEA: Institute Françoise D'Etudes Andines.
PUCP: Pontificia Universidad Católica del Perú.

ANCIENT AND EARLY-MODERN SCHOLARSHIP

Note: Italicized dates between brackets indicate that the text was published right after or close to its finishing date.

Acosta, José de. [*1590*] 2002. *Historia natural y moral de las Indias*. Edited by José Alcina Franch. Madrid: Dastin.

Acosta, José de. [*1588*] 1987. *De procuranda Indorum salute*. Edited by Luciano Pereña et al. Madrid: CSIC.

Agía, Miguel. 1604. *Tratado que contiene tres pareceres graves en derecho*. Lima: Antonio Ricardo.

Alvarez, Bartolomé. [*1588*] 1998. *De las costumbres y conversión de los indios del Perú: Memorial a Felipe II*. Edited by María del Carmen Martín Rubio, Juan J. R. Villarías Robles, and Fermín del Pino Díaz. Madrid: Ediciones Polifemo.

Aristotle. 1996. *The Politics and the Constitution of Athens*. Edited by Stephen Everson. New York: Cambridge University Press.

Arriaga, José de. [1621] 1999. *La extirpación de la idolatría en el Piru.* Edited by Henrique Urbano. Cuzco: CBC.

Biblia del oso. 1569. Traducción de Casiodoro de Reina. Facsimile edition. Los Angeles: Mestiza Press.

Cabello Valboa, Miguel. [1586] 2011. *Miscelánea antártica.* University of Texas manuscript. Edited by Isaías Lerner. Seville: Fundación José Manuel Lara.

Chaves, Hierónimo de. 1584. *Chronographia o repertorio de tiempos, el mas copioso y precisso, que hasta ahora ha salido a luz.* Seville: Fernando Diaz.

Cieza de León. [1553] 1984. *La crónica del Perú.* Edited by Manuel Ballesteros. Madrid: Historia 16.

Colón, Cristóbal. [1493] 1989. "Diario del primer viaje." In *Cristóbal Colón: Textos y documentos completos,* edited by Consuelo Varela. Madrid: Alianza Editorial.

Colón, Cristóbal. [1493] 1989 . "Carta a Luis de Santangel." In *Cristóbal Colón: Textos y documentos completos,* edited by Consuelo Varela, 139–46. Madrid: Alianza Editorial.

Cortés, Hernán. [1519] 2002. "Primera Carta-Relación." In *Cartas de relación,* edited by Mario Hernández Sánchez-Barba, 43–81. Madrid: Dastin.

Covarrubias Horozco, Sebastián de. [1611] 2006. *Tesoro de la lengua castellana o española.* Edited by Ignacio Arellano and Rafael Zafra. Madrid: Iberoamericana Vervuert— Universidad de Navarra.

D'Avalos y Figeroa, Diego de. 1602. *Primera parte de la miscelanea avstral.* Lima: Antonio Ricardo.

García, Gregorio. [1607] 2005. *Origen de los indios del Nuevo Mundo e Indias Occidentales.* Edited by Carlos Baciero et al. Madrid: CSIC.

Garcilaso de la Vega, el Inca. [1609] 2002. *Comentarios reales de los incas.* Facsimile edition. Edited by José Luis Rivarola. Madrid: Agencia Española de Cooperación Internacional.

Garcilaso de la Vega, el Inca. [1609] 1995. *Comentarios reales de los incas.* Edited by Carlos Araníbar. Mexico: FCE.

Garcilaso de la Vega, el Inca. [1590] 1989 . *Diálogos de amor de León Hebreo (La tradvzion del indio de los tres Dialogos de Amor de Leon Hebreo).* Facsimile edition. Edited by Miguel de Burgos Núñez. Seville: Padilla Libros.

Gómara, Francisco López de. [1552] 2004 . *Historia general de las Indias.* Barcelona: Linkgua Ediciones.

Granada, Luis de. [1565] 1994 -95. *Memorial de la vida cristiana.* In *Obras completas,* edited by Alvaro Huerga, vols. IV–V. Madrid: Fundación Universitaria Española.

Granada, Luis de. [1567] 1994. *Segunda guía de pecadores.* In *Obras completas,* edited by Manuel Arroyo Stephens, 531–1081. Madrid: Fundación José Antonio de Castro.

Granada, Luis de. [1583] 1989. *Introducción del símbolo de la fe.* Edited by José María Balcells. Madrid: Cátedra.

Granada, Luis de. [1574] 1788. *Meditaciones muy devotas sobre algunos passos y misterios principales de la vida de nuestro Salvador.* In *Obras del Venerable Padre Maestro Fray Luis de Granada,* edited by Alvaro Marín, 405–582. Madrid: Real Compañía de Impressores y Libreros del Reyno.

Guaman Poma de Ayala, Felipe. [ca. 1614] 1987. *Nueva crónica y buen gobierno.* Edited by John V. Murra, Rolena Adorno, and Jorge L. Urioste. Madrid: Historia 16.

Huarte de San Juan, Juan. [1575] 2005. *Examen de ingenios para las ciencias.* Edited by Guillermo Serés. Madrid: Cátedra.

Las Casas, Bartolomé de. [1522 -36?] 1990. *De unico vocationis modo.* In *Obras Completas,* edited by Paulino C. Delgado and Antonio García del Moral, vol. 2. Madrid: Alianza Editorial.

Las Casas, Bartolomé de.[1550 -56?] 1992. *Apologética historia sumaria.* Edited by Vidal Abril Castelló et al. In *Obras Completas,* edited by Paulino C. Delgado and Antonio García del Moral, vols. 7–9. Madrid: Alianza Editorial.

Las Casas, Bartolomé de. [1552] 1992. *Brevísima relación de la destrucción de las Indias.* Edited by Ramón Hernández. In *Obras Completas,* edited by Paulino C. Delgado and Antonio García del Moral, vol. 10, 29–94. Madrid: Alianza Editorial.

Las Casas, Bartolomé de. [ca. 1561] 1994. *Historia de las indias.* In *Obras Completas,* edited by Miguel A. Medina et al., vols. 3–6. Madrid: Alianza Editorial.

Molina, Cristóbal de (el almagrista) [Bartolomé de Segovia]. [ca. 1553] 1968 . *Relación de muchas cosas acaescidas en el Perú.* In *Crónicas peruanas de interés indígena,* edited by Francisco Esteve Barba, Biblioteca de Autores Españoles (cont.), vol. 209, 59–95. Madrid: Ediciones Atlas.

Montayés, Jaume. 1557. *Libro intitulado espejo de bien biuir.* Madrid: Francisco Sánchez.

Montesclaros, Marqués de. [ca. 1615] 1990. "Deduzido de los papeles del Marqués de Montesclaros." In *El gobierno americano del Marqués de Montesclaros,* edited by Antonio Herrera Casado, 112–54. Guadalajara: Institución Provincial de Cultura "Marqués de Santillana."

Oré, Luis Jerónimo de. [1598] 1992. *Symbolo catholico indiano.* Facsimile edition. Edited by Antonine Tibesar. Lima: Australis.

Ortiz de Ceruantes, Juan. 1619. *Memorial que presenta a Su Magestad el Licenciado Juan Ortiz de Ceruantes . . . la perpetuidad de Encomiendas.* Madrid: N.p

Polo Ondegardo, Juan. [1571] 2012. "Las razones que movieron a sacar esta relación y notable daño que resulta de no guardar a estos indios sus fueros." In *Pensamiento colonial crítico: Textos y actos de Polo Ondegardo,* edited by Gonzalo Lamana, 217–330. Lima-Cuzco: IFEA–CBC.

Real Cédula dada en Aranjuez el 25 de mayo de 1609 sobre el servicio de indios y la mita minera. Biblioteca Nacional de España, R/16127, ff. 211–218.

Roman, Hieronimo. 1575. *Republicas del mundo.* Medina del Campo: Francisco del Canto.

Salinas y Cordova, Buenaventura de. [1630] 1957. *Memorial de las historias del nvevo mvndo Pirv.* Edited by Luis E. Valcárcel and Warren L. Cook. Lima: Universidad Mayor de San Marcos.

Santo Tomás, Domingo de. [1560] 1995. *Grammatica o arte de la lengua general de los indios de los reynos del Peru.* Edited by Rodrigo Cerrón Palomino. Cuzco: CBC.

Sepúlveda, Juan Ginés de. [ca. 1551] 1975 . "Apología de Juan Ginés de Sepúlveda." In *Apología de Juan Ginés de Sepúlveda contra Fray Bartolomé de las Casas y de Fray Bartolomé de las Casas contra Juan Ginés de Sepúlveda,* edited by Angel Losada, 57–82. Madrid: Editora Nacional."

Tercero catecismo y exposición de la doctrina cristiana, por sermones." [1585] 1990. In *Monumenta catechetica hispanoamericana (siglos XVI–XVIII)*, edited by Juan Guillermo Durán, vol. II, 613–741. Buenos Aires: Pontificia Universidad Católica Argentina.

Thamara, Francisco. 1556. *El libro de las costvmbres de todas las gentes del mvndo, y de las indias.* Anvers: Martín Nucio.

Torquemada, Juan de. [1615] 1986. *Monarquía indiana.* Edited by Miguel León Portilla. México: Editorial Porrúa S.A.

Xerez, Francisco de. [1534] 1985. *Verdadera relación de la conquista del Perú.* Edited by Concepción Bravo Guerreira. Madrid: Historia 16.

Vitoria, Francisco de. [1539] 1989. *Relectio de Indis.* Edited by Luciano Pereña et al. Madrid: CSIC.

CURRENT SCHOLARSHIP

Acosta, Antonio. 1987a. "La extirpación de las idolatrías en el Perú. Origen y desarrollo de las campañas. A propósito de *Cultura andina y represión*, de Pierre Duviols." *Revista Andina* 1: 171–95.

Acosta, Antonio. 1987b. "Francisco de Avila. Cusco 1573 (?)—Lima 1647." In *Ritos y relaciones de Huarochirí*, edited by Gerald Taylor, 553–616. Lima: Instituto de Estudios Peruanos-IFEA.

Adorno, Rolena. 2008a. *De Guancané a Macondo.* Seville: Renacimiento.

Adorno, Rolena. 2008b. *The Polemics of Possession in Spanish American Narrative.* New Haven, Conn.: Yale University Press.

Adorno, Rolena. 2000. *Guaman Poma: Writing and Resistance in Colonial Peru.* 2nd ed. Austin: University of Texas Press.

Adorno, Rolena. 1993. "La censura y su evasión. Jerónimo Román y Bartolomé de las Casas." *Estudios de Cultura Náhualt* 23:263–96.

Adorno, Rolena. 1989. *Cronista y príncipe.* Lima: PUCP.

Adorno, Rolena. 1987. "Waman Puma: El autor y su obra." In *Nueva crónica y buen gobierno*, by Felipe Guaman Poma de Ayala, xvii<en-dash>xlvii. Madrid: Historia 16.

Agamben, Giorgio. 2005. *State of Exception.* Chicago: University of Chicago Press.

Alberdi Vallejo, Alfredo. 2010. *El mundo al revés.* Berlin: WVB.

Alberro, Solange. 1994. "Acerca de la primera evangelización en México." In *La venida del reino*, edited by Gabriela Ramos, 11–30. Cuzco: CBC.

Aldea Vaquero, Quintín. 1993. *El indio peruano y la defensa de sus derechos.* Lima-Madrid: PUCP-CSIC.

Alfaro, Juan. 1952. *Lo natural y lo sobrenatural.* Madrid: CSIC.

Anzaldúa, Gloria. 1987. *Borderlands/La Frontera: The New Mestiza.* San Francisco: Aunt Lute Books.

Arrom, Juan J. 1991. *Imaginación del nuevo mundo.* Mexico: Siglo XXI Editores.

Assadourian, Carlos. 1994. *Transiciones hacia el sistema colonial andino.* Lima: Instituto de Estudios Peruanos; Mexico City: El Colegio de México.

Assadourian, Carlos. 1993. "Dominio colonial y señores étnicos en el espacio andino." *HISLA* 1:7–20.

Bakhtin, Mikhail M. 1986. *Speech Genres and Other Late Essays*. Austin: University of Texas Press.

Bakewell, Peter. 1984. *Miners of the Red Mountain: Indian Labor in Potosí, 1545<en-dash>1650*. Albuquerque: University of New Mexico Press.

Baldwin, James. 2010. *The Cross of Redemption*. Edited by Randall Kenan. New York: Vintage International.

Baldwin, James. 1998. *Baldwin: Collected Essays*. Edited by Toni Morrison. New York: The Library of America.

Baldwin, James. 1993[. *The Fire Next Time*. New York: Vintage International.

Barnadas, Josep M. 1993. "Idolatría en Charcas (1560–1620)." In *Catolicismo y extirpación de idolatrías*, edited by Gabriela Ramos and Henrique Urbano, 89–103. Cuzco: CBC.

Barnes, Mónica. 1995. "Las edades del hombre y del mundo según Hierónimo Chaues, de Sevilla y Guaman Poma de Ayala, del Perú." In *Humanismo Siglo XX: Estudios dedicados al Dr. Juan Adolfo Vázquez*, edited by Juan Schobinger, 291–97. San Juan: Editorial Fundación Universidad Nacional de San Juan.

Belda Plans, Juan. 2000. *La Escuela de Salamanca y la renovación de la teología en el siglo XVI*. Madrid: Biblioteca de Autores Católicos.

Beltrán de Heredia, Vicente. 1949. "Los alumbrados de Jaén." *Revista española de teología* 9 (35): 162–221, 446–88.

Bhabha, Homi. 1994. *The Location of Culture*. London: Routledge.

Boone, Elizabeth H., and Gary Urton, eds. 2011. *Their Way of Writing. Scripts, Signs, and Pictographies in Pre-Columbian America*. Washington, D.C.: Dumbarton Oaks Research Library and Collection.

Brading, David A. 1993. *First America*. Cambridge: Cambridge University Press.

Brading, David A. 1986. "The Incas and the Renaissance: *The Royal Commentaries* of Inca Garcilaso de la Vega." *Journal of Latin American Studies* 18:1–23.

Breva-Claramonte, Manuel. 2008a. "Grammatization of Indigenous Languages in Spanish America: The Mental Language, Language Origin and Cultural Factors." *Histoire Epistémologie Langage* 30 (2): 11–24.

Breva-Claramonte, Manuel. 2008b. "El marco doctrinal de la tradición lingüística europea y los primeros misioneros de la Colonia." *Bulletin hispanique* 110:25–59.

Brokaw, Galen. 2010. *A History of the Khipu*. Cambridge: Cambridge University Press.

Burns, Kathryn. 2010. *Into the Archive: Writing and Power in Colonial Peru*. Durham, N.C.: Duke University Press.

Burns, Kathryn. 2007. "Unfixing Race." In *Rereading the Black Legend: The Discourses of Religious and Racial Difference in the Renaissance Empires*, edited by Margaret R. Greer, Walter D. Mignolo, and Maureen Quilligan, 188–202. Chicago: University of Chicago Press.

Cantú, Francesca. 2001. *Guaman Poma y Blas Valera*. Rome: A. Pellicani.

Carroll, Lewis. 2015. *The Annotated Alice*. Edited by Martin Gardner. Expanded and Updated by Mark Burstein. New York: W. W. Norton & Co.

Cartledge, Mark J., and David Cheetham. 2011. *Intercultural Theology*. London: SCM Press.

Casanovas, González. 2000. *Las dudas de la corona: La política de repartimientos para la minería de Potosí (1680–1731)*. Madrid: CISC.

Castanien, Donald. 1969. *El Inca Garcilaso de la Vega*. New York: Twayne Publishers.

Castañeda Delgado, Paulino. 1971. "La condición miserable del indio y sus privilegios." *Anuario de estudios americanos* 28:245–334.

Castañeda Delgado, Paulino. 1983. *Los memoriales del padre Silva sobre la predicación pacífica y los repartimientos*. Madrid: CSIC.

Castro-Gómez, Santiago, and Ramón Grosfoguel. 2007. "Giro decolonial, teoría política y pensamiento heterárquico." In *El giro decolonial*, edited by Santiago Castro-Gómez and Ramón Grosfoguel, 9–23. Bogotá: Siglo del Hombre Ediciones, Universidad Central-Pontificia Universidad Javeriana.

Castro-Klarén, Sara. 2016. "For It Is but a Single World." In *Inca Garcilaso and Contemporary World-Making*, edited by Sara Castro-Klarén and Walter Fernández, 195–228. Pittsburgh, Pa.: Pittsburgh University Press.

Castro-Klarén, Sara. 2011. *The Narrow Path of Our Nerves*. Madrid: Iberoamericana Vervuert.

Cerrón Palomino, Rodolfo. 2013a. *Tras las huellas del inca Garcilaso*. Boston: Latinoamericana Editores, CELACP, Revista de Crítica Literaria Latinoamericana.

Cerrón Palomino, Rodolfo. 2013b. *Las lenguas de los incas: El puquina, el aimara y el quechua*. Frankfurt am Main: PL Academic Research.

Cerrón Palomino, Rodolfo. 1998. "El cantar de Inca Yupanqui y la lengua secreta de los incas." *Revista andina* 32:417–52.

Cerrón Palomino, Rodolfo. 1995. "Estudio introductorio." In *Grammatica o arte de la lengua general de los indios de los reynos del Peru*, by Domingo de Santo Tomás, vlxvi. Cuzco: CBC.

Chang-Rodríguez, Raquel. 1977. "Elaboración de fuentes en 'Carta Canta' y 'Papelito Jabla Lengua.'" *Kentucky Romance Quarterly* 24 (3): 433–39.

Charles, John. 2010. *Allies at Odds: The Andean Church and its Indigenous Agents, 1583<en-dash>1671*. Albuquerque: University of New Mexico Press.

Chartier, Roger. 1992. *L'ordre des livres*. Aix-en-Provence: Alinea.

Chartier, Roger. 1987. *Lectures et lecteurs dans la France d'ancien régime*. Paris: Éditions du Seuil.

Chartier, Roger, and Alain Paire. 1993. *Pratiques de la lecture*. Paris: Payot.

Coello de la Rosa, Alexandre. 2014. "Los *Memoriales* de don Juan Ortiz de Cervantes y la cuestión de la perpetuidad de las encomiendas en el Perú (siglo XVII)." *Colonial Latin American Review* 23 (3): 360–83.

Cohen Suarez, Ananda. 2016. *Heaven, Hell, and Everything In Between: Heaven, Hell, and Everything In Between* . Austin: University of Texas Press.

Cornejo-Polar, Antonio. 1993. "El discurso de la harmonía imposible (El Inca Garcilaso de la Vega: Discurso y recepción social)." *Revista de crítica literaria latinoamericana* 19 (38): 73–80.

Cornejo-Polar, Antonio. 2003. *Escribir en el aire*. Lima: CELAP, Latinoamericana Editores.

Cummins, Thomas B. 2002. *Toasts with the Inca: Andean Abstraction and Colonial Images on Quero Vessels*. Ann Arbor: University of Michigan Press.

Cunill, Caroline. 2011. "El indio miserable: nacimiento de la teoría legal en la América colonial del siglo XVI." *Cuadernos Intercambio* 8 (9): 229–48.

De Certeau, Michel. 1990. *L'invention du quotidien: 1 Arts de faire*. Paris: Gallimard.

Dedenbach-Salazar Sáenz, Sabine. 2013. *Entrelazando dos mundos*. Quito: Abya-Yala.

Degregori, Carlos Iván. 1991. "Educación y mundo andino." In *Educación bilingüe intercultural*, edited by Madeleine Zúñiga et al., 13–26. Lima: Fomciencias.

De la Cadena, Marisol. 2000. *Indigenous Mestizos: The Politics of Race and Culture in Cuzco, Peru, 1919–1991*. Durham, N.C.: Duke University Press.

Deloria, Philip. 2004. *Indians in Unexpected Places*. Lawrence: University Press of Kansas.

Deloria, Philip. 1999. *Playing Indian*. New Haven, Conn.: Yale University Press.

Demarest, Arthur A. [1981] 2004. *Viracocha: The Nature and Antiquity of the Andean High God*. Cambridge, Mass.: Peabody Museum Monographs.

Denery II, Dallas G. 2005. *Seeing and Being Seen in the Later Medieval World*. Cambridge: Cambridge University Press.

Díaz, Mónica. 2017. *To Be Indio in Colonial Spanish America*. Albuquerque: University of New Mexico Press.

Du Bois, W. E. B. [1920] 2015. "The Souls of White Folk." In *Darkwater: Voices from within the Veil*, 17–29. New York: Dover Publications.

Du Bois, W. E. B. [1903] 1990. *The Souls of Black Folk*. New York: Vintage Books.

Durand, José. 1976. *El Inca Garcilaso, clásico de América*. Mexico: Secretaría de Educación Pública.

Durand, José. 1963. "El nombre de los Comentarios Reales." *Revista del Museo Nacional* 32:322–32.

Durand, José. 1949. "Dos notas sobre el Inca Garcilaso." *NuevaRevista de Flología Hispánica* 3:278–90.

Durkheim, Emile. 1995. *The Elementary Forms of Religious Life*. New York: Free Press.

Durston, Alan. 2007. *Pastoral Quechua: The History of Christian Translation in Colonial Peru, 1550<en-dash>1650*. Notre Dame, Ind.: University of Notre Dame Press.

Duviols, Pierre. 1997a. "La interpretación del dibujo de Pachacuti-Yamqui." In *Saberes y memorias en los Andes*, edited by Thérèse Bouysse Cassagne, 101–23. Paris: Éditions de l'IHEAL.

Duviols, Pierre. 1997b. "Respuesta de Pierre Duviols a la crítica de Tom Zuidema." In *Saberes y memorias en los Andes*, edited by Thérèse Bouysse Cassagne, 125–48. Paris: Éditions de l'IHEAL.

Duviols, Pierre. 1993. "Estudio y comentario etnohistórico." In *Relación de antigüedades deste reyno del Piru*, by Joan de Santa Cruz Pachacuti Yamqui Salcamaygua, 11–126. Cuzco: CBC.

Duviols, Pierre. 1988. "Introducción." In *Fábulas y mitos de los incas*, edited by Henrique Urbano and Pierre Duviols, 137–58. Madrid: Historia 16.

Duviols, Pierre. 1983. "Guaman Poma, historiador del Perú antiguo: Una nueva pista." *Revista Andina* 1:103–15.

Duviols, Pierre. 1980. "Periodización y política: La historia prehispánica del Perú según Guaman Poma de Ayala." *Bulletin l'Institut Français d'Etudes Andines* 9 (3–4): 1–18.

Duviols, Pierre. 1977. *La destrucción de las religiones andinas.* Mexico: Universidad Nacional Autónoma de México.

Duviols, Pierre. 1964. "The Inca Garcilaso de la Vega, Humanist Interpreter of the Inca Religion." *Diogenes* 44:36–52.

Duviols, Pierre. 1963. "Sur le système religieux des *Comentarios reales de los incas.*" *Annales de la Faculté des Lettres et Sciences Humaines d'Aix* 37:227–41.

Duviols, Pierre. 1962. "Les traditions miraculeuses du siège du Cuzco (1536) et leur fortune littéraire" *Bulletin de la Faculté des Lettres de Strasbourg* 40 (7): 1–7.

Eco, Umberto. 1997. *The Search for the Perfect Language.* Oxford: Blackwell Publishing.

Eire, Carlos M. 2002. *From Madrid to Purgatory: The Art and Craft of Dying in Sixteenth-Century Spain.* Cambridge: Cambridge University Press.

Eliav-Feldon, Miriam, Benjamin Isaac, and Joseph Ziegler, eds. 2009. The Origins of Racism in the West. Cambridge: Cambridge University Press

Escobar, Alberto. 1971. "Lenguaje e historia en los Comentarios Reales." In *Patio de Letras,* 7–44. Caracas: Monte Avila Editores C.A.

Estenssoro Fuchs, Juan C. 2003. *Del paganismo a la santidad.* Lima: IFEA.

Fabian, Johaness. 1983. *Time and the Other.* New York: Columbia University Press.

Fanon, Frantz. [1952] 2008. Black Skin, White Masks. Translated by Richard Philcox. New York: Grove Press.

Farías, Fernando A. 2008. *Indio y cristiano en condiciones coloniales.* Quito: ABYA-YALA.

Fernández-Palacios, Christian. 2016. "Inca Garcilaso's Biography." In *Inca Garcilaso and Contemporary World-Making,* edited by Sara Castro-Klarén and Walter Fernández, 20–32. Pittsburgh, Pa.: Pittsburgh University Press.

Fernández-Palacios, Christian. 2004. *Inca Garcilaso: Imaginación, memoria e identidad.* Lima: Universidad Mayor de San Marcos.

Feros, Antonio. 2017. *Speaking of Spain: The Evolution of Race and Nation in the Hispanic World.* Cambridge, Mass.: Harvard University Press.

Fisher, Andrew B., and Matthew F. O'Hara, eds. 2009. *Imperial Subjects: Race and Identity in Colonial Latin America.* Durham, N.C.: Duke University Press.

Fleming, David. 1994. "Guaman Poma, Hieronymo de Chaves and the Kings of Persia." *Latin American Indian Literatures Journal* 1:46–60.

Foucault, Michel. 1975. *Surveiller et punir.* Paris: Gallimard.

Gates, Henry L. Jr. 1988. *The Signifying Monkey.* Oxford: Oxford University Press.

Geertz, Clifford. 1973. *The Interpretation of Cultures.* New York: Basic Books.

Genette, Gérard. 1997. *Paratexts.* Cambridge: Cambridge University Press.

Genette, Gérard. 1980. *Narrative Discourse.* Ithaca: Cornell University Press.

Gera, Deborah. 2003. *Ancient Greek Ideas on Speech, Language and Civilization.* Oxford: Oxford University Press.

Goldwert, Marvin. 1957–58. "La lucha por la perpetuidad de las encomiendas en el Perú virreinal, 1550–1560 (continuación)." *Revista Histórica* (Lima) 23:207–45.

Goldwert, Marvin. 1955–56. "La lucha por la perpetuidad de las encomiendas en el Perú virreinal, 1550–1560." *Revista Histórica* (Lima) 22:336–60.

González Díaz, Soledad. 2012. "Guaman Poma y el *Repertorio* anónimo (1554): Una nueva fuente para las edades del mundo en la *Nueva corónica y buen gobierno.*" *Chungará* 44 (3): 377–88.

Gose, Peter. 2008. *Invaders as Ancestors: On the Intercultural Making and Unmaking of Spanish Colonialism in the Andes.* Toronto: University of Toronto Press.

Graulich, Michel, and Serge Núñez Tolin. 2000. "Les contenus subliminaux de l'image chez Felipe Guaman Poma de Ayala." *Journal de la Société des Américanistes* 86:67–93.

Griffiths, Nicholas. 1995. *The Cross and the Serpent: Religious Repression and Resurgence in Colonial Peru.* Norman: University of Oklahoma Press.

Gutiérrez, Gustavo. 1992. *En busca de los pobres de Jesucristo.* Lima: Instituto Bartolomé de Las Casas, Centro de Estudios y Publicaciones.

Gutiérrez, Gustavo. 1971. *Teología de la liberación.* Lima: Centro de estudios y publicaciones.

Hanke, Lewis. 1949. *The Spanish Struggle for Justice in the Conquest of America.* Philadelphia: University of Pennsylvania Press.

Hanke, Lewis. 1946. "Viceroy Francisco de Toledo and the Just Titles of Spain to the Inca Empire." *The Americas* 3 (1): 3–19.

Harrison, Regina. 1994. *Signos, cantos y memoria en los Andes.* Cayambe: Abya-Yala.

Havel, Václav. 1987. *Vaclav Havel, Or Living in Truth.* Boston: Faber and Faber.

Heng, Geraldine. 2018. *The Invention of Race in the European Middle Ages.* Cambridge: Cambridge University Press.

Hering Torres, Max S., María Elena Martínez, and David Nirenberg, eds. 2012. *Race and Blood in the Iberian World.* Berlin-Zurich: LIT Verlag.

Hernández, Max. 1991. *Memoria del bien perdido.* Madrid: Sociedad Estatal Quinto Centenario.

Hill, Cristopher. 1972. *The World Turned Upside Down: Radical Ideas During the English Revolution.* London: Penguin.

Holland, Augusta E. 2008. *Nueva Corónica: Tradiciones artísticas europeas en el virreinato del Perú.* Cuzco: CBC.

Huerga, Alvaro. 1978. *Historia de los alumbrados (1570–1630).* Madrid: Fundación Universitaria Española.

Husson, Jean-Philippe. 1995. "En busca de las fuentes indígenas de Waman Puma de Ayala:Las raíces incas y Yaruwillka del cronista indio: ¿invención o realidad?" *Revista Histórica* 19:29–71.

Hyland, Sabine. 2003. *The Jesuit and the Incas: The Extraordinary Life of Padre Blas Valera, S.J..* Ann Arbor: University of Michigan Press.

Imbelloni, José. 1939. *Los vocablos "pachacuti" y "pachacutec" de los cronistas del Perú y sus determinantes gramaticales y semánticas.* Buenos Aires: Imprenta y Casa Editorial Coni.

Itier, César. 1993. "Estudio y comentario lingüístico." In *Relación de antigüedades deste reyno del Piru,* by Joan de Santa Cruz Pachacuti Yamqui Salcamaygua, 127–78. Cuzco: CBC.

Jericó Bermejo, Ignacio. 2005. *La escuela de Salamanca del siglo XVI.* Guadarrama, Spain: Editorial Revista Agustiniana.

Jurado, Carolina. 2013. "Memorial cerca de las congruencias de la perpetuidad de las encomiendas de los indios." *Revista de Historia del Derecho* 46:45–72.

Keller, CatherineKeller, Michael Nausner, Mayra Rivera eds. 2004. *Postcolonial Theologies: Divinity and Empire*. Saint Louis, Mo.: Chalice Press.

Kelly, L. G. 2002. *The Mirror of Grammar: Theology, philosophy and the Modistae*. Amsterdam-Philadelphia: John Benjamins.

Lamana, Gonzalo. 2012. "Pensamiento colonial crítico: Polo Ondegardo, los Andes y los estudios andinos." In *Pensamiento colonial crítico: Textos y actos de Polo Ondegardo*, edited by Gonzalo Lamana, 49–87. Lima-Cuzco: IFEA, CBC.

Lamana, Gonzalo. 2010. "What Makes a Story Amusing: Magic, Occidentalism and Overfetishization in a Colonial Setting." *Journal of Latin American Cultural Studies* 19 (1): 87–102.

Lamana, Gonzalo. 2008. *Domination without Dominance: Inca-Spanish Encounters in Early Colonial Peru*. Durham, N.C.: Duke University Press.

Lamana, Gonzalo. 2007. "Of Books, Popes, and *Huacas*; or, the Dilemmas of Being Christian." In *Rereading the Black Legend: The Discourses of Religious and Racial Difference in the Renaissance Empires*, edited by Margaret R. Greer, Walter D. Mignolo, and Maureen Quilligan, 117–49. Chicago: University of Chicago Press.

Larson, Broke. 1995. "Andean Communities, Political Cultures, and Markets: The Changing Contours of a Field." In *Ethnicity, Markets, and Migration in the Andes: At the Crossroads of History and Anthropology*, edited by Brooke Larsonand Olivia Harris, 5–53. Durham, N.C.: Duke University Press.

Latasa Vassallo, Pilar. 1997. *Administración virreinal en el Perú: Gobierno del marqués de Montesclaros (1607–1615)*. Madrid: Editorial Centro de Estudios Ramón Areces.

Laurencich Minelli, Laura. 2005. *Exsul Immeritus Blas Valera Populo Suo e Historia et Rudimenta Linguae Piruanorum: Indios, gesuiti e spagnoli in due documenti segreti sul Perù del XVII secolo*. Bologna: CLUEB.

Law, Vivien. 2003. *The History of Linguistics in Europe from Plato to 1600*. Cambridge: Cambridge University Press.

Lohmann Villena, Guillermo. 1966. *Juan de Matienzo, autor del "Gobierno del Perú" (su personalidad y su obra)*. Publicaciones de la Escuela de Estudios Hispano-Americanos de Sevilla, no. 170. Seville: Escuela de Estudios Hispano-Americanos.

López-Baralt, Mercedes. 2011. *El Inca Garcilaso, traductor de culturas*. Madrid: IberoamericanaVervuert.

López-Baralt, Mercedes. 2003. Introducción. In *El Inca Garcilaso de la Vega*, edited by Mercedes López Baralt, xilxxix. Madrid: Espasa-Calpe.

López-Baralt, Mercedes. 1988. *Icono y conquista: Guaman Poma de Ayala*. Madrid: Iperión.

López-Baralt, Mercedes. 1992. "From Looking to Seeing. The Image as Text and the Author as Artist." In *Guaman Poma de Ayala: The Colonial Art of an Andean Author*, edited by Rolena Adorno et al., 14–31. New York: Americas Society.

López-Baralt, Mercedes. 1993. *Guaman Poma, autor y artista*. Lima: PUCP.

López Díaz-Valentín, Patricio. 2012. "La condición jurídica del indígena americano en hispanoamérica durante los siglos XVI y XVII." *Fuego y Raya* 4:123–49.

Mannheim, Bruce. 1991. *The Language of the Inka since the European Invasion*. Austin: University of Texas Press.

MacCormack, Sabine. 1991. *Religion in the Andes: Vision and Imagination in Early Colonial Peru*. Princeton, N.J.: Princeton University Press.

MacCormack, Sabine. 1989. "Atahualpa and the Book." *Dispositio* 14 (36–38): 141–68.

MacCormack, Sabine. 1988. "Pachacuti: Miracles, Punishments, and Last Judgment: Visionary Past and Prophetic Future in Early Colonial Peru." *American Historical Review* 93 (4): 960–1006.

MacCormack, Sabine. 1985. "'The heart has its reasons': Predicaments of Missionary Christianity in Early Colonial Peru." *Hispanic American Historical Review* 65 (3): 443–66.

Martín Rubio, María del Carmen. 1998. "Aullagas, un pueblo muy ruico del atiplano boliviano." In *De las costumbres y conversión de los indios del Perú*, by Bartolomé Alvarez, xxxvlix. Madrid: Ediciones Polifemo.

Martínez Gil, Fernando. 1996. *La muerte vivida: Muerte y sociedad en Castilla durante la Baja Edad Media*. Toledo, Spain: Diputación provincial de Toledo, Universidad de Castilla, La Mancha.

Mazzotti, José A. 2016. "A Synchretic Tropology." In *Inca Garcilaso and Contemporary World-Making*, edited by Sara Castro-Klarén and Walter Fernández, 62–128. Pittsburgh, Pa.: Pittsburgh University Press.

Mazzotti, José A. 2010. "Intellectuals and Mestizaje: Inca Garcilaso, Blas Valera, and the Organic Function of Colonial *Letrados*." In *Rethinking Intellectuals in Latin America*, edited by Mabel Moraña and Bret Gustafson, 29–48. Madrid : Iberoamericana Vervuert.

Mazzotti, José A. 1996. *Coros mestizos del Inca Garcilaso*. Lima: FCE.

Meiklejohn, Norman. 1988. *La Iglesia y los Lupacas de Chucuito durante la colonia*. Cuzco: CBC.

Méndez Fernández, Benito. 1993. *El problema de la salvación de los "infieles" en Francisco de Vitoria*. Rome: Iglesia Nacional Española.

Merluzzi, Manfredi. 2014. *Gobernando los Andes*. Lima: Roma TRE and PUCP.

Miccinelli, Clara, and Carlo Animato. 1999. "Missionari gesuiti nella terra degli Incas." *Societaties Rivista dei Gesuiti Dell'Italia Meridionale* 47 (5–6): 191–201.

Mignolo, Walter D. 2011. *The Darker Side of Western Modernity: Global Futures, Decolonial Options*. Durham, N.C.: Duke University Press.

Mignolo, Walter D. 2007a. "Afterword: What Does the Black Legend Have to Do with Race?" In *Rereading the Black Legend: The Discourses of Religious and Racial Difference in the Renaissance Empires*, edited by Margaret R. Greer, Walter D. Mignolo, and Maureen Quilligan, 312–24. Chicago: University of Chicago Press.

Mignolo, Walter D. 2007b. "Delinking. The Rhetoric of Modernity, the Logic of Coloniality and Grammar of De-coloniality." *Cultural Studies* 21 (2): 449–514.

Mignolo, Walter D. 2000. *Local Histories/Global Designs: Coloniality, Subaltern Knowledges, and Border Thinking*. Princeton, N.J.: Princeton University Press.

Mignolo, Walter D. 1999. "Philosophy and the Colonial Difference." *Philosophy Today* 43:36–41.

Mignolo, Walter D. 1995. *The Darker Side of the Renaissance: Literacy, Territoriality, and Colonization*. Ann Arbor: University of Michigan Press.

Mills, Kenneth. 1997. *Idolatry and Its Enemies: Colonial Andean Religion and Extirpation, 1640<en-dash>1750*. Princeton, N.J.: Princeton University Press.

Miró Quesada, Aurelio. 1994. *El Inca Garcilaso de la Vega*. Lima: PUCP.

Miró Quesada, Aurelio. 1974. "Las ideas lingüísticas del Inca Garcilaso." *Boletín de la academia peruana de la lengua* 9:27–64.

Miró Quesada, Aurelio. 1945. *El Inca Garcilaso*. Lima: Las EE.AA.

Modrak, Deborah K. W. 2001. *Aristotle's Theory of Language and Meaning*. New York: Cambridge University Press.

Morong Reyes, Germán. 2016. *Saberes hegemónicos y dominio colonial*. Rosario: Prohistoria Ediciones.

Mumford, Jeremy. 2000. "Clara Miccinelli's Cabinet of Wonders." *Lingua Franca* 10 (1): 36–45.

Nelson, Diane. 1999. *A Finger in the Wound: Body Politics in Quincentennial Guatemala*. Berkeley: University of California Press.

Ortega, Julio. 2003. "Trauma and Narrative in Early Modernity: Garcilaso's *Comentarios Reales* (1609–1616)." *MLN* 118:393–426.

Ortega, Julio. 1992a. "The Discourse of Abundance." *American Literary History* 4 (3):369–85.

Ortega, Julio. 1992b. "Garcilaso y el modelo de la nueva cultura." *Nueva Revista de Filología Hispánica* 40 (1):199–215.

Orwell, George. 1946. *A Collection of Essays*. New York: Harcourt.

Ossio, Juan M. 2008. *En busca del orden perdido*. Lima: PUCP.

Ossio, Juan M. 1977. "Myth and History: The Seventeenth-Century Chronicle of Guaman Poma de Ayala." In *Text and Context: The Social Anthropology of Tradition*, edited by Ravindra K. Jain, 51–93. Philadelphia: Institute for the Study of Human Issues.

O'Gorman, Edmundo. [1958] 2006. *La invención de América*. Mexico: FCE.

O'Toole, Rachel. 2012. *Bound Lives: Africans, Indians, and the Making of Race in Colonial Peru*. Pittsburgh: University of Pittsburgh Press.

Padrón, Ricardo. 2010. "Ideología y naufragio: El Inca Garcilaso frente a José de Acosta." In *400 años de Comentarios reales*, edited by Elena Romiti and Song No, 129–53. Montevideo: Aitana Ediciones.

Pagden, Anthony. 1987. *The Fall of Natural Man: The American Indian and the Origins of Comparative Ethnology*. Cambridge: Cambridge University Press.

Pavlić, Ed. 2016. *Who Can Afford to Improvise? James Baldwin and Black Music, the Lyric and the Listener* New York: Fordham University Press.

Pietschmann, Horst. 1989. *El estado y su evolución al principio de la colonización española de América*. México: FCE.

Plas, Sophie. 1996. "Un source européenne de la *Nueva coronica y buen gobierno* de Guaman Poma." *Journal de la Société des Américanistes* 82:97–116.

Pollack, Aaron. 2016. "Hacia una historia social del tributo de indios y castas en hispanoamérica: Notas en torno a su creación, desarrollo y abolición." *Historia Mexicana* 66 (1): 65–160.

Porras Barrenechea, Raúl. 1955. *El Inca Garcilaso en Montilla (1561–1614)*. Lima: Instituto de Historia.

Poupeney Hart, Catherine. 1996. "Diálogos y sátira en la 'Crónica' de Felipe Guaman Poma de Ayala." *Scriptura* 11: 191–202.

Quijano, Aníbal. 2014. "Colonialidad y modernidad/racionalidad." In *Anibal Quijano: Textos de fundación*, edited by Zulma Palermo and Pablo Quintero, 56–66. Buenos Aires: Ediciones del Signo.

Quijano, Aníbal. 2000. "Colonialidad del poder, eurocentrismo y América Latina." In *La colonialidad del saber: Eurocentrismo y ciencias sociales*, compiled by Edgardo Langer, 201–46. Buenos Aires: CLACSO.

Quijano, Aníbal. 1992. "'Raza,' 'etnia' y 'nación' en Mariátegui: Cuestiones abiertas." In *José Carlos Mariátegui y Europa*, edited by Roland Forgues, 757–75. Lima: Amauta.

Quijano, Aníbal, and Immanuel Wallerstein. 1992. "Americanity as a Concept, or the Americas in the Modern World-System." *ISSAI* 134:549–57.

Quilter, Jeffrey, and Gary Urton, eds. 2002. *Narrative Threads: Accounting and Recounting in Andean Khipu*. Austin: University of Texas Press.

Quispe-Agnoli, Rocío. 2006. *La fe andina en la escritura*. Lima: Universidad Nacional Mayor de San Marcos.

Rabasa, José. 1993. "Writing and Evangelization in Sixteenth-Century Mexico." In *Early Images of the Americas: Transfer and Invention*, edited by Jerry M. Williams and Robert E. Lewis, 65–92. Tucson: University of Arizona Press.

Raibmon, Paige. 2005. *Authentic Indians: Episodes of Encounter from the Late-Nineteenth-Century Northwest Coast*. Durham, N.C.: Duke University Press.

Rama, Angel. [1984] 1996 . *The Lettered City*. Translated and edited by John Charles Chasteen.Durham, N.C.: Duke University Press.

Ramos, Gabriela, and Yanna Yannakakis, eds. 2014. *Indigenous Intellectuals: Knowledge, Power, and Colonial Culture in Mexico and the Andes*. Durham, N.C.: Duke University Press.

Rappaport, Joanne. 2014. *The Disappearing Mestizo: Configuring Difference in the Colonial New Kingdom of Granada*. Durham, N.C.: Duke University Press.

Rappaport, Joanne, and Tom Cummins. 2012. *Beyond the Lettered City: Indigenous Literacies in the Andes*. Durham, N.C.: Duke University Press.

Rey, Agapito. 1952. *Castigos e documentos para bien vivir ordenados por el rey don Sancho IV*. Bloomington: Indiana University Press.

Rey Hazas, Antonio. 2003. *Artes de bien morir*. Madrid: Lengua de Trapo.

Rivarola, José Luis. 2001. *Comentarios reales de los incas: Estudio*. Madrid: Ediciones de Cultura Hispánica-AECI.

Romano, John. 1979. "James Baldwin Writing and Talking." *New York Times*, September 23, 1979.

Rosenblat, Angel. 1977. *Sentido mágico de la palabra y otros estudios*. Caracas: Universidad Central de Venezuela.

Rowe, Kavin. 2010. *World Upside Down: Reading Acts in the Graeco-Roman Age*. Oxford: Oxford University Press.

Saignes, Thierry. 1999. "The Colonial Condition in the Quechua-Aymara Heartland (1570–1590)." In *The Cambridge History of the Native Peoples of the Americas*, edited by Frank Salomon and Stuart Schwartz, vol. 3, 59–137. Cambridge: Cambridge University Press.

Saignes, Thierry. 1995. "Indian Migration and Social Change in Seventeenth-Century Charcas." In *Ethnicity, Markets, and Migration in the Andes: At the Crossroads of History and Anthropology*, edited by Brooke Larson and Olivia Harris, 167–95. Durham, N.C.: Duke University Press.

Salomon, Frank, and Mercedes Niño-Murcia. 2011. *The Lettered Mountain: A Peruvian Village's Way with Writing*. Durham, N.C.: Duke University Press.

Samuels, Gabriel. 2016. "Jeremy Hunt Told Off for 'Fiddling Ostentatiously' with Phone during Debate on Cutting Nurses' Bursaries." Independent, May 4, 2016. https:// www.independent.co.uk/news/uk/politics/jeremy-hunt-told-off-parliament-fiddling -phone-bercow-a7013156.html.

Sánchez-Concha Barrios, Rafael. 1996. "De la miserable condición de los indios a las reducciones." *Revista Teológica Limense* 30 (1): 95–104.

Scott, James C. 1990. *Domination and the Arts of Resistance: Hidden Transcripts*. New Haven, Conn.: Yale University Press.

Seed, Patricia. 2001. *American Pentimento: The Invention of Indians and the Pursuit of Riches*. Minneapolis: University of Minnesota Press.

Seed, Patricia. 1995. *Ceremonies of Possession in Europe's Conquest of the New World, 1492–1640*. Cambridge: Cambridge University Press

Seed, Patricia. 1991. "'Failing to Marvel': Atahualpa's Encounter with the Word." *Latin American Research Review* 26 (1): 7–32.

Shorter, Aylward. 2006. *Toward a Theology of Inculturation*. Eugene, Ore.: Wipf and Stock.

Silverblatt, Irene. 2009. Foreword. In *Imperial Subjects: Race and Identity in Colonial Latin America*, edited by Andrew B. Fisher and Matthew F. O'Hara, ixxii. Durham, N.C.: Duke University Press.

Silverblatt, Irene. 2004. *Modern Inquisitions: Peru and the Colonial Origins of the Civilized World*. Durham , N.C.: Duke University Press.

Silverblatt, Irene. 1987. *Moon, Sun, and Witches: Gender Ideologies and Class in Inca and Colonial Peru*. Princeton, N.J.: Princeton University Press.

Silverblatt, Irene. 2009. "Foreword." In *Imperial Subjects: Race and Identity in Colonial Latin America*, edited by Andrew B. Fisher and Matthew D. O'Hara, ixxiv. Durham, N.C.: Duke University Press.

Smith, Paul Chaat. 2009. *Everything You Know about Indians Is Wrong*. Minneapolis: University of Minnesota Press.

Smith, Shawn Michelle. 2004. *Photography on the Color Line: W. E. B. Du Bois, Race, and Visual Culture*. Durham, N.C.: Duke University Press.

Stern, Steve. 1995. "The Variety and Ambiguity of Native Andean Intervention in European Colonial Markets." In *Ethnicity, Markets, and Migration in the Andes: At the*

Crossroads of History and Anthropology, edited by Brooke Larsonand Olivia Harris, 73–100. Durham, N.C.: Duke University Press.

Stern, Steve. 1992. "Paradigms of Conquest: History, Historiography, and Politics." *Journal of Latin American Studies* 24:1–34.

Stern, Steve. 1986. *Peru's Indian Peoples and the Challenge of Spanish Conquest: : Huamanga to 1640*. Madison: University of Wisconsin Press.

Spalding, Karen. 1988. *Huarochirí: An Andean Society Under Inca and Spanish Rule*. Stanford, Calif.: Stanford University Press.

Szemiński, Ian. 1983. "Las generaciones del mundo según Guaman Poma de Ayala." *Histórica* 7 (1): 69–109.

Tandeter, Enrique. 1992. *Coacción y mercado: La mineria de plata en el Potosi colonial, 1692<en-dash>1826*. Buenos Aires: Sudamericana.

Taussig, Michael. 1993. *Mimesis and Alterity: A Particular History of the Senses*. New York: Routledge

Taylor, Gerald. 2003. *El sol, la luna y las estrellas no son Dios: La evangelización en quechua (siglo XVI)*. Lima: IFEA.

Taylor, Gerald. 2000. *Camac, camay y camasca y otros ensayos sobre Huarochirí y Yauyos*. Cuzco: CBC.

Telechea Idígoras, Ignacio J. 1977. *Tiempos recios: Inquisición y heterodoxias*. Salamanca: Ediciones Sígueme.

Thomson, Sinclair. 2011. "Was There Race in Colonial Latin America? Identifying Selves and Others in the Insurgent Andes." In *Histories of Race and Racism: The Andes and Mesoamerica from Colonial Times to the Present*, edited by Laura Gotowitz, 72–91. Durham, N.C.: Duke University Press.

Thurner, Mark. 2011. *History's Peru: The Poetics of Colonial and Postcolonial Historiography*. Gainesville: University Press of Florida.

Trouillot, Michel-Rolph. 1995. *Silencing the Past: Power and the Production of History*. Boston: Beacon Press.

Urbano, Henrique, ed. 1999. "Estudio preliminar." In *La extirpación de la idolatría en el Piru*, by José de Arriaga, xicxxxi. Cuzco: CBC.

Urbano, Henrique. 1993. "Idolos, figuras, imágenes. La representación como discurso ideológico." In *Catolicismo y extirpación de idolatrías*, edited by Gabriela Ramos and Henrique Urbano, 7–30. Cuzco: CBC.

Van de Guche, Marteen. 1992. "Invention and Assimilation. European Engravings as Models for the Drawings of Felipe Guaman Poma de Ayala." In *Guaman Poma de Ayala: The Colonial Art of an Andean Author*, edited by Rolena Adorno et al., 92–109. New York: Americas Society.

Van Deusen, Nancy E. 2015. *Global Indios: The Indigenous Struggle for Justice in Sixteenth-Century Spain*. Durham, N.C.: Duke University Press.

Vargas Ugarte, Rubén. 1951. *Pareceres jurídicos en asuntos de Indias*. Lima: C.I.P.

Varner, John Grier. 1968. *El Inca: The life and times of Garcilaso de la Vega*. Austin: University of Texas Press.

Villarías Robles, Juan J. R., and María del Carmen Martín Rubio. 1998. "Sobre el autor." In *De las costumbres y conversión de los indios del Perú: Memorial a Felipe II (1588)*, by Bartolomé Alvarez, xiiLxxiii. Madrid: Ediciones Polifemo.

Vizenor, Gerald. 2009. *Native Liberty: Natural Reason and Cultural Survivance.* Lincoln: University of Nebraska Press.

Vizenor, Gerald. 1999. *Manifest Manners: Narratives on Postindian Survivanc.* Lincoln: University of Nebraska Press.

Vizenor, Gerald. 1998. *FugitivePoses: Native American Indian Scenes of Absence and Presence.* Lincoln: University of Nebraska Press.

Vizenor, Gerald, and A. Robert Lee. 1999. *Postindian Conversations.* Lincoln: University of Nebraska Press.

Wachtel, Nathan. 1973. "Pensamiento salvaje y aculturación: El espacio y el tiempo en Felipe Guaman Poma de Ayala y el inca Garcilaso de la Vega." In *Sociedad e ideología: Ensayos de historia y antropología Andinas*, 163–228. Lima: Instituto de Estudios Peruanos.

Wafula, R. S., Esther Mombo, and Joseph Wandera, eds. 2016. *The Postcolonial Church: Bible, Theology, and Mission.* Alameda, Calif.: Borderless Press.

Zamora, Margarita. 1988. *Language, Authority, and Indigenous History in the* Comentarios reales de los incas. Cambridge: Cambridge University Press.

Zanelli, Carmela. 2016. "Las fábulas de Garcilaso ¿Alegoría, historia o ficción en los *Comentarios reales?" Lexis* 40 (2):421–33.

Zuidema, Tom. 1997a. "Pachacuti Ymqui andino: Respuesta de Tom Zuidema a Pierre Duviols." In *Saberes y memorias en los Andes*, edited by Thérèse Bouysse Cassagne, 115–23. Paris: Éditions de l'IHEAL.

Zuidema, Tom. 1997b. "Segunda respuesta de Tom Zuidema a Pierre Duviols." In *Saberes y memorias en los Andes*, edited by Thérèse Bouysse Cassagne, 149–54. Paris: Éditions de l'IHEAL.

INDEX

Note: Pages in italic type refer to illustrative matter.

double consciousness, 15, 124, 126–131, 142, 148–149, 176–178, 207n2, 207n6
Du Bois, W.E.B., 14, 15, 165, 181, 187, 194n12

evangelization, first and second, 29–31, 36–43, 46, 153–155, 160–166, 183
La extirpación de la idolatría en el Piru (Arriaga), 55–57, 199n34

Fabian, Johannes, 48, 197n19
fable, 10, 142–147
fable and allegory, 142–147
Filosofía Nahuatl (Portilla), 145
forced labor. *See* mining and labor

García, Gregorio, 208n14, 212n14
Garcilaso de la Vega, el Inca, 8–14, 123. *See also Comentarios reales de los Incas*, *"CRI"* (Garcilaso)
Geertz, Clifford, 158
Ginés de Sepúlveda, Juan, 27
Gómara, Francisco López de, 131, 132–139, 150, 168–171, 175–176, 208n13, 209n18, 214n26
grace, 69, 71, 73, 78, 86–89, 91. *See also* divine intervention
Grammatica o arte de la lengua general de los indios de los reynos del Perú (Santo Tomás), 31–32, 33, 35, 44, 158, 200n4
Granada, Luis de: *Introducción al símbolo de la fe*, 70–71; *Meditaciones muy devotas*, 117–118; *Memorial de la vida cristiana*, 64–65, 91, 95, 111, 112, 116–117, 205n16
Greek (language), 196n7
Guaman Poma de Ayala, Felipe, 8–14, 123. *See also Nueva corónica y buen gobierno*, *"NCBG"* (Guaman Poma)

hand of God, 86–97. *See also* divine intervention
Hebrew (language), 196n7
hidden meanings, 30–31, 36. *See also* irony; material intelligence

Hispania Victrix. See Historia general de las Indias (López de Gómara)
Hispaniola, 27–28
Historia de Indias (Las Casas), 73
Historia general de las Indias (López de Gómara), 131, 169–171, 209n18
Historia natural y moral de las Indias (Acosta), 29, 43, 72–73, 131, 133, 139, 202n29
huacas, 40, 56, 89, 161, 202n27
Huarochirí, 189
Huiracocha, 168, 172, 214n29

idolatry: accusations of, 20, 197n21, 198n32; Acosta on, 72–74, 212n15; Arriaga on, 55–57; extirpation of, 55–57, 74, 112–113, 116; Garcilaso on, 13, 19, 160, 179–180; Granada on, 71; Guaman Poma on, 13, 19, 80, 89–90; Las Casas, 71, 73; origin of, 49. *See also* conversion and material intelligence
ignorance. *See* material intelligence
ignorancia invencible, 71, 201n12
imagination, meaning of, 151–152, 211n6
Incan origin story and history, 8–10, 140–146, 175
Indian, as concept, ix–x, 14–18, 178–179, 194n10. *See also* absent presence, Indians as; active presence, Indians as; postindian, as concept
Indigenous activist intellectuals, x, 8–14, 15, 18, 28, 181, 193n4, 193n6. *See also* Garcilaso de la Vega, el Inca; Guaman Poma de Ayala, Felipe
Indigenous knowledge: abstract meaning and, 29–31, 38, 40, 151–152; *Lettered City, Lettered Mountain*, 11–12, 13; overview of Spanish colonialism on, 4–8, 21; schooling systems of, 12. *See also* language and writing systems; material intelligence
inteligencia material. See material intelligence

202n27; sermon rhetoric in, 98–100, 114–118; on whiteness, 20–21, 21–22, 62. *See also* Guaman Poma de Ayala, Felipe Núñez Vela, Blanco, 67

Oré, Luis Jerónimo de, 55, 70, 78–79
Origen de los indios del nuevo mundo e indias occidentales (García), 208n14
Ortega, Julio, 177
Ossio, Juan, 99
"Our Spiritual Strivings" (Du Bois), 15

Panopticon model, 171
paternalism, 31–38, 65–66. *See also* material intelligence
Paul (saint), 40, 113, 114, 116–117
pecheros, 102, 103, 104
perception, 5–7, 116–117, 184–187. *See also* colonial difference; whiteness
Perú, origin of name, 149–151
Pizarro, Francisco, 5, 82, 84, 85, 106
Plato, 9, 33
Polo Ondegardo, Juan, 198nn29–30, 203n31
Portilla, León, 145
postindian, as concept, 17–18, 125, 149, 188. *See also* absent presence, Indians as; active presence, Indians as; Indian, as concept; survivance
praeparatio evangelica, 142–143
pride, 5
problema del indio, 74, 109, 182–183
De procuranda Indorum Salute (Acosta), 29, 43, 45, 72, 212n15

Quechua, 31–34, 112, 156, 161–162, 177
Quijano, Aníbal, 13, 194n8
quipu, 193n4
Quispe-Agnoli, Rocío, 99

race: invention of concept, 13–16, 184–187; "race-thinking" and race feelings, ix, 7, 18, 21, 128, 184, 185; skin color and, 16–18,

21, 62, 105, 108, 184, 194n12. *See also* colonial difference; whiteness
Republicas del mundo (Roman), 160
El requerimiento (text), 4–5, 66, 78, 88
Roman, Hieronimo, 160

Salamanca school, 29, 71, 73, 78
Santo Tomás, Domingo de, 155; *Grammática,* 31–32, 33, 35, 44, 158, 200n4; incident with *cacique,* 6–7, 15, 16–17, 35–37; on Indigenous knowledge and intelligence, 31–38, 156; on Indigenous religious beliefs, 158–159, 195n4; on language, 51, 197n22; on Latin, 33–34; *Lexicon,* 31, 34, 35
Second Ecclesiastical Council of Lima, 30
second sight, 15, 130, 174, 176
Sepúlveda, Juan Ginés de, 27, 50, 174, 197n21
Smith, Shawn Michelle, 15
social category, 103, 204nn4–5
Solar, Antonio, 167–168, 172, 175
Spalding, Karen, 189
Spanish colonialism, 3–8; coloniality of power, as concept, 13–14, 181–187, 194n8; conflicts and Indigenous political participation against, 18–21, 195n14; on Hispaniola, 27–28; narratives, overview, 8–14
Spanish language, 193n4
state of exception, 63, 106–107
survivance, 22, 123, 160, 178. *See also* postindian, as concept
Symbolo cathólico indiano (Oré), 55

Tangatanga story, 161–165
taxation, 102–105
temporal knowledge, 47–53, 197n19
términos particulares, 34, 51, 196n8, 197n22
Tesoro de la lengua castellana o española (Covarrubias), 126–127, 151, 152
Thamara, Francisco de, 131, 134
theory of universal harmonization, 177, 207n2, 208n7

ABOUT THE AUTHOR

Gonzalo Lamana is an associate professor in the Department of Hispanic Languages and Literatures at the University of Pittsburgh. His publications include *Domination without Dominance: Inca–Spanish Encounters in Early Colonial Peru* and *Pensamiento colonial crítico: Textos y actos de Polo Ondegardo*.